Irish Fiction and Postmodern Doubt—
An Analysis of the Epistemological
Crisis in Modern Fiction

IRISH FICTION AND POSTMODERN DOUBT–
AN ANALYSIS OF THE EPISTEMOLOGICAL
CRISIS IN MODERN FICTION

Neil Murphy

Studies in Irish Literature
Volume 12

The Edwin Mellen Press
Lewiston•Queenston•Lampeter

Library of Congress Cataloging-in-Publication Data

Murphy, Neil.
  Irish fiction and postmodern doubt : an analysis of the epistemological crisis in modern fiction / Neil Murphy.
    p. cm. -- (Studies in Irish literature ; v. 12)
  Includes bibliographical references (p.   ) and index.
  ISBN 0-7734-6518-9
  1. English fiction--Irish authors--History and criticism. 2. Knowledge, Theory of, in literature. 3. English fiction--20th century--History and criticism. 4. Higgins, Aidan, 1927--Criticism and interpretation. 5. Jordan, Neil, 1951--Criticism and interpretation. 6. Banville, John--Criticism and interpretation. 7. Ireland--Intellectual life--20th century. 8. Postmodernism (Literature)--Ireland. 9. Belief and doubt in literature. 10. Ireland--In literature. I. Title. II. Studies in Irish literature (Lewiston, N.Y.) ; v. 12.

PR8807.K56M87 2004
823'.914099417--dc22

2003066109

This is volume 12 in the continuing series
Studies in Irish Literature
Volume 12 ISBN 0-7734-6518-9
SIrL Series ISBN 0-7734-7983-X

A CIP catalog record for this book is available from the British Library.

Studies in Irish Literature: General Editor Eugene O'Brien
Front cover image by Su, © 2002

Copyright © 2004 Neil Murphy

All rights reserved. For information contact

The Edwin Mellen Press
Box 450
Lewiston, New York
USA 14092-0450

The Edwin Mellen Press
Box 67
Queenston, Ontario
CANADA L0S 1L0

The Edwin Mellen Press, Ltd.
Lampeter, Ceredigion, Wales
UNITED KINGDOM SA48 8LT

Printed in the United States of America

for Rose and Ted

CONTENTS

Acknowledgements ix

Preface xi

Chapter 1 Detecting the Boundaries 1

    1.1 Beginnings 1
    1.2 Towards a Critical Heritage 6
    1.3 Irish Literary Precedents: Joyce and Beckett 11
    1.4 Into the Postmodern 20

Chapter 2 Aidan Higgins: The Fragility of Form 37

    2.1 Prelude 37
    2.2 The Constraints of Form 39
    2.3 Existential Irrelevance and the Big House 43
    2.4 *Real* Fiction 50
    2.5 The Mutability of Form 54
    2.6 Dissolving Scenes 64
    2.7 Love as Linguistic Abstraction 69
    2.8 Fictional Realities 74
    2.9 Dissolving Ontologies 82
    2.10 The Fictionalisation of Memory 92
    2.11 Conclusion 98

Chapter 3 John Banville: Out of the Postmodern Abyss 103

    3.1 Prelude 103
    3.2 The Postmodern Big House 107
    3.3 Uncertain Gazings: Scientific Ontologies and Historical Fantasies 114
    3.4 Intertextual Ontologies 131
    3.5 Nietzsche and the Reformulation of Reality 156
    3.6 Reconstructing Artistic Reality 171
    3.7 Conclusion 187

Chapter 4 Neil Jordan: Dissolving Selves 193
    4.1 Prelude 193
    4.2 Spatial Form and the Rejection of Temporal Sequence 196
    4.3 The Past as Imagined Ontology 204
    4.4 Reconstructing the Self 210
    4.5 Mythic Gateways and the Retreat from Realism 216
    4.6 Visual Ontology 224
    4.7 Conclusion 227

Conclusion 231

Notes 239

Bibliography 245

Index 257

ACKNOWLEDGEMENTS

Oceans of gratitude are owed to the many people who have significantly shaped this study. Particular credit lies with the warmth and expert guidance of Declan Kiberd, who never ceases to be my teacher. Tom Kilroy planted the initial seeds and Sean Ryder oversaw their early growth. Pat Sheeran, sadly no longer among us, was a central and inspirational influence: echoes of him are everywhere in these pages. The scholarship and generosity of spirit of Rüdiger Imhof and Joe McMinn made this journey a little less hazardous, while an illuminating trail of postcards and letters from Aidan Higgins left a deep imprint. Peter van de Kamp's exemplary scholarship and incisive advice was almost as welcome as his friendship. Thanks too to Peter Sirr for his endless assistance and his publication, in *Graph*, of an early short piece on Higgins that grew into the chapter on Higgins in this volume. Another less detailed precursor to the finished book chapter on Higgins has appeared in *The Review of Contemporary Fiction*, Autumn 2003, with thanks to Robert McLaughlin (ed.). Thanks too to the editors of *The Irish Review* and the *Irish University Review* for publishing embryonic short pieces on Banville and Higgins. And of course, to Eugene, *der magister ludi*, many many thanks.

Special mention must be made of Keith Hopper and Roberta Gefter, who have frequently helped with bibliographical information and offered much valued assistance, and of John Moriarty who has been a trusty guide in ways that cannot even begin to be named. Former colleagues at the American University of Beirut, particularly James Wackett, were a constant source of advice and diverse expertise, while my undergraduate and graduate students in the same university continually provoked further thought, especially Faten Beydoun, Khaled Naim and Jasmine Masri. Students at Stansfield, Singapore, too, made a significant input via their enthusiastic engagement, none more so than Rosita Abrew, Manjeet Dhillon, Lim Lee Ching, Liz Matthews, Geraldine Song and Wong Kai Cheng. Thank you all, adventurers every one.

Without Rose's and Ted's support and love, quite simply this would not exist. There is no way to thank you enough. Similarly so with Con, the rock upon which so much has always depended – uncle, brother, friend, no description will suffice. And to attempt to describe the myriad ways that this work has been informed, prepared, and made at all possible by my wife Su, is simply not possible. Her strength, resilience, assistance and presence makes this hers as much as it is mine; mo chroí, kesayangan ku. Final mention goes to my daughters Maya and Nadia Roisín who brighten every shade, and never fail to offer a welcome refuge from the labyrinths of print.

The front cover illustration is by Su © 2002, with many thanks.

Singapore 2003

PREFACE

Over twenty years ago, halfway through what was to become his tetralogy on the scientific revolution which undermined humanity's sense of centrality and security within the known universe, John Banville reflected upon the literary and imaginative consequences of that loss:

> Modernism has run its course. So also, for that matter, has post-modernism. I believe, at least I hope, that we are on the threshold of a new *ism*, a new synthesis. What will it be? I do not know. But I hope it will be an art which is honest enough to despair and yet go on; rigorous and controlled, cool and yet passionate, without delusions, aware of its own possibilities and its own limits; an art which knows that truth is arbitrary, that reality is multifarious, that language is not a clear lens. Did I say *new*? What I have defined is as old as Homer.

The end, or the exhaustion, of modernism and post-modernism may, it seems, lead us back to the future, to a realisation that literature has always been a kind of parallel, or virtual, reality. The tension and the contest between realistic and non-realistic narratives, and their respective claims to a superior understanding and knowledge of the world in which we live, suddenly seem to propose a false or misleading set of issues and principles: alternatively, the loss of old certainties and paradigms offers new imaginative possibilities, and a release from the need for certainties. The phoney war between convention and experimentation is perhaps drawing to a close. Heisenberg's 'uncertainty principle', a phrase from the most speculative end of quantum mechanics, now seems a most decisive and comforting metaphor for an art which accepts the ineffable and unknowable world of human desire and ambition.

Too many post-modern narratives seem written with the academy of theory in mind, often too intellectually clever for their own fictional good. Neil Murphy's study of three important Irish post-modernists, Banville, Higgins and Jordan, shows a most discriminating engagement with the intellectual and philosophical dimension to the fictions, while never losing sight of their interest and their challenge as literary narratives. Just as the old distinctions between realistic and metafictional forms or traces are increasingly difficult to explain or defend, so too the separation of theory and fiction has become harder to understand or sustain, or at least is often blurred. Theory about fiction is not always immune to its own fictions, and fiction about theory is often more tied to history than it cares to admit. Murphy is constantly alert to the paradoxical logic of this kind of chiasmus, and defers to the non-programmatic character of the stories he reads for us, while all the time suggesting how they belong to a special kind of history which moves back and forth between the dominant features of modernism and post-modernism.

Banville, Higgins and Jordan represent three important landmarks on the map of late twentieth century Irish post-modernism, each in his own way bringing a radical, adventurous and playful change into the novel, the short story and the cinema. They are daring artists who require daring readers, constantly challenging audiences to reimagine the past through a series of supreme fictions which represent it as both familiar and strange, ancestral yet alien. With a masterly, but modest, command of the Irish and international contexts which help us understand the cultural, literary and philosophical background of post-modern writing, Murphy offers a reasoned and readable account of how these three writers continue and transform the legacy of Joyce, Flann O'Brien and Beckett. In a self-aware and self-critical kind of criticism in sympathy with the narrative frankness of post-modernism, he acknowledges what he calls the 'anaemic' quality of much criticism, and then goes on to give us a most imaginative tour of a reimagined past.

If, as Murphy suggests, there has been an 'epistemological crisis' in contemporary Irish fiction, then something similar has been happening in Irish literary studies over the last decade: where the literature has gone, the criticism must follow. In both cases, the 'crisis' turns out to be quite good news. The pioneering work of Seamus Deane and Declan Kiberd, in particular, has inspired a whole new generation of critics to reconsider the ways in which we might regard and understand Irish studies; with Dr. Murphy's work we have firm evidence of the critical and imaginative fruit of that imaginative revolution.

Professor Joseph McMinn
University of Ulster
Jordanstown

CHAPTER 1

Detecting the Boundaries

'No one, wise Kublai, knows better than you that the city must never be confused with the words that describe it'. Italo Calvino, *Invisible Cities*

1.1 Beginnings

Being a first book, the ghosts of many formative moments reside within these covers. Attempting to trace a line, or lines, of continuity is a hazardous, monumental task, one that is likely to offer up, at best, fragile glimpses at the development of an analytical schema. Certain moments must suffice, like Gabriel's assertion in Joyce's 'The Dead' that 'literature is above politics'. An important juncture, no doubt. As was first sight of Yeats's golden Byzantine bird, and later, the unnerving, tremulous echo of Beckett's *perhapses*. Later still, Barthes transformed all of those texts into tissues of quotations, only for Eliot to pronounce those tissues a tradition of talent. The sequence, of course, is all mine. What gradually emerged was a two-fold conviction. First, that at the heart of great literature lies a spirit of questioning, rather than answering, and second, that the social and historical impetus of much of contemporary criticism seems oddly anaemic when one considers the majesty of form and the complex fabric of any work of art. The spirit of the New Critics, and the Modernity with which they symbiotically interacted, is ever-present in this study. That John Banville, Aidan Higgins and Neil Jordan all transcend the surface dressing of the social and historical, is crucial to this study and central to the mode of analysis which I endeavour to execute. The strength of this trio of contemporary Irish writers is illustrated by virtue of the fact that their work dictates the analysis, to a large extent. I have sought, in this study, to allow the multiplicity of voices in each text to be heard, above the clamour of modish social and historical theory.

The analysis of history, sociology and other branches of the social sciences reveals that all literary texts originate in a specific culture, all bear traces of the cultural codes and practices which define their historical moment, in the broadest possible sense. However, it is also obvious that literature engages a diversity of other intellectual forces in the process of its construction, ranging from the implications of form to the particular philosophical and literary models to which any author may be subjectively drawn. Furthermore, great literature offers a multiplicity of linguistic discourses, which inevitably defines the way that the author represents, or responds to, his/her cultural reality. Thus, the relationship between culture and writing may be inevitable, but equally inevitable is that the relationship between writing and culture is extremely complex and contemporary assumptions that all writing is directly representative of a specific culture are extremely hazardous as a practice of reading. Furthermore it is a fragile presumption that the literary model any writer constructs will offer a lucid cultural vision and, secondly, that the author even intended to offer a cultural vision, that is, of course, if it is even possible to speak of an author's intention in the current critical landscape. Ultimately, this study resists any temptation to contextualise literary works in the social or historical moment unless, of course, the dominant emphasis of the text appeals for such an act.

A number of other considerations underpin the content and direction of this study. The primary critical assumption is that the relationship between text and life is deeply problematic for a variety of reasons, which will be considered hereafter. Engaging this assumption within the context of Irish fiction largely defines the writers who receive most of my critical attention. The work of Aidan Higgins, John Banville, and Neil Jordan has consistently confronted what is, in many respects, the legacy of literary Modernism and Postmodernism and thus, these writers, in significantly divergent ways, have drawn their readers into fictional landscapes where human knowledge, articulation and experience is debated. This is not to suggest that they are the only Irish prose writers who confront such issues or that they are the most important contemporary Irish writers. Rather, their work reflects a diversity which characterises some of the significant literary concerns found in both Irish and international contemporary fiction. As such their work acts as a representative body of writing with which this study can debate wider issues. That none of these writers specifically attempts to represent modern Ireland in any political sense is also central to the aforementioned assumption that the relationship between text and society is a troubled one.

Much of the contemporary literary criticism of Irish writing is effectively a response to the images of Irishness, both modern and historical, which serves to confirm various expressions of a unique cultural consciousness within the writing of Ireland. This is understandably a reflection of the social and historical concerns of writers like McGahern, Bolger, Doyle, Colm Toibin as well as the Irish academic responsiveness to postcolonialism and other politicised modes of reading[1] but it is important to remember that Yeats, Joyce, Beckett and Flann O'Brien are primarily valuable not simply for offering visions of Ireland to literature but for contributing significantly to Modernism and Postmodernism. Their primary value to literature is formal and if they did offer visions of Ireland, it was their literary lenses that so stunned the world. In his mature poetry Yeats elevated the status of the poetic image above all else, while Joyce powerfully identified human experience with linguistic expression in all his work from *A Portrait of the Artist as a Young Man* onwards. The relationship between Irish writing and Modernism remains a fascination for contemporary experimental writers, as is obvious from a cursory remark by John Banville, which indicates his belief in a possible underlying cause for what he sees as an Irish obsession with writing:

> Hiberno-English, as we may call it, is a wonderfully versatile, yet often treacherous literary tool. The subtlety, richness and volatility of English as written in Ireland is the result of an alchemical fusion, as it were, between two wholly dissimilar methods of linguistic interpretation of the world and our being in it. (Banville 1993, 8)

Banville proceeds to claim that all Irish writing is primarily a linguistic endeavour. Echoing Stephen in *A Portrait*, Banville claims that Irish writing is profoundly coloured by the particular variation of English that has evolved in Ireland. However, to suggest that all Irish writing is *primarily* a linguistic endeavour is questionable at best. Arguably, all writing, Irish or otherwise, is primarily a linguistic endeavour but Banville suggests that Irish writing is, in a more profound manner than other writing, a result of compulsive attentiveness to matters linguistic – in preference to the actuality of experience. This is an extravagant claim, one which reflects Banville's own work rather than that of many of his peers. However, it is here at the level of language that it is possible to discern two particular schools of thought in much of Irish literature, which in many ways reflect a wider critical debate.

When the medium, in this case language, becomes primarily important then the significance of content is diminished. Writing which allows language this primary role tends to become self-reflexive because it is the medium itself that will inevitably attract one's attention. In Irish literature there is a sceptical, experimental tradition that stems from Joyce, and includes Flann O'Brien and Beckett. Neither Beckett nor O'Brien is exclusively Joycean but they both react to the lessons taught by Joyce and Modernism in a way that affects their work deeply. This distinct strain in Irish literature perseveres in contemporary Irish fiction and it is now possible to speak of a tradition that extends beyond Joyce, Beckett and O'Brien.

The one underlying trait that authors of this tradition share, is that they all respond to the lessons taught by Modernism. These writers cannot ignore such lessons and return to the fiction practised before Joyce. Language, memory and perception are the key issues for writers of this tradition. Characters and plots tend to be less precisely drawn than in the realist novel and subject matter is increasingly non-Irish. Two critics largely responsible for formulating the negligible body of work penned on the critical tradition (or 'counter' tradition as Kearney has it) are Richard Kearney and Rüdiger Imhof. Both have offered suggestions as to the substance and significance of such a tradition and have suggested various writers as possible contributors to this diverse tradition. Though Imhof and Kearney have sought to establish sets of criteria in order to establish a specific tradition, Joseph McMinn, Keith Hopper and Anthony Cronin have also contributed much to this tradition by virtue of their valuable case studies on Banville (McMinn) and Flann O'Brien (Hopper and Cronin).

The aim of this work, initially with reference to Kearney and Imhof and later to other critical perspectives, is to elucidate the meaning of a critical tradition in terms of Irish literature and also to assign to it a wider critical significance via comparisons with international writing and critical theory. I will also offer up a study of those writers whom I perceive to be the main participants in a critical tradition in contemporary Ireland with a view to elucidating their work. Ultimately, based primarily on my studies of Higgins, Banville and Jordan, I intend to offer a variety of arguments which will consider Postmodernism in a way which will challenge the acrimonious debate that is often provoked at the mere mention of the word. The representative value of their work becomes a consideration in this respect. Thus, this study will draw together a variety of critical positions and use them to evaluate the contributions made to the Modernist and Postmodernist debate by my three primary subjects. I will position my subjects both in the context of Irish literature and in a wider international framework and in doing so indicate how, in different ways, these authors are trying to write their way out of the limitations of the novel form that they inherit from their predecessors. For practical purposes, the range of my study of Higgins, Banville and Jordan will fall between 1960 and 1996.

1.2 Towards a Critical Heritage

Contemporary Irish Novelists, edited by Rüdiger Imhof, although an extremely useful case study of selected individual authors, does not intend to posit a framing theoretical statement about contemporary Irish fiction. Nevertheless Imhof's pioneering contribution to criticism of contemporary Irish fiction is commendable, and his work is a valuable and detailed scholarly source. Having written texts on both Flann O'Brien and John Banville as well as numerous articles on what he views to be the 'fringes'[2] of Irish fiction, it is clear where Imhof's critical preference lies, since both Banville and O'Brien belong to a distinctly experimental tradition. Imhof's body of work is aimed at championing writers of this tradition and for quite some time he has been its most outspoken admirer. However, Imhof himself suggests that Sean O'Faolain's story 'The Fruitless Wife' and Fintan O'Toole's essay 'Island of Saints and Silicon: Literature and Social Change in Contemporary Irish Literature,' indicate a shift away from appreciation of stereotypical Irish narratives (Imhof 1992, 151). More valuable is his awareness of the trend towards an 'internationalisation of narrative discourse' in Irish fiction (Imhof 1992, 151). He also rightly distinguishes between attempts at experimentation of an exclusively thematic kind and experimentation with narrative. After all, experimentation of a thematic kind is not really experiment at all; it is just the expression of new experiences in the same narrative forms, and thus those experiences remain rigidified within the constraints of staid forms.

The 'fringes' with which Imhof is concerned are those fictions which attempt to be 'international' in terms of narrative technique. Although Joyce might be the grand Irish master of modern narrative experiment, Imhof argues that the critical tradition is an international one: 'The "critical" novel represents an international event that has come late to Ireland, at least, that is, in which the "critical" novel has evolved after Joyce and Beckett' (Imhof 1989, 10). Imhof's pedantic distinctions are at least helpful in diagnosing his terminology. By international Imhof means experimental in a post-Joyce, post-Beckett sense. The context of Imhof's distinction lies in his accusation that Richard Kearney seems to view his 'counter' tradition as a purely Irish phenomenon. However, Imhof's accusation, while understandable, is unwarranted. Kearney does attempt to trace the contemporary critical novel back to Joyce but nowhere does he claim that it is an indigenous Irish phenomenon. Certainly, by specifically focusing on Irish writers, there is an explicit suggestion that this is so, but it can be argued that Kearney is simply operating within an available national tradition. However, there is little doubt that Kearney's critical tradition is part of a larger international tradition.

Joyce is both an Irish and an international experimental writer, as is Beckett. To place contemporary Irish fiction in a critical framework dominated by the Joycean example is both an obvious and helpful approach. Imhof's criticism, although mild, is an example of his fastidiousness rather than any inaccurate assumption of Kearney's. Furthermore, aside from this and a few other minor differences, both critics arrive at similar conclusions. They simply utilise different literary exemplum. Imhof's short study, 'How it is on the Fringes of Irish Fiction', expresses his preferred origins. Not satisfied with relying on Beckett and Joyce as precedents, Imhof views the contemporary critical novel as symptomatic of an intertextual dialogue with other national literatures. He specifies the substance of this dialogue as follows:

> What strikes one right away is the immense variety of experimentation. This includes such diverse efforts at innovation or developing narrative discourse as these: the exploitation of Joycean techniques; the multi-faceted use of point-of-view; an attempt at what Philip Quarles, in Huxley's *Point Counter Point*, calls 'musicalisation of fiction'; the spatialisation of narrative discourse; fragmented or split narrative; the disruption of chronology; fabulation and metafiction (including, possibly, histiographic metafiction); dirty realism and hyper-realism; cubist fiction and inchoate fiction, which is to say a kind of narrative shown in the process of being created. (Imhof 1992, 153)

Much of Imhof's critical terminology echoes that which is later applied by Brian McHale, Robert Scholes and Patricia Waugh, critics whose work has been almost exclusively concerned with metafiction, fabulation or Postmodernism. And it is in this context that Imhof views the contemporary Irish critical novel.

Although Imhof states there is much experimentation in evidence in contemporary prose in Ireland he is rarely without strong reservations and rejects many works unreservedly. Apart from John Banville, Imhof seems to view experimental fiction writers in Ireland as quite a lame collection, plagued, as he sees it, by inadequacies. Although he praises Robert McLiam Wilson's efforts he ultimately claims the writing is just mildly unconventional. Sebastian Barry is dismissed, as are Aidan Matthews, Dermot Bolger and Bernard Share. These are among the few who actually receive a mention. Even Aidan Higgins whose writing Imhof has previously compared with *Finnegans Wake*, does not survive unscathed: 'With Higgins, there seems operative little that could be called an attempt at signposting, and the reader is left in the dark' (Imhof 1992, 157). However, Imhof considers many writers who, early in their careers, suffer from over-exuberance and inexperience, an accusation which can also be justly raised against Banville's first novel, *Nightspawn*. The most important aspect of Imhof's work is that he focuses on a number of extremely promising novelists who do not always write about things Irish and, furthermore, attempt to experiment with their medium, the novel. Imhof is quite correct in his belief that narrative experiment in Ireland is not widespread but it does exist and there are a select few who are experimenting with language, form and perspective to the extent that they ultimately question the nature of human existence.

Richard Kearney is quite expressive regarding the roots of what he sees as the 'counter' tradition in contemporary Irish novels. His position is lucidly expressed in a number of essays that articulate what he sees as a 'crisis of imagination',[3] initiated first by Joyce, and developed by Beckett. The basic thrust of Kearney's argument defines a crisis brought about by the Modernist dissatisfaction with the traditional novel form:

> My purpose is to indicate how their writing becomes self-reflexive as it explores fundamental tensions between imagination and memory, narration and history, self and language. In short I propose to show how these authors share, with Joyce and Beckett the basic modernist project of transforming the traditional narrative of quest into a critical narrative of self-questioning. (Kearney 1988, 83)

Thus, in Kearney's schema, self-questioning evolves as the dominant impetus of the narrative. I stress the word 'evolves,' because self-referential literature does not begin with Joyce, it can be traced back to Cervantes, Shakespeare, Sterne and Defoe. However, self-reference does not necessarily mean self-questioning and this is an important distinction. Self-referential literature is not new but the radical destabilising impulse of Modernist and Postmodernist fiction has few true predecessors, Sterne's *Tristram Shandy* being the most obvious one. The dominant feature of Kearney's critical novel then is a radical self-questioning which manifests itself in many ways.

Kearney neatly splits the counter tradition into two generations, the first comprising Beckett and Flann O'Brien, the second McGahern, Higgins, Banville, Stuart and Jordan. The first generation, he argues, 'interpreted the Joycean identification [of art with reality] as an imperialism of fiction over fact and subsequently sought to make the journey of writing possible by saving fact from the jaws of fiction' (Kearney 1988, 88). More questionable is Kearney's 'second generation' which 'interpreted the stalemate as a surrender of memory to the order of the creative imagination' (Kearney 1982, 396). Firstly, Kearney's criteria seem too clinical when dealing with such diverse talents, especially as the surrender seems far from complete. There is, of course, some accuracy to his statement but writers like Banville or Neil Jordan change direction so rapidly as to render such criteria ineffectual. Secondly, I believe Kearney's second generation to be improbable colleagues. Like Imhof, I cannot agree that John McGahern's fiction belongs in a critical tradition. Kearney suggests that McGahern's novel *The Leavetaking* attains self-reflexive status by virtue of its narrator's concern with the past: 'The cancer of the past is too resilient to be healed by a single decision of the imagination. The cloying circularity of time perpetually threatens all creative initiative' (Kearney 1982, 397). The treatment of memory in *The Leavetaking* attains little more than thematic status and, therefore, Kearney exaggerates its level of significance for narrative. The realistic impetus of *The Leavetaking* is far too dominant for it to be considered in the same light as even

Aidan Higgins's fiction which, despite considerable levels of narrative innovation, always seems reluctant to abandon some kind of representative intent. The quest structure of *The Leavetaking* too remains intact and self-questioning of the medium itself is non-existent. Therefore the novel does not even concur with Kearney's original conditions. Yes, it does prod at the issue of memory but is not in any way disruptive to the narrative. Furthermore, since *The Leavetaking*, McGahern's fiction has been the most accomplished representative of the realist novel in Irish fiction. For all McGahern's achievements and exceptional gifts he is certainly not an experimental novelist in the vein of Banville, Higgins or Jordan.

Kearney also selects Francis Stuart as a representative of the 'critical' tradition. Unfortunately, Stuart is far less innovatory than Kearney seems to initially assume. In his recent novels Stuart's characters are interested in the nature of the imagination and its role in society, or its uncomfortable relationship with society, to be more precise. However, Stuart's novels remain quite conventional in narrative terms and are not experimental despite the engaging thematic concerns. Also Kearney, despite an interesting commentary on *A Hole in the Head*, does not actually inform his readers why Stuart belongs in a Joyce/Beckett tradition.

As I have previously stated, Kearney's decision to generalise with his two generations of novelists is an unhelpful method considering the diversity of his subjects. The contemporary focus of this study naturally excludes Kearney's first generation, Beckett and Flann O'Brien. Of Kearney's second generation, I am convinced of the inclusion of John Banville, Aidan Higgins and Neil Jordan. This trio of novelists produce writing which, to avail of Kearney's words, 'is at all times fundamentally *problematic*' (Kearney 1982, 400).[4] Such a condition must be the central feature of novels of the critical tradition in contemporary Irish fiction, just as it is in the work of Joyce, Beckett and O'Brien.

Both Imhof and Kearney are concerned with how contemporary Irish novelists confront the problematic nature of the novel after it was deconstructed by Joyce and then experimented with by writers everywhere. Despite their conflicting attitudes on a number of areas the ultimate aims of both are similar; to evaluate and to highlight the 'critical' novel as it is being practised in contemporary Ireland. However, the literary ancestry of the tradition, as each of them see it, is essential to the way in which one views the Irish critical novel. Kearney's evaluation of Joyce in 'A Crisis of Imagination' is extremely valuable in terms of how he views the evolution from the traditional novel to Modernist scepticism and beyond. Imhof's work, although to date less developed regarding the literary antecedents of the critical novel, other than an analysis of the literary derivations to be found in John Banville's fiction, does offer some indications of the origins of the recent Irish experimental novel by virtue of his interest in Postmodernism and metafiction.

1.3 Irish Literary Precedents: Joyce and Beckett

Kearney traces the quest-structured traditional novel with its inherent Cartesian logic through Joyce's fiction and arrives at a position where the novel is radically questioned, to the point of silence. Kearney rightly accepts the internal quest structure of *A Portrait of the Artist as a Young Man* as an indication of the novel's essentially traditional narrative technique. However, he does consider the self-reflexivity of the novel to be significant. *A Portrait*, by its very title, informs us of the central artistic motivation behind the text. It is a novel about a young artist-figure who ponders both the meaning of his existence and of his art. Thus the novel ultimately reflects back upon itself, although not in a way that is radically self-questioning. Although essentially self-reflexive *A Portrait* retains its traditional quest-motive and does not subvert its own medium. There are moments, however, when Stephen questions the meaning of his medium, moments when the charade of linguistic mimesis is touched upon:

> Did he then love the rhythmic rise and fall of words better than their associations of legend and colour? Or was it that, being as weak of sight as he was shy of mind, he drew less pleasure from the reflection of the glowing sensible world

> through the prism of a language many-coloured and richly storied than from the contemplation of an inner world of individual emotions mirrored perfectly in a lucid supple periodic prose? (Joyce 1992, 180–81)

Although Stephen probes the meaning of language and touches upon the Kantian distinction between word and thing, the reactionary extremes of *Ulysses* have not yet fully absorbed the writing. In *A Portrait* the reality principle, though jostled with occasionally by Stephen's aestheticising mind, remains the dominant anchor in the text.

With *Ulysses* Joyce attempts to transcend the reality principle by vividly documenting both Dedalus's and Bloom's attempts to recreate themselves. Both try to disentangle themselves from the past, a past which torments them in their own particular ways. Kearney's isolation of the 'Ithaca' chapter as the expression of Dedalus's and Bloom's failure to junk history is insightful:

> The autocreative imagination proves to be sterile, devoid of all genuine creativity, all intimacy and life. And so memory reasserts itself at last when the chimes of St. George's bell at half past two makes Stephen remember the mother he thought himself rid of and makes Bloom recall the dead. The 'Ithaca' chapter concludes with an acknowledgement of the futility of any artistic creation which censures history. The point seems to be that the only valid form of imagination is one which incorporates memory, opening itself to the fluxile temporality of history as it does in the soliloquy of Molly. (Kearney 1982, 392)

The past, or reality, cannot be debunked in favour of imagination. The two must somehow collide and co-exist. The characteristic Modernist concerns with history and language are raised in *Ulysses* in an effort to comprehend the coalescence of reality and the imagination. Stephen ponders the meaning of the past:

> In the intense instant of imagination, when the mind, Shelley says, is a fading coal, that which I was is that which I am and that which in possibility I may come to be. So in the future, the sister of the past, I may see myself as I sit here now but by reflection from that which then I shall be. (Joyce 1986, 160)

Our conception of the past, that crucial part of our existence, is conditioned by the state of the imagining mind that recalls the past. But how does one communicate such a fluctuating past? By accepting the transience as an inseparable part of past, present and future. The ambiguities inherent in language further complicate the universe of the novel. Leopold Bloom ponders the act of describing his wife to Stephen at their journey's end:

> How did he elucidate the mystery of an invisible attractive person, his wife Marion (Molly) Bloom, denoted by a visible splendid sign, a lamp?
>
> With indirect and direct verbal allusions or affirmations: with subdued affection and admiration: with description: with impediment: with suggestion. (Joyce 1986, 576)

The hazardous journey from word to object is the focus of Bloom's attention, just as it is Joyce's. The difficulty of adequately writing what is meant, after discovering what is actually meant, is at the core of Bloom's confusion, echoed formally by the scientific linguistic register. As with Joyce, the process of making the leap from experience to imaginative reconstruction is of primary significance. The outcomes to Bloom's and Dedalus's journeys are less important than the probing nature of the journeys themselves. Ultimately the credibility of *Ulysses*'s representative value is disrupted and the self-parodic emphasis of the novel generates the deconstructed condition of the novel form thereafter.

Finnegans Wake represents Joyce's artistic concerns propelled to the limit, to the outer reaches of communicative fiction. As Kearney sees it, reality and the artistic motivation are no longer distinguishable:

> As in *Ulysses* the quest structure becomes a self-destructive parody of itself. Dream and facticity, language as signifier and world as signified, myth and gossip, mimic each other to the point of identity. A meaningless 'collideorscape' of 'undivided reawility' finally becomes indistinguishable from an 'epiphanised' world of artistic 'scriptsigns'. (Kearney 1982, 393)

Is this the end of the novel? Where else is there to go? After reality and the imagination merge in an 'epiphanised' super-existence, which circulates eternally, the novel, it seemed, had reached it climax, or death! Such is the legacy which has confronted fiction-writers ever since.

The ambiguities inherent in all of Joyce's work confirm the inadequacies of the exactitude of the traditional novel and he critically reduces all mimetic attempts to the status of systems of signs and the role of the artist is to read and shape those multifarious signs. Furthermore, the questioning mind which is a constituent part of the process of Joyce's fictions no longer allows the novelist to have blind faith in perception, language, memory and, ultimately, in a distinction between reality and the imagination, a distinction Joyce exposes as impossible.

Patricia Waugh, whose main preoccupation is with the significance and strategies of metafiction, considers Joyce to be the Modernist writer whose work is closest to what she perceives to be Postmodernism. She isolates Joyce's self-reflexive response to language as the prime reason for her proposition. However, she does differentiate between Joyce's Modernism and metafiction:

> *Ulysses* (1922) goes further [than *A Portrait*] in showing 'reality' to be a consequence of style. However, despite parody, stylisation and imitation of non-literary discourses, there is no overtly self-referential voice which systematically establishes, as the main focus of the novel, the problematic nature of language and 'reality'. The only strictly metafictional line is Molly's 'Oh Jamesy let me up out of this pooh!' (Waugh 1984, 25)

Thus, *Ulysses* does not merit metafictional status in Waugh's schema. Self-reflexivity is undoubtedly a condition of *Ulysses* but the necessary overt voice of metafictional novels is generally absent or avoided. Discernible in such an absence is an important distinction between Modernism and metafiction, which is essentially one of the primary distinctions between Modern and Postmodern fiction. *Ulysses*, one the most celebrated moments of Modernism, acts as an indication of the internal workings of Modernism itself. Waugh's foremost distinction between Modernism and metafiction is the former's lack of the systematic flaunting of its artifice which exists in the latter. It is therefore but a question of degrees of self-reflexivity or overtness. Waugh's general analysis considers literature since the nineteenth century to be a series of shifting emphases, away from realism, towards metafiction:

> ...as one moves from realism through modernist forms to contemporary metafiction, the shift is towards an acknowledgement of the primary reality not of this 'common-sense' context of everyday reality but of the linguistic context of the literary text. (Waugh 1984, 87)

Waugh then sees contemporary metafiction as the logical step in this shedding of the 'reality' principle. In fiction, or in all things linguistic, the world is entirely a verbal construct. Although Waugh's perspective, which suggests an inevitable motion towards contemporary metafiction away from the traditional novel, is perhaps too systematic, it is reasonably accurate. Some of her ideas are derived from Roman Jakobson's examination of 'the dominant' which is applied more potently by Brian McHale in his *Postmodernist Fiction*, an application I will presently outline.

Richard Kearney's isolation of Joyce as the precursor to his counter tradition has profound implications for much more than Joyce's own writing. Because Joyce's fiction is an international event it is more fruitful to consider his contribution in the context of some of the movements he initiated. To an extent this represents a convergence of the approaches by Kearney and Imhof. Most significant is Joyce's immense contribution to Modernism and, in turn, Modernism's direct relationship with that problematic contemporary phenomenon, Postmodernism. Joyce is inextricably implicated in these literary and cultural moments, as are the novelists of the counter tradition in contemporary Irish fiction.

The dominant artistic philosophy inherent in the novel before Modernism is that art mirrors life and thus can directly comment on morality, society and one's place in it. This comment then characteristically projects a world-view which can be harmonised and articulated. The connection between life and the sentence appears impenetrable. Therefore art is responsible to life as a kind of guide. It is forced to contribute, to make things happen, to change lives. Modernism rejects this unequivocally. David Lodge explains this shift in perspective:

> Modernism turned its back on the traditional idea of art as imitation and substituted the idea of art as an autonomous activity...The writer's prose style, however sordid and banal the experience it is supposed to be mediating, is so highly and lovingly polished that it ceases to be transparent but calls attention to itself by the brilliant reflections glancing from its surfaces...discarding the

traditional narrative structures of chronological succession and logical cause-and-effect, as being false to the essentially chaotic and problematic nature of subjective experience, the novelist finds himself relying more and more on literary strategies and devices that belong to poetry, and specifically to Symbolist poetry…(Lodge 1981, 6)

The 'literariness' of *Ulysses*, *The Waste Land* or the novels of Woolf or Faulkner is obvious to the point of distraction from the 'content'. The world in Modernist texts gives off a glittering shine that begs admiration for the quality of the artifice. However, Modernism never fully censors life or existence in the way that Postmodernism does. Lodge accurately differentiates between Modernism and Postmodernism in terms of their respective aims:

> Postmodernism continues the modernist critique of traditional realism, but it tries to go around or underneath modernism, which for all its formal experiment and complexity held out to the reader the promise of meaning, if not a meaning. (Lodge 1981, 12)

Postmodernism radically denies the validity of language in wresting meaning from life and, in particular, the past. Arguably, communication then breaks down and the world of language becomes a world of brittle, vacuous signifiers that have lost the objects they are meant to signify. Meaning is lost. I stress 'arguably' because there are perspectives other than this, which I will presently offer. Initially, I wish to investigate Beckett's relationship to these 'isms' and to clarify his position in Kearney's and my own hierarchy of the critical novel.

As early as 1931 Beckett claims 'There is no communication because there are no vehicles of communication' (Beckett 1931, 47). Already language, as a line of communication, is invalidated, for Beckett. Kearney sees Beckett's fiction as a result of his 'identification of imagination and reality as a victory of the former over the latter':

> Writing becomes problematical in that the novelist falls victim to his own fiction, bereft of all life-giving experience. In these novels the imagination reigns supreme; all external reality is only a figment of its colonising creativity. (Kearney 1982, 393)

The obsessive self-questioning, self-doubting and at times self-dismissive tone of Beckett's fiction does indeed reduce the possibility of any possible empirical, external 'reality'. His overtly self-reflexive characters are time and again reincarnated in expressions of bafflement at their own medium, past, present and future, their powers of perception and movement, and ultimately their own absurd existences from which they never manage to touch the actual world of experience, 'reality'.

Beckett's *Trilogy* perfectly illustrates the artistic movement from Modernist questioning to Postmodern fragmentation. *Molloy* has already turned the traditional quest motif on its head and the characters' quests simply act as sterile, peripheral plotted aspects to the self-reflexive inquiry which is the novel's *raison d'être*. When Molloy informs us of the condition of his story the narrative credibility is immediately threatened:

> All I know is what the words know, and the dead things, and that makes a handsome little sum, with a beginning, a middle and an end as is the well built phrase and the long sonata of the dead...Saying is inventing. Wrong, very rightly wrong. You invent nothing, you think you are inventing, you think you are escaping, and all you do is stammer out your lesson...(Beckett 1979, 31)

The opening page to *Molloy* is held together by a staccato of *perhapses*. Nothing is definite about words, truth or even inventing. It even appears that Moran and Molloy might be identical, or might not be. The internal contradictions in *Molloy* threaten to destabilise the novel's narrative and its correspondence to a 'reality'. The novel tentatively clings to the realm of meaningfulness, or the realm of Modernism. There are many unresolved tensions which almost cause the fiction to implode. Brian McHale believes that by invoking the model of the 'unreliable narrator', the projected world is stabilised (McHale 1996, 12). Stabilised is perhaps too strong a word. Better to say that *Molloy* remains tottering on the edge of stability by virtue of our efforts to prevent it from deconstructing its correspondence to life.

The equivocating narrator of *Malone Dies* quickly complicates the hard-earned significance of *Molloy* when he claims that he, Malone, is the creator of Molloy and Moran. Since we know that Malone is a fictional character himself, then Molloy's and Moran's feasibility is rendered even more complicated. After all, Malone is confused about his own substance as he stammers and babbles his way through oceans of self-doubt: 'But what matter whether I was born or not, am dead or merely dying, I shall go on doing as I have always done, not knowing what it is I do, nor who I am, nor where I am, nor if I am' (Beckett 1979, 207). Despite being the unlikely creator of Molloy and Moran, Malone's grasp on his own ontological status is weak, and grows weaker as his dialogue progresses. The title of the text refers to the narrator's death. Whilst relating his story about Macmann/Saposcat the text ends without Malone ever having resurfaced. Which then is the primary world, Malone's or Macmann's, or neither? In this way the world projected in *Malone Dies* is rendered highly ambiguous. The reader is uncertain of the ontological status of either narrative: Malone's narrative, or that of Macmann/Saposcat. Any significant relationship to actual life is therefore also disturbed in a serious way. Furthermore Malone obliquely denies Beckett's authorship. Malone pens the novel '*Malone Dies*' and continually interrupts the narrative to comment upon its quality: 'I near the goal I set myself in my young days and which prevented me from living. And on the threshold of being no more I succeeded in being another. Very pretty' (Beckett 1979, 178). Such self-reflexive antics are relatively unobtrusive in their own right but when added to Malone's other claims and denials the narrative begins to lose meaning, in the traditional sense. Malone tells us he is the author of *Molloy* and the inventor of Macmann/Saposcat. He is the narrator of his own universe, one in which he struggles to find truths, truths which are abruptly denied when approached. Malone's ultimate problem is that he, like Beckett, is trapped within the walls of his imaginative fortress with nothing but words and surreal memories. No matter how many ontological levels he constructs, no matter how many Molloys,

Morans, Merciers or Camiers he might invent, the actuality of existence cannot be reached.

At the close of *Malone Dies* Macmann is abandoned in an unstable place where the ontological stratum have collapsed. Macmann's creator, who it seems has died, cannot be his ultimate creator. Macmann is lost in a fictional Pandora's box and eventually fades out. *The Unnamable* complicates the situation further still. The unnamed narrator purports to be the creator of Malone and thus Molloy, Moran et al. *The Unnamable* displays many of Malone's creative gimmickry inventing new characters and landscapes but to a much greater extent and dismisses them as soon as they become tiresome to him. This inevitably leads him to the question of his own existence. Along the way to this self-interrogation he strips his landscape of things, of objects from the real world, as he travels nearer to the creative core of his self. Finally the unnamable asks who is it that created him. He thus admits the absolute fictional nature of his existence. His creator is Beckett who is, in a way, his God figure. The unnamable is trapped within the imaginative constraints of Beckett's creation and cannot reach the real world. The trilogy is ultimately concerned with this chasm between life and the imagining mind which perceives and then transforms. For Beckett the gap is wide, unbridgeable. But this is not necessarily a negative thing. The silence, into which Beckett's unnameable eventually lapses, occurs when the artist gazes into the chasm between word and thing, between imagination and actuality: 'I cannot be silent. About myself I need know nothing. Here all is clear. No, all is not clear. But the discourse must go on. So one invents obscurities. Rhetoric' (Beckett 1979; 269). There is no end to discourse for Beckett. He writes against logic from within the depths of creative silence. He probes the very discourse that he deconstructs. Yes, his monologues define the limitations of language and imagination in terms of their relationship to 'reality' and yes, such a practice is self-defeatist, in a sense, but there is also freedom to be discovered.

Beckett's dissent is liberating because it signals a new perspective that, arguably, offers up a relativised system of communication where the limits to language and perception are only limits in the traditional sense. If the problematic condition of communication, as Beckett sees it, is accepted not as a rejection of dialogue but as a constituent part of the communicative process perhaps then the seemingly endless prevarications of Beckett's sleepwalking heroes might be fruitful. Such is the challenge Beckett lays before contemporary practitioners of the novel, and all writing, and many contemporary Irish novelists have responded in a significant way.

1.4 Into the Postmodern

The contribution made by Joyce and Beckett to contemporary literature is immeasurable and their influence upon those revolutionary moments we label Modernism and Postmodernism cannot be stressed enough. In turn their influence upon writers writing in Ireland is also considerable. Richard Kearney has provided some valuable and cogent insights into the critical novel as penned by Joyce and Beckett and the subsequent counter-tradition, which respond to the lessons taught by the two masters of literary scepticism. He has indicated that the creative pursuits of certain contemporary Irish novelists are unavoidably linked with the writing of Joyce and Beckett and that the nineteenth century realistic novel, although still popular among some of Ireland's brightest literary lights, has been rejected by a significant number of Irish novelists. This has as much to do with Sterne, Rilke, Hoffmannstahl, Nietzsche and Proust, among others, as it does with Joyce and Beckett. John Banville is as likely to build Rilkean, Nabokovian or Nietzschean quotations or appropriations into his intertextual fictions as he is to avail of Joyce or Beckett. Aidan Higgins spikes his fictional universes with utterances from Hoffmannstahl, Proust and Defoe while the echoes of Beckett are rarely absent, and Neil Jordan's literary texts fuse Kafkaesque dream visions with Blakean prophetic echoes. All three of my primary subjects are strongly indebted to their two great Irish predecessors but the merits of a critical argument which confines itself to a national literature are few and smacks of a tribalism which neither Joyce or Beckett would have appreciated. One admittedly needs a comparative framework but with novelists like Banville, Higgins and Jordan such limitations can be as blinding as they are informative. For this reason Richard Kearney's position is somewhat restrictive in terms of this study. Rüdiger Imhof's work, alternatively, seeks to extend beyond the literary exemplum of Joyce and Beckett and considers contemporary Irish fiction in an international context specifically informed by his reading of Postmodernism, fabulation or metafiction. Both approaches are legitimate despite their implicit conceptual differences. With these differences in mind, some kind of fusion of Kearney and Imhof underpins this study.

Postmodernism is a problematic concept, not least because of the ambiguity of the word itself. It sounds like a spent version of Modernism gasping the final breaths of its more articulate predecessor. And yet the claims made for Postmodernism are equalled in their intensity only by the vehemence aroused by a mere mention of the word in certain circles. There is a need to reach an acceptable working definition, even if such a concept is essentially alien to the very idea of Postmodernism. Ihab Hassan, one of contemporary Postmodernism's most eloquent supporters, offers up the following sentiments:

> Thus we cannot simply rest – as I have sometimes done – on the assumption that postmodernism is antiformal, anarchic, or decreative; for though it is indeed all of these, and despite its fanatic will to unmaking, it also contains the need to discover a 'unitary sensibility'.[5] (Hassan 1985, 122)

Hassan's view occupies one extreme position of the debate being conducted about the significance of Postmodernism. Its detractors too have much rhetorical ammunition, which I will presently outline. Due to the specific intent behind this study I will hereafter need to confine myself to Postmodern fiction since the vast area of cultural Postmodernism is not the primary focus of this study. However, there will be obvious implications for a wider cultural context in the study of the fiction.

Patricia Waugh's study of metafiction is valuable because it attempts to differentiate between the concepts of Modernism and Postmodernism. As I have previously outlined, Waugh views the foremost difference between Modernism and Postmodernism to be the former's lack of the systematic flaunting of artifice in evidence in the latter (Waugh 1984, 22). Of course, Modernist texts are frequently self-reflexive, but in Waugh's schema they are not consumed by their own condition of artifice. Modernist texts, she claims, do not foreground the problematic process of their own creation in the way that metafictional texts do. At the heart of contemporary metafiction Waugh claims that language, as a self-conscious synthetic system, is overtly evident:

> For Sterne, as for contemporary writers, the mind is not a perfect aestheticizing instrument. It is not free, and it is as much constructed out of as constructed with, language. The substitution of a purely metaphysical system (as in the case of Proust) or mythical analogy (as with Joyce and Eliot) cannot be accepted as final structures of authority and meaning. Contemporary reflexivity implies an awareness both of language and metalanguage, of consciousness and writing. (Waugh 1984, 24)

Ultimately the issue raised by metafiction is that one cannot rely on synthetic structures to provide truth and therefore the process of utilising one's medium, writing, is scrutinised, often, as in Beckett's case, to the extreme. Contemporary metafiction explores the meaning of this actuality in many different ways. Some novels, like Richard Brautigan's *In Watermelon Sugar*, present universes in which anything is possible. Brautigan's ultimate efforts are always to preserve discourse, to set up new lines of communication in an effort to comprehend a universe which will not yield to the exactitude of language: 'Wherever you are, we must do the best we can. It is so far to travel, and we have nothing there to travel, except watermelon sugar. I hope this works out' (Brautigan 1973, 7). Brautigan's arbitrary choice of symbols is significant in that it represents an effort to renegotiate the relationship between word and thing. The primary function of Brautigan's symbolic language is to indicate the nature of the writing itself, to comment upon the process of the novel and its possibilities: 'Some of the bridges are made of wood…and some of the bridges are made of stone gathered from a great distance and built in order of that distance, and some are made of watermelon sugar' (Brautigan 1973, 2). Appropriating the traditional symbol of crossing bridges, Brautigan suggests that those bridges constructed of watermelon sugar are the ones across which he can travel most easily. The glistening invention is, for Brautigan, more potent as a vehicle of communication than representational methods. The difficulty with using traditional emblems beside arbitrary ones is that the act of communicative *rapprochement* between text and reader is sundered, or at least compromised. This reflects the ambiguity and confusion of Postmodernism. *In Watermelon Sugar*, like many Postmodern novels, concludes, or rather expires, on the threshold of expectancy. It simply falters into silence: 'The musicians were poised with their instruments. They were ready to go. It would only be a few seconds now, I wrote' (Brautigan 1973, 138). Writing against familiar forms of narrative closure, Brautigan's already unsteady text makes one final gesture of defiance against narrative order.

The strategies which Postmodern novelists employ in response to the lessons learnt from Modernism and its precursors are varied. Ultimately these writers struggle to surpass the sundered relationship between language and experience, the past and memory and perception and reality. Consumed to a far greater degree by these issues than their predecessors, contemporary artists avail of countless methods to maintain coherent discourse. Some, like Brautigan, perpetually acknowledge the rift between signifier and signified and the imagination and reality but their use of Postmodernist gimmickry tends to lead them up the same literary cul-de-sac time and again, whilst moving further away from striking up any significant thread of communication with life. Lost in a world of arbitrary symbols and increasingly barren signifiers some Postmodern novelists fail to respond in any meaningful way to Modernist scepticism. Writing in a repetitive limbo is not what Joyce or Beckett offered. They were both able to eke out correlations between art and life, however taxing their metaphorical systems may be.

Postmodernism is not necessarily a hedonistic set of anti-principles and Postmodern fiction does not always disappear into the angst-ridden abyss of self-doubt. Brian McHale's study *Postmodernist Fiction* is one of the more rational and coherent evaluations of Postmodern fiction because, as well as documenting the progression from Modernism to Postmodernism in a lucid and informed manner, McHale also provides a splendid array of the strategies used by contemporary Postmodern novelists in their efforts to surmount a potential discursive impasse. Unlike many other commentators of Postmodernism McHale does not use the familiar gestures of defiance or arrogance. Nor does he wade through the endless argument upon which others seem to thrive. Instead he simply declares his interest, displays how certain writers construct their fictional worlds, and tells us why.

The basic premise of McHale's argument for the autonomous status of Postmodernism is the most convincing argument this author has read. Tracing his thesis back to the Russian Formalist Roman Jakobson, or even earlier to Jurij Tynjanov, McHale claims there is a distinct difference between Modernist and Postmodernist texts. The source of this difference he gleans from Jakobson's 'shifting dominant'.[6] For Jakobson the 'dominant' in a piece of literature conditioned the essence of the work:

> The dominant may be defined as the focusing component of a work of art: it rules, determines, and transforms the remaining components. It is the dominant which guarantees the integrity of the structure...a poetic work [is] a structured system, a regularly ordered set of artistic devices. Poetic evolution is a shift in this hierarchy. (McHale 1996, 6)

Jakobson's dominant is a helpful insight into the evolution of literature and its influence is widespread in literary theory. Patricia Waugh, too, touches upon the 'dominant' in her efforts to trace the evolution of Postmodernism. However, it is McHale's particular application of the theory that is of significance and originality. Shifting dominants are all very well but one has to distinguish the exact nature of this shift before the theory is of any real benefit. The nature of the shifting evolutionary patterns between Modernism and Postmodernism is expressed by McHale as follows:

> This is essentially a one-idea book…That idea is simply stated: postmodernist fiction differs from modernist fiction just as a poetics dominated by ontological issues differs from one dominated by epistemological issues. (McHale 1996, XII)

Thus the Postmodernist dominant is ontological and the Modernist dominant is epistemological. McHale recalls Jakobson to emphasise that ontological elements do appear in Modernist texts also but they are not dominant. They are subsidiary and optional. It is only when they become dominant and the epistemological elements become secondary that Postmodern fiction exists. Modernism therefore is dominated by epistemological concerns, or concerns which are primarily concerned with the 'accessibility and circulation of knowledge, the different structuring imposed on the 'same' knowledge by different minds, and the problem of 'unknowability' or the limits of the knowledge' (McHale 1996, 9). Modernism is primarily consumed with the limits of knowledge and employs various devices to overcome this. Joyce's and Eliot's mythical structures are aimed at generating systems with which we can contain and comprehend life. In *Ulysses* existence itself is not doubted, at least not overtly. Knowledge is questioned and its limitations are probed but existence itself is not thrown into disarray as it is in the Postmodern world of ontological obsession.

The ontological dominant of Postmodernist fiction is persistent and interrogative. The primary obsession, that of existence itself, is expressed in many guises. McHale lists quite a few:

> What is a world? What kinds of world are there, how are they constituted, and how do they differ? What happens when different kinds of world are placed in confrontation; or when boundaries between worlds are violated? What is the mode of existence of a text, and what is the mode of existence of the world (or worlds) it projects? How is a projected world structured? (McHale 1996, 10)

These, McHale argues, are representative of questions asked by Postmodernist novels. At a certain point in the evolution of the novel, ontological issues outstrip epistemological ones. As epistemological uncertainty grows more unstable the dominant dynamic of the text becomes ontological. Because of this close relationship it is possible to conduct an epistemological reading of a Postmodern text with reasonably fruitful results. Furthermore, many Postmodern texts document the dissolution of the epistemological dominant prior to investigating the projected world on an ontological level.

In order to further clarify his argument McHale offers Thomas Pavel's definition of an ontology: 'a theoretical description of a universe' (Pavel in McHale 1996, 27). Pavel's 'theoretical description' implicitly junks realism and highlights the distinction between the 'fictional' world and the 'real' world of experience. The extension of this is apparent in many Postmodernist novels which utterly refuse to present realistic scenarios and in some cases 'reality' itself is renegotiated in terms of its relationship to man's encyclopaedic order. Italo Calvino's Marco Polo, of *Invisible Cities*, registers the problematic nature of language coupled with memory's inexactitude and in doing so jeopardises the ontological status of Venice: 'Memory's images, once they are fixed in words, are erased', Polo said. 'Perhaps I am afraid of losing Venice all at once, if I speak of it. Or perhaps, speaking of other cities I have already lost it, little by little' (Calvino 1974, 69). The more Polo tries to articulate the actuality of experience the more transparent it grows. This represents the Modernist epistemological problematic at its most extreme. Calvino, however, evolves from this position to the point of extinguishing reality, or at least imbuing it with a translucent quality. Ultimately, Marco Polo does not need to travel in order to report to Kubla Khan. Once the process of his storytelling is understood the various cities become invisible in empirical terms and Polo's shaping visions extend beyond the limits of sensual response. In this way reality is relativised in a fictional universe, which appropriately abounds in anachronisms and anomalies.

In their efforts to reflect a diversity of human imaginative responses to living, Modernist texts frequently avail of numerous narrators but reality is never obliquely destabilised as it is in Postmodernist texts. Modernism never rejects the notion of truth or reality. Postmodernism relativises reality, it presents life as a universe of shifting surfaces and the narrative tactics used in Postmodern novels reflect this intent. Much of the rest of McHale's study is occupied with presenting various examples of how Postmodernism expresses its ontological dominant. One of the primary strategies of the Postmodern novelist is to disrupt feasible universes:

> Postmodernist fictions, by contrast [with modernist fiction whose associations gel together, i.e. the snowy arctic] often strive to displace and rupture these automatic associations, parodying the encyclopaedia and substituting for 'encyclopaedic' knowledge, their own *ad hoc*, arbitrary, unsanctioned associations. (McHale 1996, 48)

This kind of rupture is common in Postmodern novels and the ways in which it is achieved are varied. In contemporary Irish fiction these ruptures are used for a variety of purposes. For example, John Banville's parody, *Birchwood*, uses numerous anachronisms. There are shotguns and telephones in Gabriel Godkin's big house but the chronological occasion of the fiction, the great famine, does not allow for such objects. There are also numerous chronological inconsistencies. One moment Gabriel is in the middle of famine-ridden Ireland and the next he is catapulted forward to the land wars. These elements conspire to undermine the realism of the projected world. Aidan Higgins's *Balcony of Europe* too disrupts its own ontological stability but in a more subtle way. By spiking his fiction with quotations from various historical figures Higgins disturbs encyclopaedic reality. The overt and intentional use of intertextual allusions places various 'worlds' in collision and by doing so the author adds a synthetic tone to the text. However, Higgins differs from Banville in that, despite the author's profound mistrust of man's epistemological systems, his work does not try to establish an ontology that is radically different to conventional 'reality'. Nevertheless, both Banville and Higgins disrupt their universes purposely and, as I will display in the forthcoming chapters, they fundamentally question the concept of reality and discuss how one confronts this concept both in fiction and in life.

McHale suggests numerous other strategies used by Postmodern novelists but the unifying factor is that all of these techniques aim to destabilise the ontological status of any given projected universe for various reasons. These techniques are too numerous to deal with in this study but the results of McHale's various disruptive narrative techniques are important. Ultimately all human articulation, as we have previously accepted it, is questioned and thus, significantly, history is considered a fiction also. This is not quite as nihilistic as it initially seems. One of McHale's most cogent claims for the importance of Postmodern fiction's role in human affairs is that related to history:

> In postmodernist revisionist historical fiction, history and fiction exchange places, history becoming fictional and fiction becoming 'true' history – and the real world seems to get lost in the shuffle. But of course this is precisely the question postmodernist fiction is designed to raise: real, compared to what? (McHale 1996, 96)

This lies at the core of McHale's argument in favour of Postmodernist fiction. Because of the epistemological cul-de-sac of Modernist fiction, Postmodernist fiction struggles to articulate reality, and therefore history. Like all other discourse, history is fictional, flickering in and out of sight depending on the quality of the memory, the medium and the reader. 'Reality' becomes subservient to these three factors and the imagining mind thus has the last say on the actuality of existence. While the real world as a fixed external proposition is radically reordered in McHale's Postmodernist universes, it is not easily relinquished by many.

In several crucial ways Postmodernism is a reaction to Modernism. The ontological dominant of Postmodernism arises only when the epistemological fragility of Modernism is exposed. Also, Modernism, in its efforts to replace sequential time and the basic quest motif, demanded such exacting levels in terms of form and language that the reactionary nature of Postmodernism is unsurprising. Ihab Hassan, claiming Postmodernism to be primarily a reaction against the preceding age, suggests a listing of what he sees to be the foremost traits of the new age. The list includes: antiform, chance, exhaustion/silence, performance/happening, antithesis, text/intertext, rhetoric, rhizome/surface, signifier and indeterminacy (Hassan 1985, 122). Hassan's criteria read like a listing of the essential elements of John Banville's fictions, which will be considered in Chapter 3. Postmodern fiction is subversive, negative and non-mimetic. It parodies, it assaults existing schools of thought and knowledge and it will not even accept the validity of its own medium, language, at least in traditional terms. David Harvey, isolating what he sees as the essential difference between Modernism and Postmodernism, warns against the excesses of the latter:

> Modernism could speak to the eternal only by freezing time and all its fleeting qualities. But postmodernism responds to the fact of that in a very particular way...Postmodernism swims, even wallows in the fragmentary and the chaotic currents of change as if that is all there is. (Harvey 1989, 21)

This is the basis of the divisive controversy surrounding the value of Postmodernism. Is such an anarchic philosophy of value outside the theoretical halls of academe or outside the safe world of art? Harvey argues that the obsessive tendency to discard all existing systems of knowledge and communication is ultimately regressive and exhaustive:

> Postmodern philosophers tell us not only to accept but even to revel in the fragmentations and the cacophony of voices through which the dilemmas of the modern world are understood. Obsessed with deconstructing and delegitimating every form of argument they encounter, they can end only in condemning their own validity claims to the point where nothing remains of any basis for reasoned action. (Harvey 1989, 44)

Deconstruction, and other related schools of thought, Harvey claims, argue until communication is unintelligible, action is impossible and living is unbearable. But Harvey's response too is obsessive. Even Postmodern philosophers believe that dialogue must continue, that Hassan's 'unitary sensibility' must be discovered. As I have earlier indicated, Hassan tells us that we cannot choose between 'the essential unity of existence and its perceived diversity'. This is very different to Harvey's fragmentation. Hassan argues that there needs to be a set of regulatory systems, despite the diversity inherent in human perception. However, these regulatory systems which man utilises to order experience must be understood in terms of their limits as well as their necessity.

The anarchic tendencies of Postmodernism, although a response to Modernism, do have historical precedents, especially in the writings of Nietzsche. David Harvey, like many other commentators on Postmodernism, isolates Nietzsche as a precursor to Postmodern thought:

> To the degree that it does legitimate itself by reference to the past, postmodernism typically harks back to that wing of thought, Nietzsche in particular, that emphasises the deep chaos of modern life and its intractability before rational thought. (Harvey 1989, 116)

Nietzsche's writings gain much of their dynamics from their inherent enmity to all systematic thought and Postmodernism often assimilates this enmity as a kind of heretical authority. Nietzsche's dominant vision foresees a revaluation of all existing values: 'Behold the good and the just! Whom do they hate most? Him who smashes their tables of values, the breaker, the law-breaker – but he is the creator' (Nietzsche 1986, 51). Nietzsche's words may be interpreted as a crude *raison d'être* for Postmodernism. Whilst demolishing the exactitudes of the preceding age Postmodernism creates a new set of values. This new *ism* has as its God not reason but uncertainty or constant flux. Appearance is of more value than 'reality' and becoming is superior to being. Nietzsche is very influential to the Postmodern suggestion that appearance is of more value to life than any ambitious quest for depth or truth, beneath the appearance: 'It is no more than a moral prejudice that truth is worth more than appearance; there would be no life at all if not on the basis of perspective evaluations and appearances' (Nietzsche 1974, 47).

The relish with which Postmodern novelists absorb Nietzsche's philosophy of appearance is exemplified by Borges's preface to his *A Universal History of Infamy* in which he admits that his text is 'no more than appearance, than a surface of images' (Borges 1985, 12). John Banville's *The Book of Evidence* and Gabriel Garcia Marquez's *Love in the Time of Cholera* both ultimately contain the same demand: that one imagines and thus creates one's daily life. Both novels side-step logic, which ultimately negates itself, and present highly inventive, linguistic super-realities through which they infuse living with meaning, a meaning that places appearance above 'reality'. Although not all Postmodern novelists respond to the primacy of appearance in such fashion, most admit that human knowledge must in some way be radically altered in response to their allegiance to the fluctuations of perception. Robbe-Grillet's reaction is very different to that of Marquez but he too recognises that our way of viewing life must be altered: '...the surface of things has ceased to be for us the mask of the heart, a sentiment that led to every kind of metaphysical transcendence' (Robbe-Grillet in Lodge 1974, 472). Nabokov's Hermann speaks of 'the invention of art containing far more intrinsic truth than life's reality' (Nabokov 1987, 106). Banville's Gabriel Swan concludes *Mefisto*, tentatively promising that he will leave things to 'chance', and in *Balcony of Europe*, Aidan Higgins's Dan Ruttle continually embraces those most painful of twins, love and transience: 'You had existed as part of the seminal substance of the universe that is always becoming and never is; and now had disappeared into that which had produced you' (Higgins 1972, 239). Postmodernism responds to the *actuality* of transience and fragmentation by rejecting the synthetic structures by which man traditionally ordered life (morality/religion, language and mathematics). In place of these systems they pin their faith in perception and creative silence, or what Hassan calls 'articulate silence' (Hassan 1987, 169). However, despite the artistic innovations which a philosophy of uncertainty and flux prompts, is it conceivable that such ideas can contribute something significant to life? Can they strike up a figurative, if not literal, relationship with life? This is the essential issue.

Dick Hebdige, discussing *The Face* magazine, denounces Postmodernism's rejection of representative art as ultimately negative:

> However, the consequences of the assault on representation for *ecrivants* and image-makers are, on the whole, rather more mundane. First the referent (the world outside the text) disappears. Then the signified and we are left in a world of

> radically 'empty' signifiers. No meaning. No classes. No history. Just a ceaseless procession of simulacra. (Hebdige 1989, 268–9)

Hebdige's terminology reveals his Marxist sentiments and his view of the process of Postmodernism is both dismissive and myopic. One cannot simply pretend that words are something other than signifiers. Rather than draining words of meaning Postmodernism points to their highly vibrant associative powers. The world outside the text does not disappear but a different method is needed to interpret an alternative kind of linguistic expression. Hebdige, in his blindness, rejects the diversity of appearance and in doing so he rejects Postmodernism's attempt to respond. More potent, however, is his rejection of Baudrillard:

> He claims that reality is nothing more than the never knowable sum of all appearances. For Baudrillard, 'reality' flickers. It will not stay still. Tossed about like Rimbaud's 'drunken boat' on a heaving sea of surfaces, we cease to exist as rational cogitos capable of standing back and totalising on the basis of our experience. (Hebdige; 1989, 269)

Terry Eagleton's similar perspective suggests that Postmodernism is not simply pointless but extremely dangerous:

> ...the death camps were among other things the upshot of a barbarous irrationalism which, like some aspects of postmodernism itself, junked history, refuted argumentation, aestheticised politics and staked all on the charisma of those who told the story. (Eagleton in Harvey 1989, 210)

Both Hebdige and Eagleton warn against the excesses of Postmodernism in an hysterical fashion, believing it to carry threats of a bleak and voiceless existence. The unfortunate difficulty for Hebdige and Eagleton is that one cannot simply unlearn the lessons taught by Modernism and return blindly faithful to human systems of communication as if they were an infallible kind of Morse code. At the close of *Mefisto*, Banville's Gabriel Swan tells us: 'Even an invented world has its rules, tedious, absurd perhaps, but not to be gainsaid' (Banville 1987, 234). Despite the inexactitude of our ordering systems of memory, mathematics, morality and what Hassan terms 'the disease of verbal systems' (Hassan 1987, 32), which ultimately lend a fragmented air to life, man still needs those synthetic systems which order life. Life must be regulated, as Gabriel Swan knows very well. In this way we avoid the paranoid horrors of which Eagleton's emotive and all-too predictable Nazi-Germany imagery warns. And as for his fear that the charisma of the tale-teller will dictate who wields power – well, was it ever any other way in democracy, one wonders, and even more so in the multimedia global village? Hebdige's fear of being unable to totalise on the basis of our experience too must be addressed – we always have and always will do this but we might understand the significance of such an act a little better now.

Perhaps one of the most insightful expressions of the significance of Postmodernism comes from one of its practitioners, in praise of one of his peers. John Barth praises Jorge Luis Borges for demonstrating, 'how an artist may paradoxically turn the felt ultimacies of our time into material and means for his work – paradoxically because by doing so he transcends what had appeared to be his refutation' (Barth in Lodge 1970, 245). After Modernism's legacy of a diseased language, an imperfect memory and subjective perception how was one to write? As Borges and other Postmodern writers have shown, the process of discourse itself must be raised to a higher status and by understanding our communicative media our understanding of life, or 'reality' can only benefit. The ultimate concerns of Richard Kearney and Rüdiger Imhof lie here. Like the subjects of their studies, Joyce, Beckett et al., their aim is to consider the texture of the relationship between empirical reality and the imagining mind. As I will demonstrate hereafter, some contemporary Irish novelists respond to Joyce and Beckett as well as to Rilke, Garcia Marquez, Nabokov and Calvino, among others. Those authors who respond to the challenge of the apparent Modern and Postmodern impasse in a constructive way form the centre of this book although they vary greatly in their particular responses. John Banville, after flirting with fabulation in his earlier work, sought to expand the horizons of the historical novel in *Doctor Copernicus* and *Kepler* before returning to his invented Ireland in *The Newton Letter*, *Mefisto* and *The Book of Evidence*, and more recently with *Ghosts* and *Athena* he presents a highly imaginative virtual reality glistening with artistic connotations. The condition of writing is always a constituent part of his fictions. Aidan Higgins too responds to his predecessors in a less formal, less obviously invented way than Banville. His novels try to comprehend reality, memory and perception almost to the point of distraction. Such difficulties undoubtedly contribute to the author's writing of travel pieces and memoirs, as well as novels. In addition, Neil Jordan admits that he finds the novel form very difficult compared to his other chosen medium, film. This is a direct result of his problem with the deconstructed form in which he inherited the novel after Modernism. His peculiar response vacillates between what Waugh would consider metafiction and an interesting, if not always successful, attempt to fuse various metamorphosis myths in an attempt to evade the problems of representational fiction.

These three writers form the focal centre of my argument that the apparent *impasse* brought about by developments in Modernist and Postmodernist thinking is only feasible in the context of a belief that one can say the world in a literal, representational way. This is a pervasive fiction in itself and is, in the context of the history of English and Irish literature, a very eccentric notion with which to begin. The dominant mode of literary discourse in medieval English literature is symbolic and non-literal, emerging as it does, largely, from the Hellenic oral tradition. The celebration of a story made valuable in the telling is an ancient tradition in western culture, irrespective of its direct representational accuracy. The following chapters will attempt not to suggest that these three writers try to repair the gap between word and thing but to imply a movement towards non-representational fictions which aims to maintain a relationship with life, an endeavour which Joyce was certainly engaged in when he parodies, not simply representational literature, but our peculiar belief in its possibility. The purpose of this opening chapter, then, is to create a critical context within which the fictions of Higgins, Banville and Jordan can be placed. I have attempted to construct a containable schema based on a diverse range of ideas and literary models in order to generate both specific and general debate hereafter. Availing of McHale's differences, Waugh's (among others) self-reflexivity, Kearney's and Imhof's literary models and comparative analysis with other practitioners of Modernist and Postmodernist fiction I will evaluate the work of three very different authors whose works share epistemological and ontological doubt, to varying degrees, and in doing so draw wider significance for contemporary fiction.

CHAPTER 2

Aidan Higgins: The Fragility of Form

'That time, that place, was it all your own invention, that you shared with me? And I too perhaps was your invention...' Aidan Higgins, *Helsingor Station and Other Departures*

2.1 Prelude

Responding to Modernism's demonstration that the narrative strategies of the nineteenth century mimetic novel constructed a specific style, rather than a simplistic correspondence with life, Aidan Higgins confronts the impasse between language and existence, experience and perception and how memory transforms historical reality into imagination. The strategies that he uses are as varied as the literary genres that he explores. While some of his texts are autobiographies and others are various mutations of the novel form, all are extremely autobiographical. As Higgins informs us: 'Most of my books, very slow to appear, follow my life, like slug trails...I don't invent anything – all the fiction happened' (Higgins 'Writer in Profile' 1971, 13). It is clear, even from the scant autobiographical detail entrusted to the dust jackets of Higgins's books that his fiction is closely related to his life. Furthermore his autobiographical work and travel writing frequently confirm and elucidate the fictional events in his novels. One of the difficulties with Higgins's work is that fiction and autobiography frequently merge to create universes of highly imaginative flickers of real life, neither fiction nor autobiography in the traditional sense. For this reason it is important to include the author's travel-writing and autobiographical pieces in this study. Also, as I will hereafter clarify, these works are as crucial to an understanding of the author's artistic endeavours as are the novels and short stories.

Aidan Higgins's work is part of the critical tradition in Irish fiction because, like Joyce and Beckett, he interrogates the meaning of language, memory, perception and existence in an effort to respond to the debate initiated by Modernism. This interrogation always involves the author's attempts to translate his own experiences into literary form and, like many of his Modernist predecessors, in so doing he discovers the intense complexity that underpins such an impulse. Unlike the mainstream of contemporary Irish fiction writers, who still practice what is essentially mimetic fiction, Higgins initially confronts epistemological issues, and later, as his work develops, ontological ones. George O'Brien sees Higgins as an heir of Joyce's and Beckett's effort to comprehend life under new rules: 'Higgins follows Joyce and Beckett in not looking away, in finding a means of saying what seldom gets said, in speaking his dissenting being' (O'Brien 1989, 92). For Higgins, discourse must prevail despite the problematic nature of his medium and his perception. There are moments of intense artistic difficulty, as there must be, and there are moments of abject failure in his writing, which perhaps there shouldn't be, but Higgins confronts the legacy of Modernism and in doing so maintains the interrogative discourse perpetrated by a short list of adventurous Irish writers since Joyce.

When viewed in retrospect, the work of most writers reveals specific characteristic concerns, which are revisited throughout their lives and Higgins is no different. Higgins's primary recurring epistemological concern has always been with the past, and how it relocates itself in memory, or imagination. Thus, the events that his various heroes recount are never as poignant as their aftermath. In the fiction this is frequently expressed in the shape of dissolved or dissolving love affairs, potent emotional themes from which the author is always able to remove himself and finger through their debris with the detachment insisted upon by Joyce's and Eliot's Modernist poetics.[7] Therefore, while the author has always been fixed on perpetrating an almost masochistic analysis of his past, the work has managed to maintain an artistic distance that allows his narrators, not always happily, to confront the immense devastation inherent in the truth of transience. What follows, then, is an analysis of Higgins work (1960–96) in the context of some of the critical perspectives outlined in Chapter 1, but the author's exploration of the past, love and, ultimately, the relationship between the mind that perceives and the world in which it finds itself, will inevitably form the nucleus of this chapter.

2.2 The Constraints of Form

Aidan Higgins's first work of fiction, *Felo De Se*, is a merciless portrait-painting exercise, merciless in that the characters he sketches in the six short stories are frequently treated with disdain by the narrator, and always presented as inadequate and absurd. Higgins's characters fumble their way through various landscapes including Ireland, England, South Africa and Germany. The plots are relatively plausible and are particularly adept at recording place-names and indigenous factual information. Fundamentally, the stories are realistic scenarios within which Higgins assembles his confused characters. Layer upon layer of description is crammed into each narrative in an effort to construct vivid pictures. In this respect Higgins succeeds, almost flawlessly. Also conspicuous, in these early stories, is the author's bleakness of vision. Emily-May Kervick, one of four sisters who inhabit Springfield House in the story 'Killachter Meadow' is one of the narrator's favourite targets:

> Her entire corporeal presence had the unknown quality of things stared at so often that they are no longer seen. Her condition was one of unrelieved embarrassment. Here was a person who had run out of enthusiasms early on in life and in the halls of her spirit, so to speak, toadstools grew. (Higgins 1960, 15)

The Spanish title to the collection of stories reveals the primary thematic design of the author and indicates the reason for the brutally satirical characterisation of Emily-May. *Felo De Se*, translated as *felons of ourselves*, elucidates the author's true target. Higgins's apparently callous evocation of his characters' flaws is not intended to randomly ridicule human frailty. Rather he accuses certain of his characters of committing felonies against themselves, the worst one being inertia. All the stories detail episodes of struggle in a world that evades comprehension. Eddie Brazill, the main protagonist of 'Asylum', is an emigrant labourer and factory worker in a world indifferent to his toils, so indifferent that it nudges him towards destitution. Mr. Vaschel, of 'Nightfall on Cape Piscator', an unsuccessful antique dealer, suffers from an advanced state of lethargy which utterly confounds him: 'By the sea Mr. Vaschel walked alone with his troubles, though what his troubles were he could not say' (Higgins 1960, 183). The Kervick sisters, Eddie Brazill and many of the characters who people *Felo De Se* invent excuses to avoid confronting the mental and physical aridity in which they wallow. This refusal to accept the 'responsibility of feeling' (Higgins 1960, 43), is their outstanding felony.

Generally, *Felo De Se* avails of the conventions of realist fiction. Higgins creates well-defined characters that suffer from credible human shortcomings but the plots tend to stray from sequential narrative. Instead the author creates spatial narratives within which the temporal sequence is subverted in order to painstakingly focus on vibrant moments. Obviously the thematic concerns are appropriate for this minimalist narrative focus and Higgins's creations appear to exist in a nauseating vacuum. Patrick O'Neill claims that Higgins's characters typically 'emerge abruptly out of nowhere, are subjected to a portrait painter's penetrating scrutiny, and disappear again into the darkness from which they came' (O'Neill 1990, 95). O' Neill's assertion implies that Higgins's creations are instances of the author's art rather than realistic characters. To a large extent, he is correct and the primary cause is the density of language used. The claustrophobic quality of the stories is intense and such a state is achieved primarily by the author's use of layered, descriptive language. Roger Garfitt locates his difficulty with *Felo De Se* in these terms:

>...the external world of experience is accurately perceived, but it is rendered into a dense, highly subjective linguistic structure which becomes finally a bulwark against the experience itself. Reality is internalised. (Garfitt 1975, 225)

Garfitt proceeds to contrast Higgins's 'linguistic structure' to John McGahern's 'bare style', asserting McGahern's approach is more courageous because it allows 'experience' to have the last word. Or the illusion of experience surely! Garfitt is accurate in his assertion that reality is internalised in *Felo De Se*, as it must be. He is also accurate in recognising that the world of experience is rendered into a dense, highly subjective linguistic structure. Because the author wishes to imprison his readers, as well as his characters, in moments of inertia, he creates dense, subjective constructs, much like Joseph Conrad's early Modernist text, *Heart of Darkness* does, in its efforts to show Marlow's difficulty in communicating a sense of his experiences. Furthermore, that Higgins creates narratives that are linguistically dense is no error. To tell a believable tale employing the sparse language and realistic devices of traditional fiction is not Higgins's aim. Unlike McGahern, Higgins's narratives are expressions of the problematic nature of communication. None of his characters communicate effectively, indeed, they strive to evade contact with others. More importantly, by avoiding sequential narration, the author's discomfort with traditional narrative modes is registered. Instead the stories of *Felo De Se* expose the barren condition of passivity by presenting surreal, linguistic instances within which the perceptive eye of their creator carries more import than that of the creations themselves. Higgins communicates his intent because the foregrounding of such elaborate, subjective language reveals that the plots themselves, although obviously important constituent parts, are subservient to the act of telling.

Thus Higgins's *Felo De Se* is not simply a collection of realistic tales despite the vivid descriptions he uses to weave his scenes. Aside from the author's polished linguistic veneer, other aspects seep through the narratives to indicate the unashamed artificiality of the stories. One of the four sisters of 'Killachter Meadow' is absent from the narrative. The narrator refuses to inform us of her whereabouts, instead tersely informing us that 'she is not in this story' (Higgins

1960, 13). Effectively, the illusion of reality is disturbed. She is not of relevance to the narratorial emphasis of the text and thus she is effectively omitted. Similarly, Fraulein Sevi Klein of 'Lebensraum' actually fades out of existence, the author having finished with her:

> He watched her evaporating, crawling into her background, not declining it, deliberately seeking it, lurching away from him to stumble into a new medium (a way she had), beating down the foreshore...for an instant longer she remained in sight, contracting and expanding in the gloom, and then she was gone. (Higgins 1960, 40)

Higgins peoples his stories with mere flickers of characters. The stories contain the genesis of his later work in that the characters evoke the author's vision of transience. Irwin Pastern, the primary figure of 'Tower and Angels' informs us: 'Perhaps nothing ends, he suggested, – only changes' (Higgins 1960, 167). Higgins's characters fade in and out of his stories in a transitory fashion and resurface again and again in different guises. That his characters may have a basis in reality is secondary to their relevance to his artistic intent.

Aidan Higgins's short fictions, especially 'Killachter Meadow' and 'Lebensraum' suffer from the sheer weight of their own ambition. The medium is simply too brief to embrace the range of themes with which he grapples. The characters transcend the status of characters because they evolve into symbols of greater issues. Sam Baneham recognises too that the stories cannot contain their characters: 'Indeed it is a feature of Mr. Higgins's short stories that, while all of the characters compel attention, some through their originality burst from the constraints of the form and seem in search of a novel' (Baneham 1983, 171–2). Higgins responds to this imbalance in his later work and re-engages some of those issues that arise in the stories. The two more accomplished stories, 'Killachter Meadow' and 'Lebensraum' prompt expansion. 'Lebensraum' symbolises the theme of travel through Sevi Klein who '...had travelled all her life and would probably continue to do so until the day of her death...so that she would be always out of reach' (Higgins 1960, 39–40). *Images of Africa*, Higgins's first travel book, is only the first of many remarkable travel pieces that contribute to and extend the scope of the author's fictions. 'Killachter Meadow' also prompts further development. The story touches upon many major issues with such brevity and alacrity that Higgins's first novel is a welcome extension to 'Killachter Meadow'.

2.3 Existential Irrelevance and the Big House

Langrishe, Go Down retains much of the narrative detail of 'Killachter Meadow'. Again, there are four spinster sisters who inhabit a big house near Celbridge. Imogen has an affair with Otto Beck, a German student. Tess is renamed as Lily and does not participate except in a peripheral role. Emily-May, who commits suicide in 'Killachter Meadow', dies of phlebitis, an inflammation of a vein, a condition that often arises from complications with varicose veins. Helen reappears, and is as lethargic and limited as in 'Killachter Meadow'. The novel retains the stereotypical big house themes of decay and inertia and much of the imagery powerfully evokes the collapse of a class. However, a few minor details change. The girls' surname changes from Kervick to Langrishe as does that of Otto from Klaefisch to Beck.

Like 'Killachter Meadow', *Langrishe, Go Down* recounts the sterile existences of the girls and in general views them with a discerning eye. The love affair between Imogen and Otto is the most obvious development. It merited only scant mention in the story. At the centre of the novel the tempestuous relationship stands like a beacon, from which many of the other ideas in the text radiate. Availing of the traditional big house emblems, Higgins creates an inspired tale of the dissolution of a culture. He depicts the passing of Ascendancy values into the modern world whose new values conflict with the old. Higgins's attempt to evoke the plight of the Langrishe family gains much of its impetus from the traditional genre of decay. The continued use of big house themes in Irish fiction has prompted Seamus Deane to identify a poverty within the tradition (Deane 1977, 317–29). Understandably, Deane views a continued dependence on what he see as the Yeatsian version of Anglo-Irish romanticism as restrictive and sterile. However, Higgins's *Langrishe* does not fit cosily into the Yeatsian ideal. Higgins avails of the genre but only in a formal sense. There are many levels of significance in the novel which resonate far beyond the traditional theme of decay. Vera Kreilkamp argues that Higgins redefines the form and reinvents it and, placing Higgins in a Joycean tradition, recognises the similarity of 'carefully particularised settings'. These settings are, in fact, the actual settings of Higgins's youth but Kreilkamp accurately suggests that the author is ultimately concerned with not just his own birthplace but with history itself:

> In its most painful moments *Langrishe Go Down* is about the loss of historical memory, and even more painfully, about living in a world where history itself has been transmuted into the debris of civilisation. For Stephen Dedalus, 'history is a nightmare', for Helen Langrishe, history consists of the dead monuments of a dead culture. (Kreilkamp 1985, 30)

The opening to *Langrishe, Go Down* contains many telling implications for the novel. Helen travels homewards on a bus reading *The Evening Herald*, and the dynamic news of violent troubles in the world greatly contrasts with the stagnation of the world we are about to enter. A new kind of civilisation is being ushered in. General Franco has spoken of a free Spain and the Italians are arming. These vibrant moments, in the evolution of humanity, contrast sharply with Helen's enclosure in the mausoleum of her own deceased culture.

Higgins weaves many levels of meaning into his fiction by utilising the big house theme, essentially a symbol of transience. Firstly, and most overtly, the history of the Langrishe estate and its position in Irish history is a source of torment, particularly to Helen. While visiting Donycomper cemetery, where her parents and her sister are buried, Helen encounters an aged workman who proceeds to provide her with his version of local history. Helen's response is pitiful:

> This old man is speaking to me, telling me all over again the history of my home that I never bothered to know; or if I did by chance know it once, did not bother to remember…No doubt irrefutable facts about dead people and places which still

exist. I hear it. In my head I hear it? Do I? No, I hear nothing, remember nothing, am nothing. (Higgins 1987, 64)

Echoing Higgins's own personal history, Helen's home is one into which the family moved and thus the history is someone else's history. Her past does not extend beyond the family itself into which she perpetually delves, having nothing else to reclaim from the past. She creates in her memory an ordered movement towards her present situation, a movement in which little changes, '…variations apart (the passing of her parents, the death of Emily), in the immutable order of events' (Higgins 1987, 23). This is the source of her ultimate tragic disintegration. Beyond experiences, which congeal into memories, there is little. Helen's memories are sparse and thus she has practically nothing. Imogen's musings on Helen, after she dies, elucidate the sad condition of her life: 'And is it not strange, most strange, that a life which can be so positive, so placed, going on for years, seemingly endless, can one day go; and which is strangest of all, leave little or no trace?' (Higgins 1987, 243) Helen's contact with the outer world is extremely limited, a condition of her heritage and her personality. More powerfully than Imogen, Helen represents the isolationism and demise of her class because she does not manage to break through the cocoon of her own history. She can do nothing but cling to her paralysed past:

> In the silence the room turns on its axis and all the sounds rush back to me…what more is there to say. It seems I have lived here all my life and will very likely die here. History begins and ends in me. In me, now, today. (Higgins 1987, 74)

Helen symbolises her class splendidly, a class that fingers through its brittle past and will not, perhaps cannot, evolve and greet the new forces that are being born. Alternatively, Imogen survives, due to her liaison, however brief or destructive, with the outer world in the shape of Otto Beck.

Otto resides in the lodge of Springfield house rent-free, a favour bestowed upon him by Imogen's father prior to his death, a favour which Mr. Beck decides to recall although the old man is dead for a considerable number of years. Otto, parodically, is completing a thesis: '…investigations into seventeenth century

Ireland and Irish customs of that time, and earlier engaged on philological studies into the story of Ossian,* with reference to the brothers Grimm, Hebbel, Hamann' (Higgins 1987, 153). Imogen initially considers the attentions of Otto to be over-familiar and to be those of an upstart who is out of his social depth. The relationship which then ensues, swiftly reverses their positions as she becomes the inferior one. She may have the superiority of class but he has knowledge and information. The modern world registers its evolution through them. Imogen quickly concedes to his superior position: 'I wouldn't mind being his trollop...he could do anything he wants with me. What else is my useless woman's flesh good for?' (Higgins 1987, 91). She desires to be pillaged by him as a woman and as a member of her class (he poaches the dwindling estate and charges goods to their account in Celbridge). Nevertheless, she believes her time with Otto to be a 'time of courage and hope' (Higgins 1987, 162). The novelty of the relationship, despite its hazardous dependence on Otto's whims, breathes through Imogen's staid life carrying a promise of hope.

Ultimately the relationship ends, Otto not being content with the charms of one woman's flesh or mind. He apparently conducts another affair with one Molly Cushen to whom we are unfortunately not exposed. Nevertheless Imogen cherishes the memory, a memory which is exclusively hers, and not that of her family: 'I was not myself, yet never have I lived more in my senses...he entered me in such a way that I forgot to be ashamed...openly I gave myself to that ardour...I partake of him, his body, his past which I know nothing of' (Higgins 1987, 171). By virtue of her relationship with Otto, Imogen is released from the prison of her uneventful past. In a fruitless life, she lives a little. The remainder of her life is deeply affected by the relationship and therefore the pain was worth enduring. Imogen grows to understand that 'nothing is ever left, abandoned, but moves on' (Higgins 1987, 229). Things do not end but they must change. Sam Baneham evaluates Imogen's relationship with Otto in a positive light: 'She finds redemption in action, whereas Helen withdraws into nostalgic isolation, which is the gateway to a kind of catatonic existence' (Baneham 1983, 174). However,

Imogen's redemption is achieved at great cost. She miscarries their child and eventually finds solace only in alcohol. When Otto departs her life falters and thereafter 'One grey drab lifeless day followed another' (Higgins 1987, 244). Nevertheless at the close of the novel Helen has died, having withered away physically and emotionally, while Imogen remains. Her prospects are bleak. She is growing old and her home is seriously threatened by outside forces. However, her closing note in the fiction registers subdued hope, a kind of hope that Helen never expresses in the entire narrative:

> On the shadowed windowsill a few dead flies remained, leftovers. Hide away here, let the days pass and hope that things will change. Clouds were slowly passing across the window. Yes, that – or nothing at all. How the wind blows today. (Higgins 1987, 271)

For Imogen, life will go on, even though the note of hope is tenuous. Either way, the wrenching and pain associated with the symbolic catastrophe that Otto represents has a devastating effect. She has lived, yes, but at the end of the narrative, the compensatory memories are anaemic fare.

That Helen's death occurs in 1938 is noteworthy. It coincides with the annexation of Austria by Hitler. With Helen's symbolic passing, the Ancestral home is truly dissolved. Totalitarian regimes are expanding and strengthening in Europe and the old order is gasping its final breath. The relevance of the headlines in *The Evening Herald* is clear. Similarly, Otto Beck's relationship with Imogen begins in 1932, the year when Hitler held most seats in the Reichstag. Also Beck admires Martin Heidegger who was to be the first Nationalist Socialist Rector to be appointed to Freiburg University. In this way he personifies the new totalitarian culture even though he voices distaste for the Nazi party. It is apt indeed that he should invade Imogen's flesh with such barbaric arrogance. Thus the events of *Langrishe, Go Down* are magnified to include a larger cultural focus. Higgins, by using Otto as the real, and symbolic, threat to the Ancestral world, expands the traditional formula of the genre. Unlike other big house novels in which the impending demise of the Ancestral home is reinforced by a Catholic peasant threat, Higgins's belligerent originates in Europe, from a new, powerful culture based on racism and hatred of inertia, which the Ascendancy had come to personify.

Otto Beck, like Helen and Imogen, reaches back into his past but with a different focus from their nostalgic yearnings. He burrows into his past in an effort to place some order on his present life. He fails because his memories are vast quantities of facts and scholarly anecdotes that cannot give coherence to his life. Helen's attempts to locate significance in the past do not progress beyond fingering through Imogen's love letters and her father's papers. Imogen's remembrances almost always settle on Otto. However, the past does not provide any of them with much more than nostalgic solace.

The basic setting of *Langrishe, Go Down* is that of Higgins's own youth. The four spinsters correspond to himself and his three brothers. So is the author too in search of his past? I think not. Richard Kearney, in analysing the post-critical novel registers the problematic nature of such a search:

> Once this distinction between word and thing was deconstructed by Joyce and Beckett, the distance between the narrator's subjective consciousness and the historical world – which motivate the narrator's quest for meaning in the first place – was greatly diminished. (Kearney 1988, 98)

While exploring his various characters' inquiries into their respective pasts, Higgins effectively undermines the possibility of gleaning any substantial meaning from one's past. The author registers what Kearney terms the 'distance between subjective consciousness and the historical world' throughout the narrative and in doing so creates the tension which lingers at the core of the novel: 'The memories of things – are they better than the things themselves?' (Higgins 1987, 71). Imogen believes so: 'Of that time, what do I remember now? What can I recall if I try? Was he good to me? Yes. He was good to me; good for me; kind and considerate' (Higgins 1987, 58). In Part Two, when Imogen's narration is replaced by that of an anonymous narrator, the reality, or implied reality of Otto's behaviour is expressed. In this way the author diminishes the gap between reality and memory and the subjective consciousness gains supremacy over a historical reality. During one of Otto's typically sensitive moments he addresses Imogen: 'You're so soft', Otto said, staring before him with a vindictive face. 'Some soft spineless insect that's been trodden on. I can feel you beginning to curl up at the sides' (Higgins 1987, 227). Indeed! The memory of things, for Imogen, is surely better than the things themselves. By depicting the actual difference between the actuality, and the mind's conception of it, he implies the necessary consolatory nature of memory which functions as a kind of automated panacea for human consciousness. Reality is relativised by the human imagination not simply in the act of telling but in the act of self-preservation.

The big house genre acts as an appropriate structure upon which the author communicates his vision of transience. The past is an evasive entity. It may affect the present but it cannot be captured and thus the lessons it can teach are indistinct at best. Patrick O'Neill incisively evaluates Higgins's approach:

> However, for Higgins, the big house theme is clearly not just a realist portrayal of the decline of a passing age of grace, beauty and culture – though it certainly is that – but also a symbol of the inevitable dissolution of all order, all form. (O'Neill 1990, 98)

O'Neill's analysis contains the kernel of Higgins's endeavours. *Langrishe, Go Down* acknowledges the example set by Joyce and Beckett. It acknowledges that the lines of communication are down between word and thing, between the individual and his/her past, between perception and reality. It also accepts the artificial nature of synthetic ordering systems and registers Higgins's allegiance to flux. O'Neill extends his view of *Langrishe, Go Down* to include such matters: 'This suggestion of the immutability and indifference of things, the essential existential irrelevance of human beings and their concerns, is repeated through the narrative in the attitudes of the Langrishe sisters' (O'Neill 1990, 99). The bleakness of Higgins's vision finds utterance in the meaningless lives of most of his characters who plod desperately on. Higgins's characters exist on the periphery in a Modernist, Godless, loveless universe, a universe where all those things with which humanity comforts itself are absent, except memory, to which they cling tenaciously.

Langrishe, Go Down acknowledges the inheritance of Beckett and Joyce, it accepts the frailty and transience of human ordering systems but ultimately evokes a message of hope, however meagre, for humanity and its ability to communicate. All of these aspects are constituent parts to a multi-faceted fiction which always retains a power to generate discourse. Its value lies in the fact that it has the power to communicate the demise of a major cultural occasion and tells a moving and often sympathetic account of the lives of the Langrishe girls, Helen and Imogen in particular, whilst also acknowledging that order and the act of recapturing the past are problematic concepts. As such, the text attempts to fuse two seemingly paradoxical arguments. It accepts and assimilates the critical heritage of Joyce and Beckett, among others, and yet attempts to maintain a high level of power for language and perception. The central significance of such an approach is that the limitations within which we exist must be named but, in those terms, dialogue and history cannot be discarded, flawed though they may be. Higgins, all too aware of Beckett's reductionist tendencies, refuses to abandon an engagement with reality despite his foregrounding of the intellectual modes and communicative methods with which we construct that engagement. Thus, with *Langrishe*, Higgins still maintains dialogue with his world and yet takes as his primary emphasis the instability of that reality, both in terms of human consciousness and in the forms we construct to contain our experience. In this, to recall McHale and Jakobson, *Langrishe*'s 'dominant' is still an epistemological rather than an ontological one. The author is still primarily concerned with how our modes of knowledge respond to experience.

2.4 *Real* Fiction

Images of Africa relates Higgins's experiences while travelling with a marionette theatre company in Africa and, although technically travel writing, it confirms and develops the ideas already expressed in his fiction. The title of the work is informative in that the work presents the author's subjective images gleaned from his travels and does not attempt to present a realist portrayal of the actuality of Africa. The opening to *Images of Africa* reveals the linguistic emphasis of the account:

> The plunge over the equator. Flying fish sink, porpoises rise, and evening after evening the sun goes down in formations of cloud, furnace-like, dramatic as anything in Dore's illustrations to Dante. The approaches to a new continent. Such lovely leewardings! They must lead somewhere. (Higgins 1971, 11)

The impressionistic flavour of the opening promises a poetic vision about to unfold rather than a realistic travelogue. The reference to Dore's illustrations to Dante lends a surreal imagery to Higgins's vision and instantly the possibility of realism is eroded. The image of Dore's illustrations is but one intertextual instance in the work. Literary and artistic allusions litter *Images of Africa*, including references to F. Scott Fitzgerald, Joyce, Rembrandt and many others. These images conspire to add to the unreal nature of the account, shifting the focus away from reality to another realm. Clearly the author's response to his surroundings is informed as much by the rich fabric of his literary and artistic consciousness as it is by the African landscape. To further imbue the work with a non-realist texture the author tells of a talking snake that appears in a dreamlike moment to the narrator. Indeed the tone of the piece is frequently that of a dream interspersed with a longing for more dramatic or vivid life: 'One grows weary of the long sameness of the days here' (Higgins 1971, 36), and again: 'we dream of living elsewhere...on St. Helena, in the Seychelles. Endless life, endless choice' (Higgins 1971, 41).

The author's diary technique is based upon a system of imaginative flashes which create a vivid, pictorial series of images. However the narrative reports its subjective experiences without judging its surroundings, again revealing Higgins's ability to disassociate himself from personal experience. The most obvious characteristic of *Images of Africa* is the condition and substance of the author's subjective imagination and not, except in an oblique way, the terrain through which the marionette theatre travels. Far more powerfully than in *Langrishe* events, half-formed characters and dreamlike sensations all demand our attention to the extent that the outer world is of little significance.

The narrator of Higgins's story 'Lebensraum', in *Felo De Se*, assures us that 'the traveller is perpetually in the wrong context' (Higgins 1971, 39). In a sense this accounts for the impressionistic and non-committal qualities of *Images of Africa*. The narrator/Higgins glides swiftly through the landscape of Africa and touches lightly the lives of its people. To pretend to be in context or anything more than an interested, but culturally ignorant onlooker would yield little worth. The implications of Higgins's images are more profound though, than such an obvious limitation as this. More significant is that the author accepts that realist descriptions of any situations are essentially illusory, highly subjective impressions:

> Two African customs men in khaki uniforms; one sitting on a chair outside the post having his hair clipped, his dusty tufts. Flash of the scissors. The Union Jack wrapped about his neck. These are figures cut loose from a frieze; what you see of them – the little you can see of them – it's only a very small part of their existence; their existence in my eyes. It is nothing. These are unknowable shapes. (Higgins 1971, 24–5)

The incidental moments are Higgins's forte; a soldier getting his hair clipped, the disrespectful use of Britain's defunct Union Jack, the flash of scissors. Instantly the author dilutes the significance of this snapshot. It is nothing but a sliver of their lives conditioned by his discerning and exclusively subjective eye. The unknowable shapes fade into the internalised impressionism of Higgins's vision and disappear into the linguistic portrait. The ability to captivate reality in our own eyes, let alone in a word picture, is dismissed as the author reaffirms his acceptance of the discrepancy between perspective and reality and the hazardous nature of communicating reality. This is a Modernist perspective revisited and is perhaps informed by Rainer Maria Rilke. Rilke has the principal character of his novel *The Notebooks of Malte Laurids Brigge* (a text encountered by Higgins during his journey through Africa) declare:

> Is it possible that the past is false, because we have always spoken about its masses, just as if we are talking about a gathering of many people, instead of talking about the person they were standing around because he was a stranger and was dying. (Rilke, 1988; 23)

Beyond the focal point of the perceiver's attention, life carries on and thus all that one can write are flickers of life conditioned by our preconceptions, by chance, and ultimately by the language with which we attempt to transfix those flickers of experience. Higgins is not dismissing the possibility of seeing life or forming opinions. He does not dismiss man's power to enquire into life or form opinions and make decisions. Rather he is attempting to create new criteria with which one views one's surroundings. *Images of Africa* is a linguistic construct based on the author's autobiographical experience. Seeping through this experience, in a way more forceful than is possible in a novel, is the notion that chaotic unstable reality will always upset the formal structures, whether linguistic or simply preconceived expectations, which we attempt to place upon it. The 'Grey ghosts of human speech' (Higgins 1971, 38), will provide nothing more than an impression. Higgins's ultimate aim is not to dismiss these ghosts but to accept their imperfections.

That *Images of Africa* is an autobiographical piece of travel writing is extremely significant. Unlike a novel, *Images of Africa* confronts reality without the buffer zones of ordering devices and fictionalised characters and events. In the traditional sense, this is not a fiction. Yet, when Higgins's subjective imagination encounters the actuality of the African landscape it can provide only 'unknowable shapes' upon which the author imposes his poetic vision. This is not a novel and therefore it displays, in a more vivid way, that all experience is essentially appearance and the linguistic medium enforces the fictive nature of the experience. The narrator's response to this is not a positive one. Living in a state of uncertainty is a difficult condition: 'Morning air of forgotten childhood mingled with premonitions of one's lost end. Evening Benediction begins...knowing nothing, believing nothing; live a little longer, if you can' (Higgins 1971, 59). Echoing the intense epistemological doubt of Beckett's anti-heroes of the *Trilogy*, Higgins, confronted with his epistemological cul-de-sac, resolves to continue. He travels to the edge of artistic failure and then pulls back and continues to speak. Dialogue does not falter if the structures we employ to investigate life prove ineffectual in our attempts to transfix life. The conditions change. That Higgins insists on continuing his discourse at least indicates an artistic courage to confront such a vast dilemma but also proves that dialogue does not die, it simply places more faith in appearances and acknowledges that language is an ordering system and must be exploited to the fullest. *Images of Africa* clearly shows that the epistemological puzzles inherent in *Langrishe*'s fictional form, are every bit as relevant in the writing of a travel diary. *Images* reinforces the author's mistrust of 'reality' as a stable set of linguistic conventions and given truths and the ramifications for human communication are obvious. The privacy of Higgins's narratorial stream of consciousness in *Images* speaks from outside the recognisable codes of everyday discourse and thus the author discovers a voice that is unfettered by conventional practices. Furthermore, confronted with the alien landscape of Africa, it is interesting to witness the mind grappling with literary and artistic conventions that were born for a different landscape. Like Conrad's Marlow in *Heart of Darkness*, he learns that the landscape remains passively unconcerned by the imagining consciousness that attempts to 'plant[s] its grammar' to use Thomas Kinsella's phrase in the poem 'Another September' (Kinsella 1969, 198). Higgins's sceptical Modernist consciousness had already probed deeply.

2.5 The Mutability of Form

Aidan Higgins's major themes, the big house, the transience of love, dissolving cultures and the unavoidable absurdity of the human condition, are firmly established in *Langrishe, Go Down*. After his brief flirtation with travel writing, the author returns to the novel genre and revisits his characteristic themes with the ambitious and elaborate *Balcony of Europe*. In this sprawling fiction Dan Ruttle, artist, husband and illicit lover, observes and grasps at moments of his past in an effort to comprehend their significance and, in turn, his existence. Beginning in Dun Laoghaire in 1961, the narrator attempts to recall his family's past. Through Ruttle's memory we observe his parents, victims of former greatness and subsequent social decline. His embittered mother is freed from the past only in death whilst his father, amid bouts of optimistic gambling and drinking, cannot find any release: 'There was only this tenacious clinging to the old useless things. There was nothing else to cling on to. Tenacious memory could not let go' (Higgins 1972, 34). Higgins again propels his characters stumbling through the past. In Ruttle's father's case, it is because he has nothing but the glories of a past which have finally ceased with the death of his wife, who never allowed him forget the ebb in their fortunes.

After his mother's drawn-out demise, Ruttle and his wife Olivia leave for Andalusia where much of the novel is situated and where we are swiftly informed of the author's extramarital affair with Charlotte Bayless, an American Jewess and wife of one Bob Bayless. Dan and Olivia live in a part of Spain inhabited by a colony of expatriate artists, writers and various motley figures who languish on the beaches and participate in various romantic entanglements. The central impetus behind Dan Ruttle's existence is his obsessive love for Charlotte, a love which is in a constant state of turbulence and is really a series of failed beginnings. Ruttle's relationship with Charlotte provides the author with ample opportunity for expanding his more heady themes.

Balcony of Europe recollects Dan Ruttle's experiences and, inevitably, the problem of memory surfaces. Of his early life Dan is uncertain: 'All that seems to have happened, if it ever happened, long ago, belonging to someone else's past, not mine' (Higgins 1972, 43). Dan is severed, unavoidably, from his past and thus the act of recollection is problematic. Furthermore, consideration of the past inevitably leads to grief: 'That which is past is past; that which is wished for may not (cannot) come again. Certain scents imply: *a longing for what cannot come again*' (Higgins 1972, 160). The closest one can be to one's past is through the incidental things; scents and longings. Such is the nature of our connection to the past; scents which subtly recall and longings which colour our memories.

Ruttle's evasive past is but a part of his difficulty. His ability to communicate is also tenuous: 'I had no means to describe it, the world, myself, the world before myself' (Higgins 1972, 45). In a moment of despair, Ruttle tells of a moment from his youth when he couldn't articulate what he felt. Thus, the linguistic medium is complicated and this, added to his difficulty with memory, conspires to form a very uncertain base from which to tell his story. Ultimately memory becomes synonymous with imagination. The past, as we see it, is a fiction. Dan's fumbling with his memories reveals this clearly. Memory is not lost, it is transformed necessarily. Richard Kearney isolates the central theme of *Balcony of Europe* as, 'the attempt to wrest imagination from the vortex of memory' (Kearney 1982, 401). The author does not simply create Ruttle's memoirs. He probes the condition of their creation. Memory is initially questioned and then accepted, but only as a fluid entity forged from imagination as much as the reality from which the memory originally springs. The complex tissue of experience which Dan Ruttle gathers into his account registers his particular attempt to reclaim the past via his imagination.

The convoluted form of *Balcony of Europe* has been the focus of much negative criticism. Many have hastened to dismiss it unconditionally, with one critic rejecting it as 'an intelligent tourist's notebook jottings' (Lubbers 1987, 242). Similarly, John Banville asserts that the form of *Balcony of Europe* is its major flaw: 'So much fine writing is blurred and even lost in the formlessness of the book...Mr. Higgins has no sense of form' (Banville 1972, 18). Banville, however, is cautious enough to admit that form is an 'elusive quality' and refers to Joyce's *Ulysses* as the famous precedent. Alternatively the adventurous form of the novel has also been praised. Rudiger Imhof, comparing Higgins's writing to that of Proust is clearly impressed:

> ...its curious collage form is not least the result of its fundamental *raison d'être*: a ruminating narratorial consciousness trying to come to grips with the past, one that in the process of recollecting makes use of everything that comes to hand – impressions of people, places, events, biographical detail, epiphanies; semantic play...(Imhof 1992, 258–9)

Imhof proceeds to suggest that the aim of such an approach may be to transcend the Proustian *recherché* heritage 'in the direction of what may be termed a "total book"'. Robin Skelton too claims that there is a cohesive power in *Balcony of Europe* that lends to the novel an intricate unity:

> ...Higgins creates connections and correspondences, a web of echo and allusion which run underneath his novels. They are part of the sensibility of the narrator, whose mind, whose mirroring mind is composed of so many fragments of myth, of poetry, of learning, and of experience; they are also, however, the mind, the consciousness of the novel itself. (Skelton 1976, 35)

If Skelton's evaluation of Higgins's novel is even relatively accurate then there is something of rare quality in *Balcony of Europe*. Does Skelton's 'consciousness of the novel itself' suggest that Higgins has achieved what Imhof calls the 'total book'? Perhaps. How well this consciousness adapts to the psychosis inevitable when imagination confronts reality, or the reality of memory, is central to the success of Higgins's endeavours.

How well does Higgins's collage hold together? Higgins claims of the novel: 'I wanted to dispense with plot, do it that way: tenuous associations that would ramify, could be built upon, would stay in the mind better than the plotted thing – all lies anyway' (Higgins in Beja 1973, 163). So the author, rejecting sequential plotted narrative for spatial narrative, refuses to avail of chronological order in an attempt to surpass the intrinsic inaccuracy of that order. To impose sequential narrative on his fiction would be to ignore the Modernist rejection of nineteenth century fiction. Similarly, it would imply that the past is an ordered structure. Dan Ruttle is aware that this is inaccurate from an early age: '...the

Jesuit fiction of the world's order and essential goodness, stretching out ahead like the white guide lines. No' (Higgins 1972, 43). So what is the alternative? Higgins's fiction strives to a form but not to an order in the traditional sense. The secret to his aim can be found in one of the rejected epigraphs to *Balcony of Europe*. The epigraph, taken from Edmund Husserl, although rejected, is nevertheless printed at the rear of the text with a number of others:

> This world now present to me, and every waking 'now' obviously so, has its temporal horizon, infinite in both directions, its known and unknown, its intimately alive and its unalive past and future. Moving freely with the movement of experience which brings what is present into my intuitional grasp, I can follow up these connections of the reality which immediately surrounds me, I can shift my standpoint in space and time, look this way and that, turn temporarily forward and backwards; I can provide for myself constantly new and more or less clear and meaningful perceptions and representations, and images more or less clear, in which I make intuitable to myself whatever can possibly exist really or supposedly in the steadfast order of space and time. In this way, when consciously awake, I find myself at all times, and without ever being unable to change this, set in relation to a world which though its constants change, remains one and ever the same. (Higgins 1972, 461)

Higgins's spatial narrative is aimed at achieving Husserl's state of perception. His success is, however, not determined simply by the inclusion of an epigraph which might hope to act as a gelling agent for an otherwise disparate collection of elements. Charlotte Bayless acts as a focal point for many of the associations and implications generated in the novel. She is an American Jewess with whom Dan conducts a quasi-affair. Each of these aspects is cultivated in an effort to broaden the perspective of the narrator. Dan, caught up in the throes of his obsession, allows his imagination to roam freely through history. Within a few lines Dan likens Charlotte to the American gangster, Dillinger (because of her childhood nickname, Dilly), refers to her Jewishness, and claims she has high Slav cheekbones and a Byzantine nose. All these flashes of experience converge in Charlotte who 'comes from the dark plains of American sexual experience where the bison still roam' (Higgins 1972, 77). Dan, of tired 'forty-six Christian Old World years' marvels at Charlotte's 'bright twenty-four Jewish New World years'(Higgins 1972, 78). In her, many moments of history meet. Dan's imagination tries to discover Charlotte's past and dreams up many scenarios: 'She might have ended her days as a Jewess in Auschwitz. As a child holding on to her mother's skirt, an actress from an old silent movie' (Higgins 1972, 289). Dan juxtaposes history, reality and film and then forms an image which adds further dimensions to Charlotte. Her character, salvaged from Jewish and Polish heritage, Auschwitz, America and Spain, becomes for Ruttle a symbol of historical reality itself. In her the past converges and he imagines that he can witness her as such: 'She speaks from the back of the throat, the epiglottis, a complex human being's speech, made up of all her ancestors and past' (Higgins 1972, 78). In this way the narrator conjures up history; by gathering fragments from many areas he imagines a past life for Charlotte and in doing so creates her: 'I dreamed her as she dreamed me' (Higgins 1972, 390). Charlotte exists in the novel only in this way. She does not exist as a character in traditional terms. All her movements and dialogue are imbued with associations which generate a kind of super-reality throbbing in Dan's consciousness.

The collage of history that erupts in Dan's account, prompted by images of Charlotte and his imagining mind, resonates throughout the novel. The figure of Baron von Gerhar, an ex-Nazi with whom Dan drinks on one occasion, powerfully lingers in the fiction as a constant reminder of the atrocities committed against the Jews. Although not a central figure in the narrative, the Baron symbolises a whole era by his presence. Dan's direct discussion about the Jews, concentration camps and Hitler, and his choice of imagery, does much to charge the incident with significance: '…fixing me with his red-rimmed killer's eyes, he put it point blank' (Higgins 1972, 110). All this occurs while American warplanes slice the skies over Andalusia and while Dan Ruttle's mind acts as a focal point for movements in the past and present. From the aptly named *Balcon de Europa* bar, Dan observes past and present images coalescing and in doing so his vision emerges. There are numerous other incidents that contain associations that knit the fiction together, without availing of a recognisable arrangement of cause and effect, so much so that many of Higgins's critics are unable to perceive a form to the text. The only real structure in the fiction is Ruttle's mind which eagerly brings these strands of meaning together, and his mind does not always work in familiar patterns. Imagination, it is implied, generates its own order.

The ramifications, coaxed into existence, do not end here. Dan's love for Charlotte eventually expresses the central concern of the author. Their love is a doomed, romantic affair, as are all truly romantic literary affairs. Initially Charlotte makes Dan feel rejuvenated and perhaps this is the part of their relationship that matters most: 'Being with her, I felt lifted out of my lethargy and sloth, from the banality that encumbered my life; this small bright-faced person had that effect on me'(Higgins 1972, 126). Because of this new enthusiasm Dan's imagination is freed to recreate her in the context of his dreams and impressions. When recollecting, however, Dan realises she is utterly lost to him: 'Two dead actors, a cinema that no longer existed in a narrow street so changed I hardly knew it, as dead and non-existent as my own youth. Non-existent as any touch I ever had with her' (Higgins 1972, 120). In the realm that is Ruttle's mind, the past is transformed into a vague image, directly informed by the cinema and dead actors. The past may be reclaimed, recollected, coloured by imagination but essentially it is non-existent. It remains like the blurred images on a cinema screen, remote and unreal despite what it might whisper to us in moments of nostalgia or longing. Dan learns valuable lessons from his recollections. Once those images which the past communicates are accepted as just images then one's perspectives on living alter correspondingly. Primarily through Charlotte, Dan responds to this understanding: 'She had pale Polish eyes. She is there. She is my opposite, yet part of me. She who appears so permanent, is transitory – a souvenir' (Higgins 1972, 290). Life is altered. The past teaches us that living is transitory as are all the moments which contribute to that life. She who consumed Dan's existence for a time has vanished. All that remains is the souvenir of memory. Ruttle learns that there are no constants, only impermanence. Armed with the lessons of his youth he realises even when the affair is being conducted that Charlotte is not a fixed shape: 'So she would always escape me, changing shapes, changing clothes as she changed her lovers, changing her style as she changed her admirers' (Higgins 1972, 203). The imaginative power of Ruttle's account of Spain lingers in the reader, but for him, late in the text, everything of that time has evaporated: 'I thought of the time in Spain: those transient friends which events bring and events take away' (Higgins 1972, 455). The former intimacy of those dissolved days is cast aside by the passing of time, just as with all his past. Life, then, is emphatically shown to be a volatile construct in the narrator's mind. Impermanence is the dominant characteristic of life for Dan. It is not an ordered construct where things exist but a fluid series of beginnings which never cease. He finally realises that his experiences exist only in his mind. Of Charlotte he claims, '[y]ou had existed as part of the seminal substance of the universe that is always becoming and never is: and now had disappeared into that which produced you' (Higgins 1972, 239). Via his love of Charlotte and his attempt to recollect it, Dan realises that living is essentially fluid and the universe he comes to understand is constantly becoming. There is no stasis. Each day our lives change and move unalterably forward leaving behind a trail of memory. This is the kernel of Higgins's fiction. Life, Dan tells us, must be accepted as such: 'There are no fixtures in nature. The universe is fluid and volatile. Permanence is but a word of degrees. Our globe seen by god is a transparent law, not a mass of fact' (Higgins 1972, 352). *Balcony of Europe* registers, through its amassing of historical detail and impending wars, coupled with the account of Ruttle's failed love and acute awareness of his own transience, the chaos of living; it is ultimately a lament for what Higgins sees as the unavoidable breakdown of order. However, although a lament, *Balcony of Europe* suggests, in its optimistic moments, that impermanence is not necessarily a destructive element. If one accepts transience and the true nature of our memories then our present lives may become bearable, or at least understandable. During a meditative moment near the close of his account Dan considers the folklore of Aran: 'Aran, it is said, is the strangest place on earth. Sometimes for an hour you are, the rest is history; sometimes the two culminate in a dream' (Higgins 1972, 446). The present and the past converge and the dream born from such a union constitutes life in its fullest sense. Higgins moves towards an understanding of the intimate relationship between past and present. The past is knowable only through our present discourses and it is from this perpetually shifting vantage point that we inevitably reconstruct our pasts. In many respects this is the vision of existence that *Balcony of Europe* strives to be.

The complex patterns of association woven into *Balcony of Europe* combine to evoke Higgins's major themes; the transience of living and the chaotic state of human existence; but these very themes contain intrinsic implications on another level. Patrick O'Neill suggests that the novel operates on two levels: '...it is also, and overtly, a highly Modernist text, a way of presenting that world and a way of presenting its own discourse' (O'Neill 1990, 101). Any account of past events which raises the problematic issue of memory invariably challenges the validity of its own writing. Higgins's particular response to memory, and therefore to life, directly conditions the nature of his fictions. If the universe is in a state of flux, if life is ephemeral and refuses to be imprisoned by man's powers of communication, then the act of writing must respond accordingly. Not only do events alter in one's memory, but so too does the mind that remembers. Dan informs us that: 'Everything is only for a day, both that which remembers and that which is remembered' (Higgins 1972, 239). Thus, if both the present and the past are in flux then how is it possible to transcribe events or states of feeling? Higgins's fiction insists that it is not possible to transcribe life: 'To seek to paint that which cannot be painted – the Deity's human form – was considered by the wise ancients to be human imbecility' (Higgins 1972, 166–7). Upon this artistic principle, the text is built. Dan accepts the true nature of memory and in doing so he refrains from a realist portrayal of life. His account implicitly suggests that flux is a constituent part of memory. Therefore the text must be constructed in a way that rejects the traditional realist novel. Higgins declares his attitude towards realistic fiction openly in the novel: 'The rule of desire for realistic possession: to hold a great power within a small volume' (Higgins 1972, 325). The role of realism, it is implied in fiction, is a possessive one, an attempt to possess in its entirety. Framed, as they were, in such realistic, possessive narrative forms, many nineteenth century novels embraced moral and political agendas which relegated 'reality' to an inferior role, in their desire to take possession of that reality. *Balcony of Europe* seeks to redress that situation in its evocation of a landscape that is not subjected to any agenda by the author. Alternatively, the author constructs an image of the world which evades all such arrogant attempts to name the world with such certainty.

Balcony of Europe registers a connection with the real world even if not in the same way as realist fiction. The novel attempts to invent a new type of discourse, within which the author can speak about human existence. One of the ways he does so is by rendering the novel self-reflexive. Richard Kearney views the epigraphs to be of major significance in this regard: '...they render the novel' self-reflexive: the epigraphs turn the writing back on itself, they mirror the attempt of the novel itself to write back itself, against time' (Kearney 1982, 401). The rejected epigraphs are especially significant because, although discarded, they are printed at the rear of the novel and thus form part of the available text. Already quoted is Husserl's visionary epigraph which mirrors Higgins's formal aim. Kafka too is included and, like Higgins, his difficulty is with the past:

> Nothing is granted to me, everything has to be earned, not only the present and the future, but the past too – something after all which perhaps every human being has inherited, this too must be earned, and it is perhaps the hardest work. When the earth turns to the right – I am not sure that it does – I would have to turn to the left to make up for the past. (Higgins 1972, 462)

Obviously Kafka's sentiments translate directly into the forging of *Balcony of Europe*, and in its most despairing moments, when Dan grapples with the ghosts of his past in an effort to reclaim them, or earn them, Kafka's words ring through. The sentiments that the epigraphs contain, writerly or historical, turn the writing back on itself and render it self-reflexive and, in doing so, Higgins earns his own past, he learns to comprehend the meaning of his past. By foregrounding the textual nature of his account, partly through the use of the epigraphs, the author emphasises that the intellectual comprehension of one's own past must be accompanied by a transfiguration of the events that make up that past. The discourse, that is one's understanding of the past, must be considered in the act of *earning* the past.

Balcony of Europe is a composite of many associated elements. It questions communication, history, the transience of living, memory and the meaning of human perception. Combined with these powerful elements, it questions the process of its own formation. Its own discourse becomes one of the primary subjects of the text itself. This does not destabilise the fiction in any way, except perhaps to subtly alter the reader's perspective. There are no overt, grandiose statements concerning the nature of art in the novel, which is essentially about life. The nature of the medium simply demands that some response must be made to the problem of memory and what it means. Higgins primarily allows his artistic motivation to unfold within the narrative itself and in doing so creates a novel that addresses the condition of living while, simultaneously, being committed to his aesthetic endeavours. Each aspect complements and reinforces the other, instead of reacting against each other, and it is for this reason that *Balcony of Europe* is a truly important novel. It insists on working on two levels, refusing to operate in the highly problematic realm of the mimetic novel and refraining from the excesses of some extreme Postmodern novels which deconstruct their universes of dialogue to the point of nihilism.

2.6 Dissolving Scenes

With Higgins's third novel, *Scenes from a Receding Past*, fiction and overt autobiography meet.[9] The fiction is thus immediately compromised by the reality of Higgins's youth and birthplace. In addition, Dan Ruttle is resurrected to play the major role. Higgins has Dan plunge backwards in time to pre-*Balcony of Europe* times, even on occasion to pre-natal times. Dan's wife in *Balcony of Europe* also reappears as does Molly Cushen with whom Otto Beck has an affair in *Langrishe*. Not only do fiction and autobiography collide, so too do fictional worlds themselves. Many of the author's previous themes resurface especially, as is indicated by the novel's title, those of memory and transience.

Of the novel's two epigraphs (by Yves Berger and Richard Brautigan), Brautigan's best illustrates the tone of the novel and Dan's approach to the past:

> I do not long for the world as it was when I was a child. I do not long for the person I was in that world. I do not want to be the person I am now in that world then. I've been examining half-scraps of my childhood. They are pieces of distant life that have no form or meaning. They are things that just happened like lint. (Higgins, 1977, 10)

In *Scenes from a Receding Past* the treatment of the past is similar to that expressed in *Balcony of Europe* and the author also returns to the big house genre. In many ways *Scenes from a Receding Past* regroups many of Higgins's previous concerns and expresses them in another way.

The opening of the novel recalls *A Portrait of the Artist as a Young Man* in that Dan's youthful wonder is similar to that of Stephen. Both try to comprehend their youthful surroundings, both have problems with their names and both attend Clongowes (Dan's Clongowes wears a fictional cloak). Dan's status as an upper class Catholic denies him the privilege of being a member of either of the two traditional factions in his community and thus he struggles with his identity. He pursues the usual adolescent sexual frustrations until quite suddenly he has grown up: 'Little by little, day by day, the years go by, until they are all gone, used up, and my childhood is over, with the things of childhood. Jack Horner and Jack Spratt' (Higgins 1977, 102). The narrator attempts to reconstruct his youth, primarily to explicate the transience of it. The reconstruction is created by means of Higgins's by now familiar reliance on spatial narrative that renders the past into a selection of random vignettes. There is much pathos in Dan's reconstruction, the sketch of his brother Wally in a mental institution being the foremost example. Both his brother and his mother experience mental breakdowns which, while utilising the big house motif, create an unsettling tone of despair in the early part of the text. Later, when Dan meets Olivia the reality of his lost youth is expressed clearly in terms of her life: 'Her past, obscure enough, had become more real than my own' (Higgins 1977, 192).

Dan's fixation with the past, and his attempts to perceive it, are of major significance regarding his relationship with Olivia. Through his desire to possess her in totality, he learns the limitations of communicating past events: 'From my own imperfect memory, from no notes, from distractions and places, from my love of her, from her own retellings, emerges this rigmarole: her past that is more real than my own' (Higgins 1977, 156); more real than his own, so it seems, and yet it too is a fabrication synthesised from all the means he has available to him. Through Olivia, the assumptions of traditional realism are exposed: 'That was her past, part of it, as she told it to me, as I remember it, or what I remember of it' (Higgins 1977, 167). Olivia's past is qualified three times, questioned three times. Her version is a qualification, as is his memory, as is the possible defective nature of his memory. The inability to locate the past is a cause of grief to Dan, but nevertheless he continues piecing together the hazardous shreds of memory. In doing so Dan demonstrates how his attempt to write her biography is essentially a work of imagination. The veracity of Dan's account is thrown into disarray by virtue of his insistence on recreating whole scenes from Olivia's past: 'That place, your home, I cannot imagine it. You lived there in a house I can't quite see, walking in an overgrown garden in the heat' (Higgins 1977, 157). He cannot imagine it, yet he proceeds to build elaborate scenarios about her past. The implications that such a pursuit have for the reconstruction of his own receding past are clear. The realistic status of the story is thrown into relief. However, from the author's opening note that refers to, 'those gentle times, those guileless gossoons, [which] are now consigned to oblivion' (Higgins 1977, 10), the realistic aims of the narrative are intentionally deflated. Furthermore the nature of the narrative itself, first person present, renders the story non-realistic. Does an eleven year old boy think in terms as exotic as those espoused by the young Dan Ruttle? 'Overhead huge white clouds are piled up, vasty citadels, white castles loom'

(Higgins 1977, 37). Unlike *Scenes from a Receding Past*, *Balcony of Europe* is not a realist novel, at least in the traditional sense of the term. Ironically though, it may be closer to reality than traditional mimetic fiction which aims to preserve the illusion of truth and exactitude in reconstructing past events.

The extension of Higgins's receding past is an interrogation of human existence. When Dan first spends time away from his home, Nullamore, he imagines it to be an intransient place, a source of unchanging order: 'I miss Nullamore. I think: the place that never changes' (Higgins 1977, 107). As with everything else, time dismantles the cosy certainties of his home and real life seeps in: 'It is vacation. Nullamore seems to have shrunk' (Higgins 1977, 107). Dan's education begins here. That first certainty, that first sensing of order, one's home, wilts or Dan's imagining mind dreams Nullamore into a kind of super-reality which the actuality cannot match. Dan's desire for certainty emerges frequently in the narrative, as does his dismay when he cannot achieve it. The only fixed reality he discovers is a photograph: 'Nothing can change or disturb her. She is perfect, naked and coolly regarding me. Her expression does not change. She watches me' (Higgins 1977, 77). The certainty he cherishes is not to be found in reality and it is unsurprising that one who cherishes order becomes obsessed with chaos. By the conclusion of the novel Dan has grown to accept life in all its impermanence:

> Hold onto nothing; nothing lasts. Long ago I was this, was that, twisting and turning, incredulous, baffled, believing nothing, believing all. Now I am, what? I feel frightened, sometimes, but may be just tired. I feel depressed quite often, but may just be hungry.
> All but blind
> In his chambered hole
> Gropes for worms. (Higgins 1977, 204)

The closing image of an almost blind mole groping for worms vividly reveals Higgins's bleak vision. The author burrows deep into the past in an effort to comprehend his life and in doing so confronts the opaque reality of memory. All but blind, he understands the volatility of life and records it as such.

In many ways *Scenes from a Receding Past* interrogates the same problems as Higgins's previous novels. Higgins's major themes of transience, memory and decay emerge once again, although, arguably, *Scenes from a Receding Past* responds to the issues of memory and transience in a more direct way than its predecessors, because it is less restrained by their concessions to form, however innovative those styles might be. Fundamentally, *Scenes from a Receding Past* is an autobiography coloured lightly with the process of imaginative recollection and the nominal alteration of some details. In formal terms it is less strictly literary than *Balcony of Europe* or *Langrishe, Go Down* in that the author seems less concerned with interweaving binding associations and images. Higgins presents much incidental detail, including lists of boarding school requirements, cricket scores and many particularised geographical data. The only binding force is the narrator himself. George O'Brien recognises these qualities in the novel:

> All that Higgins unrhetorically intends to claim, it seems, is that certain materials insist on presenting themselves – memories, vignettes, moments, quotations, gossip, arcana, rage, pleasure, boredom, love...Higgins seems to say there is only the world, the other; the writer, clerk-like (attentive rather than subservient), takes – rather than raises – its stock. He proceeds in the direction of that nakedness which is more familiarly the painter's objective. Simplicity and directness unveils while leaving intact...(O'Brien 1989, 90–1)

The author allows the chaos, or those moments that demand attention, to reveal itself. Much is omitted from what might constitute the actuality of a life story. Thus the form of the novel depends on the interrelation of the moments presented. The threads of association are not strong, and beyond Ruttle's selective consciousness there is little in the way of unity. There are only 'impressions' which 'offer themselves, focus, slip away' (Higgins 1977, 200). Is this sufficient to bind a work of art? In a rare moment of overt self-reflexive advice the narrator reveals his views: 'Do as I tell you and you will find out my shape. There are no pure substances in nature. Each is contained in each' (Higgins 1977, 200). The essential unity in nature, he implies, is the source of his shape. The artist who allows landscapes to reveal themselves rather than attempt to interrogate their meaning, lets the chaos of the past life and the universe seep into the fiction. Freeing itself from the formal restraints of the novel form, *Scenes from a Receding Past* exposes itself to be just what its title suggests; scenes, and not a life bound together by illusory sequential narrative or imposing synthetic structures in search of imposed unity. In *Scenes from a Receding Past* Higgins begins to remove the frame from his pictures, an activity which reaches greater expression in his subsequent texts.

2.7 Love as Linguistic Abstraction

In *Bornholm Night-Ferry* love once again acts as the mode of experience within which Higgins's characters interrogate human lines of communication and probe the meaning of their lives. Elin, a Danish poetess, and Fitzy, an Irish novelist, conduct an illicit five-year relationship during which time they spend just forty-seven days together. The rest of the time they nurture their dramatic love with letters. Both are married parents and impecunious, thus rendering their relationship more difficult than even their geographical estrangement suggests. The fiction is an epistolary novel within which both narrators roam freely across their imaginative landscapes, declaring love, jealousy, rejuvenated love, interest, hatred and ultimately rejection. The fiction is also a fond nod towards tradition – *Bornholm Night-Ferry* contains sixty-five letters, exactly the same as are contained in Swift's *Journal to Stella* and Fitzy mentions Swift's work directly in one of his letters to Elin. The use of Swift's framework imbues the work with a vaguely tragic tone and again the framing process of the lives of Fitzy and Elin adopts a literary shape.

The linguistic density of the epistolary novel means that the nature of language is invariably probed. Secondly, because much of the content of the relationship is conducted through letter writing, and their time together is limited, the letters themselves invariably deal with reminiscences. In this regard we are on familiar Higgins territory: the search for the past and the conditioning power of memory. To say that Higgins turns the same sod each time is not altogether untrue but his understanding of his piece of soil is more refined with each plunge of his literary spade and he continually experiments with new forms to house his concerns. In a fiction comprising sixty-five letters and a few short diary pieces the issues of language, imagination and remembrance form one sustained dismissal of traditional narrative and attempt to formulate a unique way of focusing on the world in which we live. *Bornholm Night-Ferry* is a highly self-reflexive fiction, because it directly informs us of the process of its creation, and what more forceful means are there than letters between lovers/writers who struggle to keep their love, almost exclusively a linguistic one, alive.

The love letters between Elin and Fitzy trace the progression of each of their responses to memory and language. Initially, their responses to their first meeting are, inevitably, acceptances of the blurring of their sensual memories. Elin differentiates between the words she uses to recall their time together and the actuality of the experience: 'Not forgotten in words but in action. The sensual memory of you is going to disappear, replaced by reflections' (Higgins 1983, 17). Elin knows that outside of the actuality, outside of her fading sensual memory there are but '"figments of imagination", monologues' (Higgins 1983, 18). Thus, the epistolary love affair is conducted solely in their respective imaginative responses to both memory and language. Furthermore, because they are from different countries and speak different languages, they grapple with each other's tongues in an effort to create a love-language.

Initially, Elin responds to the barriers between them by gleefully pursuing her imaginative response:

> We don't know each other, no. We exited to a high degree each others' dreams. We don't know each other, we are dreaming. Everything depends on if we are clever enough to dream. And believe in our dreams. And realise our dreams so fervently we are able to (sic). (Higgins 1983, 21)

She plunges into a landscape of dreams wherein the constraints of time, language, and geography are diminished, but retained. Any other reaction is doomed to failure. To attempt to recall exactitudes or to force language up to a level of precision is to encase their love in a brittle casing. However, dreaming itself is not sustainable. The actuality of their relationship must be admitted. Neither the dream nor the actuality can be ignored. Elin pleads with Fitzy to confront this: 'Please, my beloved let us save our dream by naming the reality, let us say awfull things so the rest can be true. The ghosts grow and grow when you never face them' (sic) (Higgins 1983, 92). Let us name the reality of the limitations of our dreams, and thus save the dream. Neither the dream nor the reality can survive without acceptance of the other. Fitzy responds to this plea by refusing to accept a distinction between the two: 'As to dream (perhaps the only word we cannot put quotation marks around) and "reality", whatever that may be, well they are for me one and the same' (Higgins 1983, 93). For Fitzy, the gulf between them, between any two people, is too great to cross. The lines of communication for him provide only a dream reality. 'Does not a child', Fitzy asks, 'who knows nothing, invent the whole world?' (Higgins 1983, 94). Perhaps, but surely a child uses reason to order his inventions. Richard Kearney argues for an acceptance of both imagination and reason: 'Imagination and reason, mythos and logos, are the indispensable Siamese twins of the mind. Their surgical separation can only result in the death of both' (Kearney 1985, 179). It is questionable whether Fitzy's vision of reality constitutes a surgical separation of imagination and reason, in favour of imagination, or is the true marriage of both. However, what is certain is that if one does not recognise a distinction between Kearney's twins of the mind, psychosis is inevitable. The reality principle must remain as a constituent part of the imagination and vice-versa in order for coherent dialogue to persevere. Ultimately Fitzy falters: 'It has been going on for some time. I am dreaming it, or it is dreaming me, for some time, particulars forgotten' (Higgins 1983, 174). Reality departs, the pure dream remains and dialogue ends with the novel. The struggle to articulate the actuality of their struggle ends. Fitzy is silent and Elin is consigned to some extra-linguistic universe.

Elin refuses to dissolve her reality principle into pure imagination except in moments of extreme longing. She never loses sight of rationality, allowing herself to dream but constantly aware that she is dreaming. She warns Fitzy: 'I tell you Fitzy, I imagine you so you would die from it if you were here' (Higgins 1983, 68). Her vision of him is excessive but she knows that the actuality cannot compare to it, cannot hope to compare to it. This distinction prevails in Elin's letters and her need for sensual experience, and subsequent lack of it, leads to her estrangement. The 'unreal correspondence' (Higgins 1983, 146), cannot satisfy her as it can Fitzy. She learns to see the difference between them from this perspective:

> You never divide hope from reality, and you are not a happy person. I always divide hope from reality (try to) and am not a happy being. You refuse to see reality and I am hoping wrong hopes. This goes on: Wrong moves, failured gestures. Will it ever change? (sic). (Higgins 1983, 153)

Conducted through a linguistic medium, their love cannot survive the rigours of two opposing visions. Being separated, writing in a love language and imagining each other, hope is essential. However, for Fitzy, hope, imagination and reality all converge and express themselves in a linguistic dream world. Elin's last letter does not even conclude the relationship, meaning has long since been lost in a sea of imagination and language, and finality is a forgotten concept.

The alternate poles which Elin and Fitzy come to represent correspond to the self-reflexive discourse of the novel itself. Conveniently, the two narrators comment on each other's letters and the novel itself is in totality a commentary on the nature of fiction and the imaginative process. Initially, one experiences, then remembers, and then transforms. The two lovers lose sensual memory and conjure up many desperate methods of regaining it: 'If I cannot have you all in one piece, mail me bits of you. Du' (Higgins 1983, 73). Such ploys are, of course, little more than futile love games. Soon they grow to rely on memory with all its consequent vagaries and thus we have imaginings. Inherent in all of this is the suggestion that any attempt to linguistically apprehend a life, or the storm of emotions that frequently accompanies life, must ultimately work according to these principles. It is what one does with such knowledge within a problematic linguistic structure that is central to *Bornholm Night-Ferry*.

Bornholm Night-Ferry is one of Higgins's most overtly self-reflexive novels because it directly confronts its own medium, and in doing so interrogates the meaning of memory and the limitations of language. Furthermore it openly exposes the hazardous transformative process that is art. Elin and Fitzy both create fictions forged from their imperfect memories, language and their different responses to these aspects. 'Reality' is lost along the path to the creation of the letters. Elin registers the inadequacy of the reality principle in one of her letters: 'Your memories of us are too full of "unreliableness" but mostly more true than the reality' (Higgins 1983, 65). Reality is expressed as a collage of moving surfaces rather than a static empirically attainable actuality. The actual expression of this fact is the transformative agent. Thus, reality is raised to the level of Fitzy's and Elin's imaginings via memory and language. In this way *Bornholm Night-Ferry* comments on its own formation and its own relationship to Higgins's 'reality'.

Despite the author's obvious acceptance of the artificial nature of man's medium, language, he also acknowledges that a breakdown in dialogue is directly related to over-reliance on imagination. The affair falters and dies because the 'real', the sensual, is forsaken and replaced by a purely synthetic world of language, memory and imagination. Humanity cannot survive in such a limited framework. The sensual and the imaginative cannot survive if sundered. *Bornholm Night-Ferry* accepts that human communication is at best problematic. There are many chasms which render communication hazardous; between word and thing, memory and actuality, thought and gesture. In *Bornholm Night-Ferry*, the linguistic lovers interrogate these chasms but for them the gaps are too great and communication falters. Communication is always difficult, perhaps even impossible, in concrete terms but if the true nature of the web of human dialogue is comprehended then perhaps communication can evolve. For this reason

Higgins's self-reflexive epistolary novel is valuable. The formal fabric of *Balcony of Europe* and *Langrishe, Go Down* is relinquished, and the innards of the work are exposed. Life is a fiction that must be interpreted, or imagined, in conjunction with comprehension, however problematic, of one's sensual experience, and it is not a mass of exactitudes that we can simply name with our synthetic modes of expression.

2.8 Fictional Realities

With Ronda Gorge and Other Precipices (Travels and Autobiographies 1956–89) and Helsingor Station and Other Departures (Fictions and Autobiographies 1956–89),[10] the reader is confronted with fiction, autobiography and travel writing. Firstly, the technical demarcations between travel writing and autobiography are fine, if they exist at all. Secondly, Higgins's previous fiction tends to overlap with both travel writing and autobiography to such a degree that the lines between the genres are blurred. And thirdly, the very basis of the author's artistic vision in his previous work clearly indicates an unwillingness or inability to wholly distinguish between reality and the imagination. As Fitzy tells Elin in Bornholm Night-Ferry: 'As to dream (perhaps the only word we cannot put quotation marks around) and "reality", whatever that may be, well they are for me one and the same' (Higgins 1983, 93). Is the very idea of transforming reality into a work of art then a redundant one? If the landscapes are already shifting surfaces for the author, then the idea of fixing them in some kind of formal expression seems absurd, or arbitrarily formal. This assumption underlies both of these works and it must be carefully considered because this, ultimately, is the crux of Higgins's work.

All of Higgins's fiction tends to be autobiographical to some extent even *Langrishe, Go Down*, the author's most formal fiction, contains much autobiographical detail. It is wise to remember that Higgins's two works *Ronda Gorge* and *Helsingor Station* are selections from his previous writings and yet they still indicate the author's gradual evolution towards autobiography as a literary form which might respond to life in a more direct way than the novel. However, compiled works from a thirty-three year period must be treated with caution.

Ronda Gorge opens with a reprint of *Images of Africa*, which is, as I have previously indicated, a piece of travel writing which exposes the innate representative difficulties of the medium itself. The narrator fumbles through his versions of events providing the reader with 'unknowable shapes' (Higgins *RG* 1989, 20), upon a highly impressionistic landscape. Travel writing it may be, but the narrator's idiosyncratic contribution is the most outstanding aspect of the text. Travel writing and autobiography merge in *Ronda Gorge* as they must when the author is in perpetual motion. The response Higgins forms to his surroundings is remarkable in that it holds firm over more than a thirty-year temporal frame. The exterior world is at best indistinct but more often illusory. The familiar Higgins obsession with reality and the imagination is much in evidence. In 'Berlin Days and Nights (1969–70)' we witness the author 'throwing away reality, finding a new one' (Higgins *RG* 1989, 77). Reality is dispensable, because it is dependent on imagination, fluctuating at the whim of he who perceives: 'It is not as I had imagined it. But what ever is?' (Higgins *RG* 1989, 171) The past throws up few monuments to the author save inert relics that mean little: '"In a little time places begin to seem the only hieroglyphs that cannot be forgotten" (Yeats). Too true. A round tower, a path worn across a field by cattle, a standing stone. Wake up in golden sunshine. My past. Yours too. Go on' (Higgins *RG* 1989, 203). Such is the reality of the author's past. Living among the debris of a lost past seems to be Higgins's lot, as it must be for one who rummages so insistently among one's memories. The consequent response to his world is bleak: 'The globe and its wretched burden of history was only a dream, a bad dream only in God's head, on an off day long past, now whirled into space, nothingness' (Higgins *RG* 1989, 125). Higgins's vision extends to the other creatures who inhabit his universe. Most frequently he is indifferent or objective but occasionally he comments on the quality of life, as when he puzzles about the cinema:

> One fine summer evening, in Malaga and Athens, Copenhagen and Munich, long cinema queues waited to watch a violent surrogate existence run on huge screens, the sound monstrously distorted...Their own life had ceased to interest them. (Higgins *RG* 1989, 102)

Their own lives having ceased to interest them they turn to the constant drama and super-reality of the cinematic. Life suffers because it cannot be raised to such an extreme constant pitch. Film is a way to achieve or be close to those things, or to moments which cannot be. For Higgins's imagination this means the past: 'On fine summer evenings the long cinema queues waited silently in the north. To flee the world and dream, the past, was their intent; a sourceless craving now externalised, brought close' (Higgins *RG* 1989, 103). The tenuous grasp people have on reality is vividly enforced in the tragic vision of queues of souls in vain search of lost dreams or memories. Such, Higgins suggests, is the very substance of reality for many people.

In *Ronda Gorge* worlds continually collide. The author's impressionistic pictures perpetually drift away from the actuality that they struggle to describe. Past and present collide, painfully, as do the illusions thrown upon the movie screen with the world outside the cinema. Characters and phrases from his fictions appear in autobiographical writing, most notably from *Bornholm Night-Ferry*. Are such moments real, or not? Do they exist in the author's autobiographical world and, if so, what are the implications for his fictions? What is certain is that Higgins has, at least, lost sight of the boundaries which usually exist between fiction and autobiography. The level of confusion is more extreme than this simple generic quandary suggests. The author does not even seem to be able to grasp his own self: 'Am I or am I not the same person whom I have always taken myself to be? A hundred times no' (Higgins *RG* 1989, 182). The text is a multifarious collection of shifting surfaces upon which the ghost of what was once reality sways precariously. The strangeness of Higgins's universe is named in *Ronda Gorge* and in doing so the author blurs any remaining frontiers between fiction, autobiography and travel writing. Harry White recognises this quality in Higgins's writing:

> For Higgins, the fictional process is a restless transformation and not a finished verbal analogue of experience; it consists of a fluid accumulation of images which convey the past rather than a static composite of structural prose organised around a tangible plot. (White 1990, 212)

Because the fictional process is such a restless transformation for Higgins the divisions between genres are less explicit. Because language and memory are problematic, in a literal, representative way, travel writing and autobiography are retrieved from their historical actuality and fictionalised by the imagination. The structures normally associated with fictional narrative are also absent in *Ronda Gorge* but then they are absent from much of Higgins's nominal fiction.

The problematic nature of Higgins's *Ronda Gorge* is further accentuated by its sister text, *Helsingor Station*. Unlike *Ronda Gorge*, much of *Helsingor Station* is nominally fiction. 'Killachter Meadow' and 'Lebensraum', two of the more successful stories from *Felo De Se*, are reprinted. Everything else has previously appeared in various states of development in magazines and anthologies over the years, since 1956. The short fictions and autobiographical snapshots of *Helsingor Station* are more explicitly self-reflexive than those of *Ronda Gorge*. 'Sodden Fields'[11] provides an interesting and unequivocal statement of artistic intent:

> Nothing is too clear, of its nature, least of all the limpidities of language...I tell you a thing. I could tell it otherwise. A few pictures emerge into the light from the shadows within me. I consider them. Quite often they fail to please me. I call them 'pictures' but you kind readers suffering from an ideal insomnia, must know otherwise. What I mean to convey is: movements from the past. (Higgins *HS* 1989, 44)

'Sodden Fields' is an autobiographical sketch and thus it is clear that what Higgins means by 'movements from the past' is a recollection of his own past. The only transformative elements here then are memory and language. Certainly influenced by Joyce's parodic treatment of form in *Ulysses*, there is no formal structure in 'Sodden Fields'. The sketch, then, lists various selected events from 1927, the year of the author's birth. The swift staccato of events from 1927 is followed by the author's musings on his own relationship to the events: 'Are we not all somebody's rearings in the wretched bric-a-brac and rigmarole, of which our life may be assigned some part, however minor, if only as passive bystander?' (Higgins *HS* 1989, 46). Immediately the listing of events resumes. The intention is to indicate the overwhelming variety in life but also to register Higgins's recognition of the essential unity of our universe. Everything is inter-connected despite apparent chaos, and everything contributes something to the rigmarole of history. Naming this interconnection is, of course, an entirely different matter. The thread of the author's vision, stretching forth from 1956 to 1989, acts as a cohesive agent upon a diversity of interests. However, the fifty-year-old Higgins traces his list of events between 1927 and 1933 and then his technique falters: 'Where am I? Where was I then? What do you do when memory begins to go? I spend much of the time looking back into the past. It is no longer there. It has moved. Where to?' (Higgins *HS* 1989, 49. Movements from the past falter. Facts from history cannot do more than place the author's historical life in a larger structure. Higgins's past, like all those other events, is consigned to history or mythology: 'Our past is most certainly dead. More than that, much more; it is unimaginable. Unthinkable as the legendary but extinct horseflesh Twohelchroo' (Higgins *HS* 1989, 56). Autobiography, it follows, is also unimaginable, at least in the traditional sense. Higgins does not dismiss dialogue or communication but his writing, whether autobiography or fiction, insists that the presumptions of traditional narrative are insufficient. He utilises the stuff of his life, or the loss of it, to emphasise this insufficiency just as he does in his short fictions and novels.

'Frere Jacques, Bruder Jacques' is an account of Higgins's father's death. The descriptions of the author's parents, especially his father, practically a replica of those of Dan Ruttle's in *Balcony of Europe* and *Scenes from a Receding Past*, and very similar to those in the later *Donkey's Years*, again blur the distinction between the author's own life and his fictions. Through his father's death the author acknowledges the flux of his life: 'That which we are must cease to be, that we may come to pass in the being of another. Exist anew! A page was turned, an old man sighed' (Higgins *HS* 1989, 91). Continuity is what the author visualises in his father's death, not cessation. He already sees his own self in his sons and the natural perpetual motion of existence is thus emphasised.

The title piece of the work, 'Helsingor Station' possibly recalls the relationship between Fitzy and Elin in *Bornholm Night-Ferry*. The piece ponders the passing of a relationship between the narrator and his lover. Typical of Higgins, it is the element of transience which is articulated in the more poignant moments of the piece: 'Things will never be the same again. No, things are the same as they always were, only you're the same too, so things will never be the same again. I say things but I may mean times and places. Times with you' (Higgins *HS* 1989, 99–100). The moments they shared are frozen in his memory, as well as his vision of her, and will forever remain in stasis. Things will never be the same because he has changed. Higgins's constant evocation of transience and flux in human lives is more than an emotional response to lost moments and friends. It is a vision of human life. He does not merely berate the vagaries of memory, he names the actuality of the human condition: 'Nothing is ever left anywhere but in the mind; impermanence is the true state of nature, deterioration and decay of the human husks' (Higgins *HS* 1989, 107). Higgins's problematic relationship with the past is the major force behind his writing. Memory, at best, preserves the past in a static limbo. Higgins sees impermanence and fluidity as the true condition of living and therefore any attempt to freeze memory is illusory. The movement must be retained. He needs to name both the actuality of memory and the impermanent nature of the human condition. In linguistic terms this represents the great contemporary dilemma: how to name the world without freeze-drying it, thereby rendering it hopelessly misrepresentative of the fluid nature of living: 'Permanence has forsaken our world and jeopardy taken its place. Age does us no favours. The past itself is probably the most potent and enduring of all known aphrodisiacs' (Higgins *HS* 1989, 186). The illusion of permanence has forsaken our world at least. There is no more pretending that the past is something to be easily retained in its essence, nor can language be unproblematically equated with its referents. Higgins's fictions and autobiographies attempt to record the process of artistic development. They try to register the nature of their media and, in doing so, retrieve art and life from the abyss of historical exactitudes.

George O'Brien's analysis of both Banville's *The Book of Evidence* and Higgins's *Ronda Gorge* is interesting in this regard: 'Both *The Book of Evidence* and *Ronda Gorge* offer such comprehensive valedictories to worlds well lost that it is difficult not to imagine somebody discovering in them not a terminus for the alienated but a place to start' (O'Brien 1989, 92). Regarding Higgins's work, O'Brien's assessment is incisive. It is easy to view *Ronda Gorge* or *Helsingor Station* as comprehensive valedictories to lost worlds, as indeed they are, just as they most certainly offer options for other writers from which to develop further. This point is not lost on Higgins himself. Arguably, Higgins may be guilty of attempting to begin that same journey many times only to return and begin again. His themes are familiar ones, his blending of autobiography and fiction recurrent and his refusal to adopt any strict formal shape a constant trait. Higgins returns to his thematic obsession continually and these themes tend to dominate each work, fiction, autobiography or travel writing. This tendency is clearly expressed in *Ronda Gorge* and *Helsingor Station*. Because the works are compilations of short episodes and fictions spanning thirty-three years, it would be easy to dismiss them as random selections but these two texts contain all of Higgins's major themes; love, language, memory and transience. Because of this the multifaceted texts blend into one evocative expression of Aidan Higgins's vision which, in the later pieces, embraces impermanence and flux as the true condition of humanity. *Ronda Gorge* and *Helsingor Station* are not simply valedictories to a lost world or lost ways of seeing and expressing things. Rather, they are attempts to convey a multifarious universe which mutates once it is named or consigned to memory. I say *attempts* because the texts are not without problems, especially with regard to form. To allow chaos into a work of art is to remove the medium, or set of rules, a reader recognises and deciphers. Higgins's sketches frequently mix languages and refuse to conform to any temporal sequence. We are presented with selected vignettes whose only connection is the author's voyeuristic eye and, of course, his memory. The effective abandonment of form is an issue which must be considered when Higgins's work is evaluated. It is certainly not accurate to imply that the author is incapable of formal expression. *Langrishe* proves otherwise. What must finally be considered is how much Higgins's innovative zest has yielded, in terms of his art.

For all their poignant expression of indeterminacy and transience, and their daring attempts to allow the chaotic nature of existence to dictate form, *Ronda Gorge* and *Helsingor Station* remain problematic texts. Higgins's autobiographical and fictional vignettes reveal the author's impressionistic eye in the act of apprehension and it is this act of revelation which best characterises his technique in those texts. However, they are uneven in the context of Higgins's other fictions because there are no sustained plots, something with which Higgins seems to have dispensed. Their central power emanates from the image, in that by vividly naming something the author allows the coherence to radiate from that very vividness. In doing this, traditional plot and characterisation are subverted, bringing with it the difficulty of how the reader might contextualise events. At times the two texts read like endless note-taking exercises connected only by the author's consciousness, a consciousness dictated more by his imagination in flux rather than by any rational structure. Even in *Finnegans Wake*, Joyce at least has the safety net of Dublin, however distant it may seem, to which his imagination is linked.[12] Higgins does not have such a geographical base, or, if he does, it is so diffuse that even the well-travelled reader cannot hope to find familiar grounding. Fascinating it may be to witness the imagination in free-fall, but the whole enterprise risks disintegration. Because Higgins's fictions are so heavily autobiographical they need an imposed structure. By this I do not mean a rigidly ordered plot and familiar character-types but Higgins's previous fictions have always attempted to tell a story, even if it was not the dominant impulse. With *Ronda Gorge* and *Helsingor Station* some, if not all, of the pieces are self-sufficient but as a whole they seem more like diary jottings (presumably what

Higgins intended) than the finished work. Despite one's admiration for the author's terse and beautiful prose, and his keen insights, one always suspects that these two works represent too severe a dismantling of the fictional artefact. Fiction cannot represent life in its actuality by mapping its strange minutiae. Fiction succeeds because it can make some sense of this strangeness, or at least question it in a coherent manner. Reading these impressive, but fragmentary, works one fears that the author has, to some extent, retreated from such a process of illumination. Acknowledging the deep chaos of human experience is one thing, allowing it to dictate form in a work of art is another.

What kind of status Higgins grants to this pair of texts is uncertain but his most recent work, *Lions of the Grunewald*, offers some insight to his artistic intent. Relocating some material from *Ronda Gorge*, the author, in an opening *Apologia* to *Lions*, writes of their being now 'set in their proper context, relocated from embryonic themes'. Although this places the two texts in a certain context, one wonders then if *Ronda Gorge* and *Helsingor* are, in fact, embryonic works. This generates a particular difficulty with Higgins's work and it is raised yet again with the appearance of the first volume of his autobiography, *Donkey's Years*, published two years later in 1995, a text which again relocates material that appears throughout his fictions.

2.9 Dissolving Ontologies

Lions of the Grunewald is Higgins's first full-length fiction in a decade, the first since *Bornholm Night-Ferry*, and it initially seems that Higgins has returned to a more structured and recognisable formal arrangement. *Lions* is more like *Balcony of Europe* than any of his previous works, situated as it is on mainland Europe and populated by Dallan Weaver, drunken writer, and his wife Nancy. Like *Balcony of Europe*'s Dan Ruttle and his wife Olivia, Weaver and Nancy are surrounded by expatriates, artists, writers and alcoholics. Like Dan Ruttle, Weaver conducts a dramatic extramarital affair which functions as the primary narrative movement in the novel. Weaver and Nancy live in Berlin at the expense of DILDO (*Deutsche Internationale Literatur Dienst Organisation*) and mingle with persons real and imaginary, including Peter Handke, Max Frisch, Sir Kenneth Clarke and a host of others. Beckett gets a mention (and an unanswered telephone-call), as do Jack Lynch and Günter Grass while Weaver drunkenly cavorts through Berlin days and nights, mostly oblivious, occasionally intensely sensitive; a recipe for disaster and much heartache.

Lions raises some questions concerning Higgins's Berlin, where the author lived for a while. Is his besotted and bibulous hero a caustic self-portrait? Did the riot of events, situated circa 1968, really happen? It seems likely but, in the end, it does not really matter. With Higgins there really is very little difference between the 'instant fictionalisation' technique (Share 1983, 167)[13] that he reputedly used in the writing of *Balcony of Europe* and the travel diary genre he chose for *Images of Africa*. The actuality of experience always lingers in his work, the only difference being how he orders that experience. Within Higgins's ordering structure in *Lions*, the love-triangle traced out between Weaver, Nancy and his lover Lore is initially treated with much irreverence but gradually, as the familiarity of sequential plot dissolves, the author's voice surfaces to reveal Higgins's familiar themes; love and its transience, the pain of the past, and ultimately, how one apprehends and lives with such strangeness.

Higgins's epigraphs to *Lions* are indicative of the author's intent.[14] The first, taken from John Cheever's *Journals*, tells of the time when the lions escaped from the zoo during the last days of the war. Not only does this indicate the relevance of the zoo imagery prevalent throughout, but it also tells of nightmarish days of a 'world that has outstripped our nightmares, our subconscious', the kind of days which the novel maps. A sense of desolation pervades all, even to the frantic coupling of two homosexual lovers in sub-zero snow, prior to one of them leaping into the uninviting freezing Spree River. Alice Munro's epigraph, from *The Progress of Love* speaks of the obvious wrenches and slashing which accompanies the parting of lovers and this predicts the marital chaos about to ensue. The final epigraph, taken from Nabokov's *Speak Memory*, himself a habitual frequenter of Berlin, is especially telling: 'In the evening there, in little cul-de-sacs, the soul seems to dissolve'. Higgins's Weaver, the dominant character in *Lions*, does indeed seem to dissolve when confronted with the impasse of naming the life he has lived. Berlin, fittingly, becomes a ghostly presence in his, and the narrator's, consciousness. Ultimately, Weaver dissolves as a character to be replaced by Higgins's own voice, or that of a narratorial substitute. This dissolution is further expressed by a disintegration of the basic cause-and-effect narrative into a rush of half-memories, dreams and the narrator's desperate urge to assign some importance to the life that's just been lived. At the core of this life is Lore, with her teasing name and symbolic role as a metaphorical expression of love.

In this, Higgins's most powerful fiction, love is an essential ingredient, not just for its thematic attractions but for the associations it offers. The pastness of the narrative offers a variety of perspectives on Weaver's rapidly receding life, and the urgent and passionate love he shared with Lore is focused upon in a poignant manner. It is the sense of impermanence that is dominant, rather than any sentimental cry from the heart of lost love. However, Weaver's painful awareness of transience is coaxed to a heightened peak because it is love that is lost, not just life. Love itself, with its frightful joys and acute pains, is presented as the central image of loss within which the author allows his other themes to take root. In this sense, love is, as in the other fictions, the centrepiece for Higgins's sensibilities. This is not to suggest that Lore is merely a functional image from which the author bemoans the loss of the past. Rather, love is presented as a way of seeing, so valuable and sacred that its loss is all the greater, and yet intimately connected to life itself. Weaver, rephrasing Proust, claims that 'love is time and space the heart can catch' (Higgins 1993, 198). Love is a state from which one can witness existence, a state somehow outside the mad swirl of life. Time spent with Lore is, for Weaver, like 'a morning outside of time' (Higgins 1993, 196). As an extended epiphany, love becomes a way of comprehension, of consolation, a kind of imaginative intensity which allows him to redeem life from that state of ineffable confusion within which he is frequently lost.

Late in the novel, when Weaver, or by now Higgins's narratorial voice (the distinction growing increasingly unclear), ponders the past, the concept of love as a key to the past is vividly expressed. Everything radiates from his memory of love, even the geography of Berlin:

> The other day I was thinking of you; or rather of *Nullgrab*, that quartered city you love so much, which amounts to the same thing. When I recall *Nullgrab* I remember you, or vice versa. Go quietly, the ghosts are listening. (Higgins 1993, 274)

A part of the past cannot simply be recalled, unimpeded by the vastness of all else connected to it. It is saturated with people, none more pervasive than old lovers. People, by their natures, are impossible to rescue from the past, a point not missed by Weaver: 'Is it even possible to think of somebody in the past? Are the memories of things better than the things themselves? Chateaubriand seemed to think so; and now he too belongs to that past' (Higgins 1993, 274). The past is Weaver's primary difficulty and yet he ultimately accepts its foibles with a kind of grace that comes only with an intimate understanding of its mesmerising transience. The only pain he expresses is in gentle moments of sadness at the loss of Lore whom he places at the nucleus of all that is gone. Metaphorically, she finds powerful expression as the power of art, replete with its imaginative associations. Weaver somehow retains the essence of her in his poetic imagination, despite the onslaught of time: 'I say things but I may mean times. I say things and times but I may mean persons and places, or may be just thinking of you. Your name at the end of the world' (Higgins 1993, 274). Love, for Higgins, is the key to the past, possibly the only one. This does not gain power over the unassailable power of the past but it does make it more manageable, more visible. Your *name* 'at the end of the world', he tellingly writes. None of Higgins's best fiction functions without the presence of love and its complicated rituals, its communicative problems, its instability, beauty and transience. A tragic note of lost love rings through in his best fiction both as a lament for the loss of such a wonderful state but also as a celebration of that state, that way of seeing which, in its finest moments, releases the imagination from the burden of reason.

The sexual act is one of Weaver's overriding fascinations. Everyone, it seems, is coupling with someone. So insistent are Weaver's tales of sex that one feels the act itself emerges to symbolise Berlin itself in the author's imagination. Like a latter-day Sodom or Gomorrah (without moral overtones) Berlin's random permissiveness is presented as a frantic survival urge, which for Weaver and Lore ultimately yields no child (Lore has an abortion). Furthermore, their frantic lovemaking grows steadily more frenetic as their parting becomes imminent. It clearly does not need the retrospective eye to confirm the passing of an extraordinary love. In fact, this love is so precious that the potency of Alice Munro's epigraph is left flailing mundanely in its wake. Weaver, because he recognises the visionary nature of being in love with her, likens their separation to death:

> So they sat together on the top step in the gloaming and sipped vodka and tasted the ice and fire and no doubt entertained (if that is the word) some considerations of those Final Things that must in time come to us all, to be recorded with all the ones who had gone before, all set down in the Great Book of Numbers. (Higgins 1993, 235)

He strikes up a connection between death itself and the passing of love because love makes death remote and the passing of love is a chilling reminder of how quickly and mercilessly one hurtles to that final moment. '[L]ove is time and space the heart can catch' (Higgins 1993, 198), Weaver tells us, but inherent in such a state is the reality of its transience and thus the tragic nature of the consciousness which seems so dependent on love as a way of seeing. None of Higgins's love 'stories' end in joy, and it is the sense of tragedy that this failure lends to the works that helps to create the profound sense of impermanence at the centre of all his work. But these are no simple, tragic love stories. *Lions* tells not just of the passing of Weaver's one true love. (His great love for Lore happens to coincide with the demise of his once great love for his wife, Nancy!) For Weaver, it is the sense of life that love affords him that is so valuable: 'It was another language of another world; you took me there. I couldn't follow you; but I followed you' (Higgins 1993, 276). Love is a way of defeating the undefeatable, a way of arresting time, of intimately knowing a place and finally knowing how to rediscover the gleam of one's past life. For Weaver the key to existence is love, Higgins's potent, enduring symbol for the imagined life, the poetic memory.

Love is the most powerful image in Higgins's *Lions*. It not only binds the narrative but it acts as the focal point through which everything else radiates. Weaver does not simply inform us that love is a way of seeing, of apprehending, he allows us to sneak a glimpse at that very world he inhabits. In a sense, here the problems begin. *Lions* differs from its immediate predecessors because the narrator's overt concerns on the opening page are similar to those at the end. In short, there is a coherent plot which does not entirely disappear along the way. There are moments, of course, when Higgins's narrator digresses to trawl through Berlin's troubled history and places various historical events beside the microcosm of Weaver's own troubled life. The effect is dizzying and sometimes hazardous to the basic thrust of the novel. Much of this rummaging in history is presented through the frame of Weaver's thoughts and one could argue that Higgins is simply trying to place his hero's life against the backdrop of historical reality. However, within the philosophical framework of this particular text it seems unlikely. Higgins expresses his understanding of history very clearly in the text in one phrase that acts as a refrain in the narrative: 'All the days are different; all the days are the same' (Higgins 1993, 175). Repeated several times it communicates Higgins's perspective quite cogently. Life, history, one's being; these things don't change, only the way we see them changes.

In a sense, the events that comprise *Lions* are secondary and yet they are deeply integrated with the most important and striking aspect of the novel, how the tale is told. Everything that happens is directed by the feasibility of Higgins's narrative form. Love, the most powerful image in the text, is likened to a way of seeing, a way of imaginative apprehension. Furthermore, the pastness of the tale means that the narrator must somehow create structures through which the past can be communicated. Like Joyce, Higgins crams his tale with topographical detail, allusions, historical references and real people but unlike Eliot's or Joyce's high Modernist work, *Lions* does not possess a mythic order as the author struggles to allow chaos to define the form of the text.

Higgins uses many different techniques to articulate the mess of experience which must be forced into a coherent form and simultaneously evade such coherence. This is an age-old artistic dilemma, possibly one which cannot ever be really resolved but Higgins succeeds in creating the illusion of resolution, perhaps as near as one can get. Initially the narrator toys with overt self-reflexive play, something Higgins has rarely done before, and never so consistently. Minor theatrical images are used abundantly: 'Quick curtains here to indicate the passage of time' (Higgins 1993, 116). These devices are more playful than radically destabilising. More familiar in Higgins's work is the way that he reveals Nancy's character. Used previously in *Balcony of Europe*, Nancy's character is partly revealed by certain key phrases that she uses frequently. This type of characterisation results not in any meaningful revelation but in contributing to Higgins's wraith-like, two-dimensional characters. It is as though the narrator does not trust himself with any more expansive description. Characterisation, for Higgins, is a problematic concept because people, like life, will always resist detailed interrogation and thus an indication must suffice.

The only character whose persona is allowed to find expression is Weaver's. In contrast to everyone else, Weaver's imagination has no limits. He is liberated from chronological sequence frequently when his imagination leaps forth from Berlin to describe past events, from Russia (where he's never been), to Dover and Hamburg. Anecdotes tumble forth from his imagination, suggestive of a life he shared with Nancy. There are no restrictions to the arrangement of events in the mind. Sequential narration is abandoned as insufficient and the result, although seemingly chaotic, is a relatively intelligible passage through Weaver's troubled consciousness. As the novel progresses this becomes increasingly erratic and the third person past tense, sequential narrative of Part I grows more reliant on alternative methods to reveal the meaning of the past, and, by implication, life itself. Although the plot is initially subverted by theatrical conventions and self-reflexive comments: 'The truncated metropolis hereinafter designated *Nullgrab* is of course very much our own invention and figures and descriptions may be more aromatic than exact. An odour of pines pervades all' (Higgins 1993, 12), the basic sequential narrative remains intact until near the end of Part I when the narrator presents fragmentary dreams by both Nancy and Lore as a chapter. Another chapter follows, which relates a tale about the Berlin poet Gottfried Benn, with little obvious connection to the plot, apart from the geographical location. Part II develops into an increasingly anecdotal account and offers little in the way of significance to plot. The binding consciousness, Weaver, loses what few reservations he has, both in terms of his extra-marital affair and his digressive consciousness. Part III confirms the radical disintegration of the sparse sequential narrative that existed at the beginning. Lore's and Weaver's relationship falters and they separate. This is the time of the Munich Olympic slaughter and when Weaver's wandering mind tires of painting surreal portraits of Munich, he recalls his trip to South Africa. The plot still exists but is no longer the dominant ontological base. The digressions form the centre of the ontological state now.

The final stages of the novel reveal Weaver's consciousness via his reminiscences, especially of his relationship with Lore, in the collage chapter of past moments, 'The Other Day I Was Thinking of You'. Furthermore, the distinction between narrator and author dissolves to be replaced by a series of letters and a short account of an imagined meeting between Günter Grass and Max Frisch. Finally, the voice that remains has not resolved the meaning of his past life. Acceptance perhaps, but this does not necessarily anaesthetise the knowledge that much of that life has evaporated. The lot of the traveller? Perhaps, but one can remain forever in one place and still live with loss of various kinds. Nearing the end of this patchwork of memory, history, comedy, and, above all, imaginative apprehension, the disconnected voice asks, 'Of all that remains what residue is there, I ask you, trapped in vertiginous Time?' (Higgins 1993, 301). Nothing remains except the author's telling exhortation: 'Stir it up' (Higgins 1993, 301). Just as he has done.

Higgins's sobering perspectives on time are supplemented by his commentary on dreams, offering a valuable insight to the novel:

> In dreams there is no time, no ages, just a seamless, tireless state of the sleeper's drifting fears...It had been a time of dire portents in Jo'burg...To remember it or have it evoked in a nightmare was to make that heart bleed again...(Higgins 1993, 258)

He instinctively likens memory to the dream-state and his narrative structure clearly echoes such fluidity. With *Lions*, Higgins has finally found a narrative structure that will accommodate his vision of existence. Form and content rest easily together. Life itself, he suggests, is less important than the evoked memory, the dream-state, and since memory, like dreams, operates in an unsystematic way, so too must his fictions.

Much of Higgins's energies are directed at creating powerful images, almost visual in their intensity and these images serve to compensate for his abandonment of sequential narrative forms. Dermot Healy recognises this aspect in Higgins's writing: 'The key to Higgins is the *image* – for him storytelling stopped there – If you told what was there visually the story would inevitably follow' (Healy 1989, B10). This accounts for the narrator's reluctance to flesh out authentic characters. We are thrown a few morsels, a few resonant phrases and a kind of world must emanate from there. The surface must somehow radiate meaning, as it must in life. There are no cheap symbolic frameworks or rigid characterisation in Higgins's *Lions*, because such things belong to the inventions of artistic form and not to life. The challenge is, of course, to allow the fiction to accommodate life.

Life is presented as a swirling mess of complexity, ordered only by the mind which perceives. And, of course, the order that Weaver's mind conjures up is itself a fiction, a vision of life which insists on remaining aloof. When Nancy, once an object of love and the mother of his child, can be expressed only by external utterances, how then can one even know one's one life. Added to this is the author's retrospective telling, which complicates everything even more. As Aidan Matthews has succinctly put it: 'So the fable becomes a fiction about fictions, about the fantasies of thirty years ago' (Matthews 1993, B12).

Since *Langrishe, Go Down* Higgins's achievement is uneven. Although none of his works deserves the lack of critical attention they receive, *Langrishe*, *Balcony* and *Bornholm* are, prior to *Lions*, his greatest works because whilst operating within the novel form, the author has managed to confront the major dilemmas of the twentieth century novelist. Higgins's works are never comfortable fictions, they never seek to ingratiate themselves with a public which demands the luxury of recognisable conventions. From *Images of Africa* onwards Higgins probes the meaning of fiction. He knows that all that the mind apprehends is a fiction and he has spent ever since attempting to articulate that knowledge, not in a staid argumentative manner but in the way all great writers express their ideas, through stories. That his fictional journey has sometimes drifted into autobiography is testament to his aesthetic conceptions of art and life. *Lions of the Grunewald* is Higgins's most complete work since *Langrishe* and it is far more ambitious and expansive than that early text. It adopts a poetic suggestion that life and art share much more than one might assume. Art is not simply a transformation of 'reality', because, for Higgins, life is already story, lacking, perhaps, the complex narrative strategies of art, but story nonetheless. Higgins's life has been used as material for his art before, but in *Lions* his life is not simply availed of as material for fiction, it *is* that fiction. It is apparent that the author believes that the life he led all those years ago in Berlin was as much a dream at the time as it is now. People and places merge with memory or Higgins's poetic imagination, to suggest a story rather than to tell it as it was, itself a great literary fraud. In *Lions* reason is abandoned and imagination is dominant. The life described is itself as near to a 'story' as a life can get with its endless complexity and contradictions, all of which evade order. The telling of events from one's life amounts to an act of possession. Unfortunately, in the act of possession life is transformed by the conventions of art. Higgins tries desperately to avoid this wilful possession. In losing a coherent narrative of his own life, he paradoxically claims it, in all its fragmentary glory.

2.10 The Fictionalisation of Memory

The inclusion of Volume One of Higgins's autobiography, *Donkey's Years: Memories of a Life as Story Told* in what is essentially a study of the author's fiction, is itself an act that needs clarification.[15] In *Donkey's Years*, Higgins effectively abandons the transformative conventions of the fictive mode and offers a straight narrative account of the first half of the author's life. Higgins has always blurred generic differences between the novel, travel writing and autobiography. Certainly he knows there is a technical difference between the masking process of autobiographical fiction and his autobiography, in which certain events 'have become my own stories again' (Higgins 1995, 324). However, the author's subtitle to *Donkey's Years* reveals his continued unwillingness to render that difference absolute. 'Memories of a Life as Story Told', implies much. One's past, irrespective of the process of authentic naming, fusing of local and personal history and candid evocation of the past lives of himself and his family, is inevitably transfigured in the telling. Narrated experience is communicated in the story, and story is style. Such a process of linguistic ordering is evident, on its simplest level, in the author's shifting of tenses for emphasis and in the careful selection of key moments of dialogue (some of which are tellingly salvaged from the fiction). Although the usual construction of resonant symbols and fusion of microcosm and macrocosm are absent here, the memoir still avails, necessarily, of narrative conventions and as such the relating of his life story is a transformation from reality to text, or from his memory to text. Of course, Higgins is aware of this rather obvious inevitability: '...this bogus autobiography, bogus as all honest autobiographies must be' (Higgins 1995, 325). Thus, despite his apparent retreat from fiction, the autobiography acknowledges its own textual nature. The author's vantage point in the present dictates the texture of *Donkey's Years*, as much as its generic and textual nature and thus, despite this work being nominally an autobiography, the familiar Modernist epistemological conditions underpin the work on the whole. This is the primary reason for including an analysis of *Donkey's Years* beside Higgins's other work. In fact, the author's attempt to write out his own life, freed from the constraints (or freedom) of fiction, is crucial to a study of his work because *Donkey's Years* adds another dimension to a debate that has raged in his work from the beginning; how can linguistic expression engage human experience?

Donkey's Years is littered with specific reference to local history, childhood experiences and financial affairs. Furthermore, in his efforts to construct a vivid image of his youth, the author provides various lists (horse racing course records, travel itinerary etc) and actual photographs of his family and early childhood home, Springfield House, Celbridge, Co. Kildare. Relocating the fictional material of *Langrishe, Go Down* to autobiography, the author tells of a life of bigotry, privilege and aimlessness, all of which eventually plummets to a basement flat in Dalkey where, living out their last days, the author's parents witness the world from the knee down, via the passers-by through their window. It is frequently a harrowing tale of fading familial glory and nervous breakdowns. These people are the leftovers of a dissolved civilisation, an aspect which has found thematic expression in the author's fiction many times in the past, but here, liberated from the fictional persona, the author's lucid and often agonising accounts of his brother's (Dodo's) breakdown and his mother's death, strike with the power of authenticity. For once, Higgins allows himself an emotional response, although he carefully checks sentimental tendencies with his customary ironic wit. The artist's habits, it seems, are difficult to lose.

Confrontation with the epistemological status of one's version of one's personal history is unavoidable in an autobiography and considering that Higgins's work has always been obsessive about the past, it is no surprise that *Donkey's Years* is, among other things, a meditation on how the past finds expression in one's narratives. From the outset, the author admits his life-long fascination with memory:

> I am consumed by memories and they form the life of me; stories that make up my life and lend it whatever veracity and purpose it may have. I suspect that even before I saw the light of day on 3rd March 1927 I was already being consumed by memories in Mumu's womb and by her memories prior to mine and by her granny's prior to her, bypassing my mother, stretching as far back as accommodating memory could reach into the past. (Higgins 1995, 3)

The flood of details, anecdotes, local history and childhood recollections (related in great detail) which swiftly follow this opening admission lend credence to his claim. The author positively rejoices in the webbed intricacy of his past life and of those who lived before him, both within and outside his immediate family. Such a zealous reconstruction of the past comes at a cost, however, especially to Higgins, who has long mistrusted his mental capacity to reclaim past events. Before long, the author reveals his mother's interpretation of the old Irish phrase, donkey's years: '"Donkey's years" meant aeons of Time (presumably Irish, meaning unreliable Time)' (Higgins 1995, 31–2). Familiar echoes return. *Time*, usually capitalised by Higgins, resumes its overwhelming presence in the author's consciousness, with all its treacheries and inexactitudes. And yet it is, of course, also a restorative balm, a 'great fixative and cure-all' (Higgins 1995, 212) capable of erasing the worst of experiences. In addition, the past's essential remoteness, despite all the author's loving and painstaking efforts, remains a constituent part of the process of autobiography:

> All of that happened in the long ago; and so remote in time it seemed to belong to someone else's past, not mine, when the three of us sat under the oldest tree in the garden and the yew berries fell about us, disturbed by the thrushes feeding. (Higgins 1995, 294–5)

Even as a youth, we're told, Higgins already felt that tidal pull of his past slipping away. Why should it be any different now, near the end of a life? Higgins desperately desires to tell his story while knowing all the while the inescapable absence of who he once was: 'I am a different person now. The me then and the me now, co-existent in two such different worlds, are two entirely different beings' (Higgins 1995, 335–6). Ultimately the artist, who Higgins has always been, insists on telling his autobiography within the context of what he knows to be the complex relationship between past and present, formal expression and lived experience. He can no more capture his past life here than he could in various mutations of fiction and autobiography written over the years. However, he once again achieves, through his construction of an elaborate autobiographical structure, a glimpse of a life used up too soon: 'I was hoping to catch some of the cadences of my mother's voice – an echo reaching back into the previous century, to the voice of my maternal grandmother; into the true darkness before my time' (Higgins 1995, 323). All the details in Higgins's account are meaningless without the imagination that drives their arrangement, and this autobiography is very much a work of imaginative reclamation.

The fascination in this text lies not so much in the historical detail, both personal and public, but in the way of seeing that emerges in the telling. And it is all about stories; local folklore, private yarns that act as belief systems, rumours, 'the greatest of all whores' (Higgins 1995, 325), and how people are sustained throughout their lives not by accurate and true versions of reality, but personal habits which help people through their days. His description of his mother's later years reveals much, despite its apparent ordinariness:

> For a while she blinded herself wearing her sister's castoff reading glasses, her eyes grown huge and froglike and confused. Study the list of runners in the Turf Accountant's, fancy the chances of certain favoured jockeys (Piggot, Scobie, Breasley, Joe Mercer), slap a bob on the Tote, win a bit, lose a bit, drink when you can, avoid people, endure life. (Higgins 1995, 287)

This is an ordinary end to a life. The author offers up scraps of his parents' later years in the hope that they will speak of their lives. There are no attempts to offer lengthy glimpses into the minds of the people who populated his life. They have long since retreated into private worlds and are seen by Higgins only through the habits and rituals with which they ordered their daily lives.

In a review of *Donkey's Years*, Dermot Healy claims that Higgins has 'for years been fighting fiction by inventing fact, and disguising his persona by going abroad', but has managed, with his autobiography, to write a 'straight narrative' (Healy 1995, 46). He is partly accurate. Undoubtedly, *Donkey's Years* is written in first person past tense, a sequential narrative with few attempts to obliquely comment on the text itself. However, Higgins's autobiography is not simply a straight narrative account of his past. I have already demonstrated several examples of the author's perspective on the nature of memory. Moreover, there are a number of layers of significance to the idea of 'story' in *Donkey's Years*, which merit attention. The version of the past offered is certainly not as things happened but as people imagined they happened. Higgins allows us to glimpse at many of the personal fictions, which define people's lives in the most curious of ways. For example, Higgins's father, Batty, like many middle-aged men, was fond of telling a tale of boyhood heroism in which he beat Eamon de Valera in the eighty-eight yards race. The tall tales of people's lives compensate for official history, which, despite the lists of facts, fails to materialise in *Donkey's Years*. What emerges is Higgins's powerful awareness of narrative in people's lives. As he says of his wife: 'Your life, as narrated by you, was to me in the highest degree fascinating' (Higgins 1995, 222). Everything is transformed into story, and that is what fascinates Higgins. The things themselves are long-gone, only the stories remain. Throughout this text, the understanding that people live in stories of themselves and others, is powerfully expressed. Higgins is frequently less concerned with the event than with the way it finds itself into people's conceptions of themselves, their stories of themselves. People live in narrative, play out their public and private conceptions of themselves in various narrative models. For example, the Bowsy Murray, local hero, is here described by Higgins with irony and humour:

> The act of throwing a stumpy-booted and gaitered leg athwart the low saddle was a grave gesture both ceremonial and heraldic, man and machine (wrapped in symbolic flame, suggesting Mercury emblazoned on some obscure escutcheon invoking Subordinacy, Humility, Obeisance, Homage, Destiny, *Victualler*!) (Higgins 1995, 47)

The world, and its inhabitants come to us as creatures who live by their own conceptions of themselves, often informed by ready-made models, like the heroic Bowsy, and Higgins's ever-discerning eye witnesses a kind of prolonged story in the process of unfolding. It is his job to communicate a sense of the grand charade. He does so, and usually with tenderness and sympathy.

Donkey's Years is an autobiography, but it is a very special kind of personal account. The author, who has grappled with the meaning of fiction for so many years, was unlikely to write an ontologically stable text. Instead he offers us a glimpse of how he views his own existence. To write out his life is to take liberties with a body of events and people, which were already in the process of transforming, wearing masks, living in fictions of themselves, suffering, living and dying. Life is essentially unsayable for Higgins, at least if one intends to tell it how it is. In reading Higgins's autobiography, we are confronted instead with a vision of a fluid existence which defies memory, language and human perception and instead rejoices in its own fictionality because, it is implied, only in fiction can truth emerge. It is not literal truth that Higgins is after, he has long since abandoned the possibility of such a pointless exercise. Even here, in his autobiography, Higgins hopes to let us glimpse at a suggestion of life, at a world dictated by transience and loss as much as by occasional moments of happiness. The power of his images, of his tableaux, achieves such an end. More than anything else, Higgins offers us a vivid story that tells of how life changes people, how things seemingly just happen, often inexplicably. There is no attempt, finally, to make sense of it, just the telling of it. The telling is Higgins's way of salvaging his art from Modernist and Postmodernist self-conscious questioning. The story must be told, albeit in the context of a deeply felt conviction in the 'bogus' nature of it all.

2.11 Conclusion

Passing, as it does, through various developmental phases, Higgins's work will inevitably challenge simplistic categorisation. In his early work he is certainly Modernist in his reaction to the dissolution he views as one of the primary characteristics of cultural Modernity. In *Langrishe* and *Felo De Se* he bears witness not simply to Irish history and his own experiences but to the demise of a culture in Europe, informed as much by the world wars as by the decline of the Ascendancy in Ireland. It is all connected for Higgins. In addition, his writing has always responded to Modernist epistemological problems, especially those of memory, language and perception. No doubt he learned valuable lessons from the Modernist identification of expression with experience and has perpetually sought to locate a fictional medium to frame his vision. However, in his quest to discover a framing narrative, Higgins has dispensed with many characteristically Modernist narrative constructions. From *Images of Africa* onwards the author has sought to avoid the mythic structural devices preferred by Modernism and rarely uses archetypal framing stories in his work. He has also generally refrained from highly stylised linguistic constructions like the dramatic interior monologues of Joyce or the informing symbolism of Woolf. Higgins's work has progressively attempted to locate a means of expression that does not simply replace sequential realist narrative with mythic, symbolic or archetypal structures in the pursuit of order. There, is of course, a cost when one seeks to dispense with recognisable narrative order. Gradually his work has blurred the generic differences between the novel, autobiography and travel writing, to the extent that it challenges the view that narrative points of recognition are necessary for the preservation of human discourse.

Ultimately, Higgins's work suggests that one can write about one's experiences but one cannot freeze those experiences in some fixed order. The human reception of experience is an intensely complex phenomenon and, literature, if it is to have any integrity, must confront that fact. Reacting against Joyce's stylised example, Higgins is certainly influenced by Beckett's desire to accommodate the fragmentary nature of life, but again, Beckett's example is only partially accepted. Unlike Beckett, Higgins has attempted to maintain a direct dialogue with human experience. Where the world is an apocalyptic memory to many of Beckett's heroes, Higgins's characters are always situated in a recognisable landscape. His characters and plots always have a corresponding referent, whereas Beckett's or, as we shall see, Banville's do not. This is a crucial difference between Higgins's work and Postmodern fiction. The world remains as a feasible presence and not just as a constructed system of signs. In this Higgins's body of work is that of a Modernist, primarily characterised by a poetics dominated by epistemological concerns (*How do I say or know the world?*) but which occasionally, in particular in *Lions*, is dominated by ontological concerns (*what is this world, how real is it?*). His work has continually probed the meaning of man's systems of knowledge and communication to the point of evolving into a poetics of Postmodern instability.

Higgins's work certainly displays many of the technical characteristics of Postmodernism. His epigraphs, allusions, overt epistemological questioning and direct addressing of writerly matters are all self-reflexive acts and as such he corresponds to Patricia Waugh's conditions for metafiction, or writing engaged in 'systematic flaunting of its own artifice' (Waugh 1984, 22). The level of flaunting gradually increases in Higgins work until, in *Lions*, the text draws attention to its own textual nature to such an extent that the ontological status of the novel is destabilised. Reality becomes a product of the artistic mind that creates. All the experiences are intentionally, and obviously, passing through a transformative process in which the only real ordering structure is the author's poetic imagination. Higgins is earning his past by inventing it according to his own artistic consciousness, and not some inherited literary form. This process of transformation is Higgins's primary fascination but it also the source of the doubts about his final worth as an artist.

One essentially Modernist preoccupation in Higgins's writing, is his desire to articulate human experience as he finds it and this is where much of Higgins's value as an artist lies. Human experience is already a fiction in the living (which includes remembering) of it. He does not differentiate between life and fiction. Life is already fiction once we apprehend it. The question is how to communicate that apprehension. In refusing to avail of recognisable literary conventions in communicating his vision, Higgins effectively breaks the coded agreement between reader and writer and, in doing so, he erases many points of recognition necessary for the reader. It is not enough to say that Higgins does not understand the necessary transformation from experience to art because there is a considerable difference between his autobiography and his most recent novel, *Lions of the Grunewald*. The outlines between the two genres may not be as defined as they are with other writers but they are still significantly different in their narrative constructions. More important is Higgins's attempt to construct a form which will accommodate his conception of a life that is characterised by fragmentation, transience and unpredictability as much as it is by moments of illumination, love and the residual effect of the past on people's lives. Traditional narrative forms always generated too much of a sense of certainty to accommodate such a vision and Modernist artistic order merely replaces one system for another, which again fails to adequately speak of the deep uncertainty in human life. Thus, Higgins risks incoherence in his writing in order to speak of a fragmentary life. Ultimately, this author's success depends on one's conception of the purpose of art. Does art impose ordered structures upon human experience, metaphorical, social or otherwise, as acts of consolation in the face of disorder? Is that the meaning of all human systems? The very essence of narratology implicitly suggests this. Thus, if Higgins, like Beckett in this, refuses to construct consolatory narratives in the face of uncertainty, does it mean he has failed as an artist? I think not. In his effort to articulate what he sees as the essence of human life in narrative form, he does what all important writers have done, he finds a form that is appropriate to his message. To berate Higgins's work for refusing what is considered a necessary transformation into art is to ignore the essence of the Postmodern debate. Higgins has maintained his efforts to strike up a meaningful dialogue with life when so many other Postmodern writers have chosen intellectual cul-de-sacs. The success of his formal arrangement of his material is dependent on the author's vision, and surely the act of reading is not simply an act of recognition, it is also an act of exploration during which we discover rather than simply recognise. Ultimately, this is the challenge that Higgins has offered us.

CHAPTER 3

John Banville: Out of the Postmodern Abyss

'When he became an expert in the use and manipulation of his instruments, he conceived a notion of space that allowed him to navigate across unknown seas, to visit uninhabited territories, and to establish relations with splendid beings without having to leave his study'. Gabriel Garcia Marquez, *One Hundred Years of Solitude*

3.1 Prelude

John Banville's fiction acts as a fascinating counterpoint to Aidan Higgins's work because, although both writers react to the formidable legacy of Modernism, their responses are quite different. Both experiment with narrative forms, both display a profound mistrust of those twin tormentors of Modernism, language and memory and, most intriguingly, both discover distinct voices which attempt to articulate meaning in very diverse fictional universes. After Modernism, the difficulties facing the novelist are enormous. Language, memory and reality itself are thrown into dizzying freefall and in attempting to overcome such difficulties Banville and Higgins respond differently. Unlike Banville, Higgins does not turn away from the primacy of experience. That all his fictions are to some degree autobiographical is not simply an indication of a need to write from his own life, though this is certainly possible. Higgins's fiction refuses to resort to the pure imaginings of much of Postmodern fiction which itself refuses to accept that language can map experience. He refuses, as I have shown, to turn away from the actuality of living and concentrates on the meaning of transience, indeterminacy and, most poignantly, on what the past means to the present, or how one imagines the past. It is no accident that love, with all its vibrant associations and sensitivities, stands as the central image in Higgins's most powerful work.

Banville's response is utterly different in that he turns away from mapping life. His early fiction suffers somewhat from an excess of Postmodern gimmickry, but as his work matures Banville partially solves the dilemma of the Postmodern writer whose very methods are the source of much anxiety. Even in Banville's later fiction the author ostensibly refrains from writing political, topical or regional literature, except in a peripheral way. This is a hazardous act because when one's fiction does not somehow designate a reality it risks floundering on a barren landscape populated by bloodless marionettes. What rescues Banville from such a fate is his movement away from the academic argument, which infects so much of Postmodern fiction and his subsequent acceptance of the significance of the imagination. Though Banville's unbridled admiration for Joyce is a matter of record,[16] even without consideration of how his work echoes his great predecessor's identification of language and experience, his fictions nevertheless all display the trappings of Postmodernism and their self-reflexivity has long been merely a constituent part of their narrative form, but Banville's celebration of, and expression of, the imaginative mind is what dignifies his art and ultimately what creates a connection with life itself. Banville's universe is indeed populated by marionettes but the imposition of the imaginative impulse on such a universe acts as an expression of hope for life itself and it celebrates communication by re-evaluating it, and in doing so redeems it from the worst excesses of Postmodern fiction.

Higgins's work is characterised by the author's incessant fascination with his own life but what makes the author's work valuable is his desire to bear witness not just to his own experiences but to how the mind responds to the daily realities of life and transforms them into narrative. Thus the subject matter of Higgins's work is derived from the primacy of experience by an imaginative process which perpetually reminds one of the disorder and instability of one's 'reality'. In this his work draws one's attention to the narrative modes with which he reassembles his experiences and he reminds us that one's existence is imagined and restructured in the acts of seeing and telling. In the process, of course, the stability of 'reality' is shaken and, like Joyce, he continually reminds us of the textual nature of our signifying systems. However, to avail of Brian McHale's differentiation between Modernism and Postmodernism, Higgins's work almost always retains a dominant of epistemological questioning and rarely allows the texture of a conventionally recognisable reality, however unstable, to vanish. Similarly, though his work is inevitably self-reflexive due to its epistemological questioning, he seldom avails of the direct self-referential tools of the Postmodernist. Instead, his reality is relativised by dint of the author forcing us to see life through various narrative modes. The familiar sequential narratives of eighteenth and nineteenth century fiction are challenged and with the abandonment of these cohesive ordering systems, his vision of life emerges as one of transient, non-sequential and erratic patterns.

Banville's work, as I shall hereafter demonstrate, shares Higgins's suspicion of conventional fictional narrative forms and he too interrogates the meaning of the ordering systems which we impose on life. From the outset, his fiction acts as an assault on conventional generic forms by using parody, self-reflexivity and a variety of Postmodern stylistic devices. However, Banville's work radically differs from that of Higgins because he constructs his fictional universes not from his life experiences but by immersing himself in a series of stock characters and archetypal plots, in an effort to construct an intertextual universe. As such the author's fictional worlds turn away from life and instead create highly ornate ontologies within which he offers us his poetic vision. It is a vision of a world of human ordering systems, linguistic, scientific, moral and artistic, which he perpetually probes and reveals to be mere systems which man has invented so that he might arrange his landscapes. From the beginning Banville's work embraces Nabokovian self-reflexive narrative modes and accepts the fallibility of language, memory and perception as constituent parts of his work. He refrains from reflecting conventional reality because such a task is an impossibility to begin with. All one can do is weave fictions, and rather than offer shoddy versions of reality he embarks on a journey of constructing fabulous fictions drawn from a variety of highly appropriate scientific, literary and artistic sources and, in doing so, strives to invent a landscape which might house his concerns.

Where Higgins's work retains an epistemological dominant, Banville's work is characterised by an ontological dominant in that his work already accepts, as part of their essence, the epistemological uncertainty of human ordering systems. They do not designate a reality which resembles commonplace reality because they are concerned with constructing their own ontologies. In addition, Banville's work is overtly self-referential because the author is unwilling to allow us to accept the validity of any of his fictions as final arbitrators of truth. His work is a process of stripping away all epistemological systems until one is confronted with the essential mystery of imagination, an issue which he tackles later in his oeuvre. Thus, in this chapter, I trace Banville's progressive reduction of various branches of human knowledge to their systematic, invented status and analyse how significant is his contribution to the apparent Postmodern impasse. Banville's work is intensely ambitious and he is a very prolific writer. Higgins's work offers us an indication of the limits of the Modernist fictional enterprise while Banville's takes one beyond those limits. His work is important because, as I will show, he attempts to write himself out of the restricting, and reductive, rationale of the Postmodern novel and discover, in the process, more fertile ground for this literary form. The value of his work ultimately depends on the status of his achievement in this respect.

In this chapter I will focus primarily on Banville's science tetralogy (*Doctor Copernicus*, *Kepler*, *The Newton Letter* and *Mefisto*) and what might be termed his trilogy of art (*The Book of Evidence*, *Ghosts* and *Athena*) because in these novels the process of Banville's development is apparent, and in the trilogy he reaches a maturity which offers a clear indication of how he has responded to the epistemological crisis of Modernism and Postmodernism. It is also fruitful to conduct a brief analysis of Banville's second novel, *Birchwood*, because this early novel establishes some of the symbols that recur in the later fiction as well as being an extremely significant point of departure on Banville's fictional journey.[17]

3.2 The Postmodern Big House

Birchwood confronts the legacy of Modernism in an assured and technically accomplished way and it inaugurates a series of novels that interrogate one's systems of perception and communication in an experimental but commendable way. It is Banville's first mature fiction because, whilst incorporating many threads of literary significance, it presents a dramatic plot which is both a result of and a cause of its own telling. It is a fiction of process. Like the earlier *Nightspawn*, *Birchwood* parodies traditional genres, most obviously the big house, but also the quest romance and the gothic thriller. The author's central aim is to explore matters that are unfamiliar to the rigid genres, while remaining within their formal frameworks. Familiar techniques and perspectives are exploited in order to create an original exploratory work. Again, the characters are scarecrows whose single function is to support a body of ideas directly related to the creative act. Like the clichéd guises out of which Ben White is constructed in *Nightspawn*,[18] the characters in *Birchwood* are filched from other literary models. Banville openly admits that all the characters were 'made' for him (Banville in Sheehan 1979, 83). *Birchwood* is thus essentially composed of other works. Part One of *Birchwood*, 'The Book of the Dead', which parodically alludes to the books of verses placed with the ancient Egyptian dead for assistance in the afterworld, relates the troubled youth of Gabriel Godkin. Clearly imitating the big house novel, his father is a drunken landlord, his mother becomes insane and his strange grandparents perish in highly improbable ways. Granny Godkin's death by instantaneous combustion is lifted directly from Dickens's *Bleak House* and there are countless other literary references, many of which serve specific constructive ends. Gabriel begins his search for an imaginary sister 'in silence', cunningly, echoing Stephen's creative quest in *A Portrait*, and in Part Two, there is a Nabokovian Ada and a host of other literary characters including a magician, Prospero, who fails to appear.

Banville utilises the big house genre more abundantly than any other in his attempt to infuse the rigidified genre with new life. Like Higgins's *Langrishe, Go Down*, *Birchwood* stretches the limits of the genre by displaying that a narrow vision of loss and decay need not be the nucleus of the form. Vera Kreilkamp argues that *Langrishe* redefines and reinvents the tradition by internalising three sisters' decay to a greater extent than in previous big house novels, with profound results (Kreilkamp 1985, 28). Similarly, Banville reinvents the form by creating a self-reflexive document and, in doing so parodically uses this most politicised of forms to indicate the indefensible presumptions of the form. Like Higgins's, Banville's emphasis is on issues removed from a socio-political perspective even though both avail of the metaphorical significance of such matters. Brian Donnelly, socio-political intent firmly in mind, describes Gabriel Godkin as a 'portrait of the crazed imagination bred of incest and ancestral insanity' (Donnelly 1975, 134). He clearly misses the point. Donnelly's perspective is perhaps dictated less by the content of the novel than by the attention-grabbing publisher's blurb on the paperback edition: 'Banville's brilliant evocation of Ireland in chaos'. The inconsistent chronology alone resists such an evaluation, as do the various anachronisms such as the shotgun and telephone in famine-ridden Ireland of the 1840s. Imhof suggests that Banville's use of anachronisms represents an attempt by the author to generalise the turmoils of Irish history (Imhof 1989, 69). How valid such a notion might be is questionable at best but, nevertheless, it is certainly peripheral to the main thrust of the novel. Donnelly's evaluation of Gabriel should be reformulated to define him as a scarecrow whose sole aim is to parody a tired genre and in doing so articulate an allegiance to the interrogative novels of Joyce and Beckett, as well as all other sceptical fictions. Banville simply avails of the big house as a framework, to accommodate an evocation of the process of his own fictional journey.

Birchwood is primarily a speculative interrogation of the novel form, replete with its inherent communicative dilemma, a dilemma Banville inherits and willingly engages. Gabriel introduces this issue at the beginning of his account with a reworking of the Cartesian premise: 'I think therefore I am'. Gabriel's version: 'I am, therefore I think' (Banville *BW* 1984, 11), foregrounds existence and coyly indicates his own existence in past literature. More crucial, however, is its implication that thinking is an extension of existence and is thus unavoidably distinct. Thinking is subsequently merged with remembrance, echoing Proust's *À la Recherche du Temps Perdu*. Gabriel informs us that 'all thinking is in a sense remembering' (Banville *BW* 1984, 11) and therefore the philosophical foundation can be read, *I am therefore I remember*. Indeed, much of Gabriel's pain stems from the pastness of his account. He proceeds to indicate that memory is the main source of his difficulty from the outset: 'We imagine that we remember things as they were, while in fact all we carry into the future are fragments which reconstruct a wholly illusory past' (Banville *BW* 1984, 12). Such is the dubious position from which the narrator relates his tale. *Birchwood*, from its opening, expounds a lucid ideological foundation which implicitly denounces the basic idea of realist fiction. Gabriel cannot recreate the past but nevertheless he attempts to do so.

Such an approach is extremely unbalancing to Gabriel's narrative. Firstly the reality he attempts to designate is, by necessity, dependent on his subjective perception. The search for 'reality' is also conditioned by Gabriel's personal awareness of its impossibility, thus invoking the necessity of perpetual self-justification of his story-telling rather than the content itself which has, after all, been banished to the realm of non-attainables. In short, his account is unavoidably self-reflexive and self-questioning. If Gabriel cannot adequately recall his past life then how does he even attempt to penetrate the wilderness of memory to even touch upon the past? Alluding to Proust, he offers as a partial solution, his 'madeleines', or unconscious recollections from which he somehow reaches life.[19] Such moments are the fragments of truth about which Gabriel weaves his narrative:

> Outside my memories, this silence and harmony, this brilliance I find again in that second silent world which exists, independent, ordered by unknown laws, in the depths of mirrors. This is how I remember such scenes. If I provide something otherwise than this, be assured I am inventing. (Banville *BW* 1984, 21)

Gabriel's tale thus depends on a Proustian-charged poetics which can help to reclaim fragments of the past. Unfortunately, this tenuous position is not the final solution that Gabriel hopes it might be.

Reliance on Proust's moments of unconscious recollection which retain the essence of the past is further complicated by Gabriel's difficulty with language. He proves unable to bridge the gap between the Kantian essence, the 'thing-in-itself' (Banville *BW* 1984, 13), echoing the Modernist Woolf's *To the Lighthouse*,[20] and the signifying agent, the word. Despite glimpses of the essence of his past he cannot invoke those glimpses in words. At the close of his tortured account, Gabriel lapses into Wittgensteinian despair: 'whereof I cannot speak, thereof I must be silent' (Banville *BW* 1984, 175). According to Wittgenstein, strict linguistic definitions are unworkable and one's use of language depends greatly upon the context in which it is used: 'We have always to take account of the context, the language game in which the words are used' (Wittgenstein in Passmore 1966, 440). Gabriel's linguistic difficulties are informed by Wittgensteinian authority, as they are by Kant and structuralism. Banville has invented his Gabriel in an intertextual universe and endowed his consciousness with a literary inheritance comprising a philosophy of linguistic doubt. Due to this, Gabriel realises the impossibility of discovering, let alone communicating, his past. However, by virtue of Gabriel's account of his quest for an imaginary sister, he does realise something valuable: '...and thought that at last I had discovered a form which would contain and order all my losses. I was wrong. There is no form, no order, only echoes and coincidences, sleight of hand, dark laughter. I accept it' (Banville *BW* 1984, 174). Gabriel discovers that his attempts to place order on life cannot succeed because man's synthetic systems of order, of which language is but one, are not capable of mapping the mutable nature of life or human relationships. Gabriel's acceptance is liberating because without understanding the capricious condition of life he would be unable to respond articulately in his future incarnations, from Copernicus to Freddie Montgomery.

Part One of *Birchwood* documents Gabriel's departure from the big house and in Part Two he joins an implausible band of circus entertainers who sell 'shoddy dreams' (Banville *BW* 1984, 108). In his use of the circus, Banville expresses an uncomfortable relationship with fiction which incessantly plays games. The antics of the circus, Gabriel tells us were: 'a game that meant nothing, was a wisp of smoke, and yet, and yet, on the tight steel cord of their careful lives we struck a dark rapturous note that left their tidy town tingling behind us' (Banville *BW* 1984, 117). *Birchwood* exhibits much of the gimmickry of Postmodern fiction with its games, intertextual worlds in collision, bloodless characters, self-reflexive questioning, hesitance and sense of betrayal at the close. The novel is a highly figurative, prosaic artefact which relies on the associative powers of language rather than its descriptive power. Ironically, unlike many Postmodern novels, *Birchwood* does achieve a level of positive expression by virtue of its fictional excesses. John Barth, a purveyor of self-reflexive antics himself, justifies his approach in a way that validates Banville's *Birchwood*: 'a different way to come to terms with the discrepancy between art and the real thing is to affirm the artificial element in art' (Barth in Scholes 1967, 137). Banville does so in *Birchwood* but he also rejects such an approach in its obviously limiting simplicity. Gabriel, again availing of the circus plot, touches on this issue: 'So we played with exaggeration as a means of keeping reality at bay. It did not work. Reality was hunger, and there was no gainsaying that' (Banville *BW* 1984, 144). Banville's awareness of the need to somehow blend reality and imagination is evident here. He does not solve the problem but he signals his dissatisfaction with the endless prevarication of the Postmodern novel whose self-indulgence is ultimately self-defeatist and destabilises its own validity as discourse. As Gabriel later reflects: 'Something was dying here...It was not the hunger that was killing us but the famine itself' (Banville *BW* 1984, 153). The hunger is only a symptom of an outward reality which always remains as a reminder of the folly of denying its importance.

Gabriel's circular journey is completed with his return to Birchwood. Stylistically too the circle is completed with a return to the abrupt artistic declarations of chapter one. Banville, via the voice of his stock protagonist, clarifies his literary position as follows:

> Perhaps I shall leave here. Where would I go? Is that why they all fought so hard for Birchwood, because there is nowhere else for them to be? Outside is destruction and decay. I do not speak the language of this wild country. I shall stay here, alone, and live a life different from any the house has ever known. (Banville *BW* 1984, 174)

Birchwood comes to symbolise not just the big house genre but realist fiction in general. Gabriel articulates the basic difficulty of writing after Joyce deconstructed the novel. Outside is destruction and decay, of which he has just persuaded us with his use of the circus metaphor, and his artistic declaration promises a return to traditional forms, if not traditional methods. Gabriel thus predicts Banville's revitalisation of the historical novel.

Although Banville expresses much admiration for Marguerite Yourcenar's historical novel, *The Abyss*, he qualifies it with a reservation: 'I feel it is a little too much the well made novel...the time in which it was set was a time of forcing of forms, and would not a little adventurous forcing of forms have been a way out of the abyss' (Banville 1977, 28). Banville's dissatisfaction with the traditional novel form is evident here, as it is in his novels but his interest in experimenting with the historical is also registered. *Birchwood* is a fiction about fiction itself and not about the demise of a once-powerful landed gentry, at least not in any dominant way. Banville faults *The Abyss* for neglecting to affirm the inadequacies of the form. After *Birchwood*, Banville avails of the basic historical novel form and transforms its basic function by shifting the emphasis away from historical reconstruction, though there is a high level of this in both *Doctor Copernicus* and *Kepler*, to that of a self-reflexive commentary on creativity itself. At the close of *Birchwood*, Gabriel eloquently enlightens us about the evolving nature of Banville's fictional journey: 'Now the white landscape was empty. Perhaps it is better thus, I said, and added, faintly, I might find some other creatures to inhabit it. And I did, and so I became my own Prospero, and yours' (Banville *BW* 1984, 172). *Birchwood* completes an important formative stage in Banville's artistic career because it vindicates its parodic treatment of existing literary forms by creating something new and, in doing so, raises some crucial questions. *Birchwood*'s images surface on many levels and yet maintain acceptable significance on each. The novel completes a meaningful circular motion, it contains productive, recurrent motifs, there is no gratuitous detail and the author manages to build a narrative humming with intertextual echoes and allusions which do not collapse under the burden of their abundance. Most importantly *Birchwood* persuades its readers rather than instructs, as is the case with the flawed novella, 'The Possessed', in *Long Lankin* and *Nightspawn*.

Seamus Deane's acknowledgement of Banville's achievement is tempered by his claim that the novel remains a 'prolegomena to a fiction' (Deane 1975, 332). Such a criticism touches upon the fundamental status of the novel of process, that is, the novel in search of its own significance and its preparatory role for future work. Can we charge *A Portrait of the Artist as a Young Man* with the same crime? Undoubtedly we cannot because there is 'real' life in it and it is not as obviously subversive, even if it leads directly to *Ulysses*. However, that Gabriel's account is also a *bildungsroman* is important. Even though he is a patchwork voice he too reaches conclusions about life in terms of man's ability to communicate. He plays more overt literary games than Stephen but at the core of his creative self he is not so different. Of course, unlike Stephen, he exists in a comic book world fraught with strange anxieties but Stephen's triumvirate of youthful anxieties, religion, family and nationalism are also greatly conditioned by his evolution towards artistic success. Stephen succeeds in purging himself whereas Gabriel fails, but his failure, like that of Beckett, is an acknowledgement of his need to formulate methods of communication to somehow extend the discourse. Gabriel's other incarnations in Banville's later fictions attempt to do just that, while always accepting the limitations voiced so lucidly in *Birchwood*.

3.3 Uncertain Gazings: Scientific Ontologies and Historical Fantasies

The movement from quest to questioning in Gabriel Godkin's narrative mirrors the Modernist movement away from the basic quest motif of nineteenth century fiction, and the echoing Wittgensteinian close to *Birchwood* clearly articulates Banville's association with the fundamental dilemma of the twentieth century artist after Modernism. However, *Birchwood* is less an interrogative novel than most Modernist texts. Instead it simply displays the limitations of human epistemological systems while attempting to display its own artificial status. As such its concerns are primarily ontological and it is the nature of Gabriel's particular ontology that is of primary interest. The silence about which Gabriel agonises must be somehow challenged. Such is the artistic inheritance that Gabriel's immediate reincarnations, Copernicus and Kepler, must explore. If one is faced with creative silence then one can only explore the silence itself and in doing so attempt to discover some meaning from it. Banville's science tetralogy is constructed on this foundation and, in its entirety, it perpetually asks what is one to do with the knowledge that human systems are just systems? How do these systems correspond to life itself, and what is the role of the imagination in apprehending life?

Doctor Copernicus and *Kepler* need to be considered together because both are historical novels, they are the first two instalments to Banville's science tetralogy but, most significantly, their narratives operate within formal generic confines in contrast to Parts Three and Four. Banville infuses these two novels with many layers of significance whilst availing of elementary historical narratives. The particular substance of these layers displays the author's evolving discourse on artistic silence. Banville's conception of the historical novel is not one which concerns itself primarily with a reconstruction of past events. The following observations by Marguerite Yourcenar are of some relevance due to Banville's qualified respect for her endeavours:

> In our day when introspection tends to dominate literary forms, the historical novel, or what may for convenience's sake be called by that name, must take the plunge into time recaptured, and must fully establish itself within some inner world. (Yourcenar 1966, 240–41)

There is a considerable distinction between Yourcenar's directive and what Banville has labelled 'Hollywood costume dramas' (Banville 1976, 26). She uses the historical novel as a vehicle through which the artist might speak and refuses to simply accept the form as a reconstruction of past events, but what this potential voice might be is another matter entirely. The novelist's concerns, she implies, need not be fundamentally historical. Rather, he/she transcends, or aims to transcend, the restriction of history which, in Banville's view, by 'necessity deals with political motive at the expense of psychology' (Banville 1976, 26). Banville's historical novels relocate this emphasis and the author's own interests become most significant. David Lodge's evaluation of Wilde's *The Ballad of Reading Gaol* eloquently states the possibilities offered by any recreation of past events: 'He is not concerned to reconstruct or explain a given event but to apprehend the event through the attributes and associations which it generates' (Lodge 1977, 24). Such attributes and associations manifest themselves in a characteristically Banvillean guise in the historical novels. Geert Lernout, appropriating Seamus Deane's view of Yeats, attempts to clarify Banville's use of history: 'We historise in order to poeticise, and Ireland, in consequence, begins increasingly to become a metaphor for the self' (Lernout 1986, 12). Banville poeticises historical fact with the same gusto that he poeticises everything his eye falls upon. The secondary status of history is certain. The author's vision must be shown and the only role of history, or anything else for that matter, is to generate a suitable basis from which his symbolic associative and, above all, artistic fiction can spring. Banville openly declares as much: 'science, history and mathematics are no more important to those books than the Odyssey is to Ulysses' (Banville in McKenna 1986, 17). Furthermore, in choosing Copernicus and Kepler as his subjects, Banville is not dealing with exclusively historical figures. Both have been subject to much attention prior to Banville's novels, so much so that their historicity has already become myth. Due to the passage of time and the fact that much of Banville's information comes from biographies, the figures he brings to us have long since ceased to be merely historical figures and thus fit comfortably into Banville's highly fictional worlds.

In both *Doctor Copernicus* and *Kepler* Banville employs a 'historical frame of reference' which offers rich symbolic parallels for his own artistic process of inquiry. Both Copernicus and Kepler are scientists who attempt to locate essential truths. Banville's novels depict these figures as creators of scientific theories who use mathematical language as their systems. In both novels the creative process and various associated issues act as the central narrative movements. Copernicus expresses the meaning of his science during one of his many epiphanic moments: 'No: astronomy was but the knife. What he was after was the deeper, the deepest thing: the kernel, the essence, the true' (Banville *DC* 1984, 90). Copernicus's distinction between his scientific system and truth itself mirrors Banville's linguistic fascination, also expressed by the pre-linguistic Copernicus at the beginning of his life: 'At first it had no name. It was the thing itself, the vivid thing. It was his friend...' (Banville *DC* 1984, 13). The meaning of Copernicus's science is thus exposed and sets the stage for much of the narrator's attempts to renegotiate the relationship between signifying systems and the world.

The historical Copernicus's vision of the universe stemmed initially from his dissatisfaction with the Ptolemaic theory of planetary motion which held precedence during Copernicus's lifetime. Ptolemy proved mathematically that the earth stood at the centre of the universe. According to Copernicus this system satisfied the formulae upon which it was based, no more. In Banville's novel, Copernicus, aware that Ptolemy's theory is basically flawed, sets out to discover truth. Ultimately, his system too fails in that it too 'saves the phenomena' but does not locate truth. He fails in his effort to locate truth through introspection whilst discarding the 'commonplace truths' (Banville *DC* 1984, 252). At the close of the novel, a vision of Andreas, syphilitic brother to Copernicus and constant reminder of base reality, informs the frustrated astronomer that:

> There is no need to search for truth. We know it already, before we ever think of setting out on our quests...we *are* the truth. The world, and ourselves, this is the truth. There is no other, or, if there is, it is of use to us only as an ideal, that brings us a little comfort, a little consolation, now and then. (Banville *DC* 1984, 252)

Copernicus is consistently portrayed as a reclusive creator whose detachment from and rejection of life contributes to his supreme fiction of the heavens. He chooses to search for truth in mathematical language. Copernicus actually only looked at amplified stars about six times in his life. Early in the novel Professor Brudzewski ironically warns the young Copernicus: 'Astronomy does not describe the universe as it is, but only as we observe it' (Banville *DC* 1984, 46). Only later does Copernicus comprehend the significance of Brudzewski's words. His mode of observation, mathematics, shapes his mechanised picture of the universe and simultaneously results in his scholarly removal from life. These are his fundamental errors. He cannot provide truth because his mathematical instrument is flawed but he also fails to recognise the extra-linguistic or extra-mathematical; the thing in itself, life:

> And this truth that we are, how may we speak it?
> It may not be spoken, brother, but perhaps it may be...shown.
> How? tell me how?
> By accepting what there is. (Banville *DC* 1984, 252)

This dialogue between Copernicus and a vision of his brother, Andreas, infers that exact definition is impossible but it is certainly not nihilistic. Truth may be shown by accepting what there is, according to Andreas. This subtle evocation of the value of fluid, transient life and the importance of surface appearances echoes throughout much of Banville's work. Girolamo Fracastro, Copernicus's unlikely, vibrant companion during his time in Italy, suggests to him, 'I believe that if there are eternal truths, and I am not convinced of it, then they can only be known, but not expressed' (Banville *DC* 1984, 92). This nears the nucleus of Copernicus's failure. He ignores the ineffable truths of life, what he calls 'this philosophy of happy ignorance, of slavery, abject acceptance of a filthy world' (Banville *DC* 1984, 251), and instead scans his mathematical skies in search of truth. He creates a fiction because, like Ptolemy, he creates a vision which is self-sustaining but does not discover truth.

Banville's Kepler too seeks truth in mathematics. Copernicus's belief that the sun is the pivotal point of the universe, and not the earth, is the basis from which Kepler's calculations emerge. He believes the 'verification of the theory', to be no more than 'mere hackwork' (Banville 1985, 96). He is aware that Copernicus's theory is loosely valid in its conception but he grows obsessed with the procedure of verifying it precisely. His self-imposed task is to mathematically map the motion of the planets and to discover the basic flaw in the Copernican system. Such a desire for exactitude is reflected in the elaborate structure of the novel, ironically based upon Kepler's most deluded work, *Harmonice Mundi*, which is also divided into five sections.

Kepler's obsession with order allows Banville to explore more facets of the creative process. The German astronomer, in Banville's fiction, believes the universe and man to be geometrically harmonious. He also believes that the 'soul is the bearer of pure harmonies; pure harmonies are innate in the soul, and so the soul and the circle are one' (Banville 1985, 174). This belief eventually proves to be one of Kepler's greatest barriers since the planets are ellipses and move in elliptical motion. His belief in geometry is unshakeable. He asserts that 'Geometry existed before the creation, is co-eternal with the mind of God, is God himself' (Banville 1985, 33). Unfortunately, geometry is only a signifying system and quite an intangible one but it is from this premise that Kepler formulates his theory of the universe. His vision is a geometrical one, through which he sees a structure he believes to be reality. Many of the historical Kepler's laws are still generally verifiable but in Banville's novel his blind obsession with geometric order prevents him from knowing life. Nearing the end of his days he considers his life:

> Suddenly now he recalled Tycho Brahe standing barefoot outside his room while a rainswept dawn broke over Hradcany, that forlorn and baffled look on his face, a dying man searching too late for the life he had missed, that his work had robbed him of. Kepler shivered. (Banville 1985, 184)

Both Copernicus and Kepler suffer from the same fate; they forfeit life in service of their scientific quests. This Faustian theme surfaces in all of Banville's science novels but it is his heroes' blind faith in their signifying systems, systems which they believe can express the thing itself, that is the cause of their losses and not the act of discovery itself. They grow to recognise that they are creators of versions of life and not discoverers of truth via man-made signifying systems.

Many of Kepler's discoveries are precise and actually yield results under scientific scrutiny but Kepler is depicted by Banville as an artist-figure only with regard to his models of the universe. Imhof isolates these models, one built around the perfect solids and the other around musical harmonies, as 'creations of the mind that have no counterpart in reality' (Imhof 1989, 129). Kepler's theory of planetary motion, which comes to him in a stylised epiphanic moment, that of five regular solids – the cube, the tetrahedron, the dodecahedron, the icosahedron and the octahedron – actually works geometrically but Kepler does not realise that there are more than six planets. With the flawed information available to Kepler, his theory works but, as with Copernicus's theory, 'truth was the missing music' (Banville *DC* 1984, 29). Kepler finally understands the significance of his life's work: 'We must take it all on trust. That's the secret. How simple! He smiled. It was not a mere book that was thus thrown away, but the foundation of a life's work. It seemed not to matter' (Banville 1985, 185). Like Copernicus, Kepler gains an understanding that all that is possible in his attempts to discover truth are self-sustaining fictions which fail to transfix reality.

However, Kepler's mathematical fictions are symptomatic of a far greater ailment. He perpetually misunderstands the events which unfold in his life and Banville appropriately describes such incidents in harmony-charged language. Of his stepdaughter, Regina, reticent symbol of truth, he claims: 'There was an air of completeness, of being, for herself, a precise sufficiency' (Banville 1985, 18). Kepler fabricates fiction from life just as he does with science, Regina being the focus of much of his misrepresentation. Later in the novel, in a letter to the by-now estranged Regina he appears confused by the actuality of her previous letter: 'This is not your tone of voice, which I remember with tenderness and love, this is not how you would speak to me, if the choice were yours. I can only believe that these words were dictated to you' (Banville 1985, 131). Confronted with a turbulent life which refuses to conform to his impossibly exact order, he immediately invents excuses to save the fiction he has built from the scraps of experience he has salvaged from life. In contrast to Copernicus's self-imposed isolation, Kepler is continually presented as a man plagued by intrusions upon his work. He is a victim of the counter-reformation, of a first marriage to a wife utterly insensitive to his work, a series of child deaths and continual financial difficulties. Even the bells, at Tycho Brahe's castle at Benatek, he fears, might disturb him. However, like with Copernicus's Italian adventure, Kepler too has an outlet in the shape of the vivacious Felix, representative of the 'splendid and exhilarating sordidness of real life' (Banville 1985, 69). Such feelings contradict his disdain for the 'clamour and confusion of other lives' (Banville 1985, 11), and the resultant tension generated by such a contrast epitomises Kepler's life. The novel concludes with the astronomer having lost interest in the 'work of his intellect' (Banville 1985, 184), and imagining a vision of Felix, finally asserting the real value of a life he had almost always tried to evade:

> I know he will meet me there, I'll recognise him by the rosy cross on his breast, and his lady with him. Are you there? If I walk to the window now I shall see you,

out there in the rain and the dark, all of you, queen and dauntless Knight. (Banville 1985, 184)

This brief analysis of *Doctor Copernicus* and *Kepler* illustrates the depth of historical reconstruction which the author felt was necessary to pursue his intentions. The unfortunate result of such depth is that the novels' primary aims have been overlooked by some critics. Seamus Deane, for example, finds fault with *Doctor Copernicus* regarding its scientific content: 'It would have been more satisfactory, if we could have had some more precise information on the process of Copernicus's discovery, even to the mathematics of it' (Deane 1977, 120). Deane's criticism clearly suggests a desire for an emphasis on scientific fact and infers that such an approach might have improved the novel. The implications of this criticism are twofold. Firstly, it inherently compliments the level of historical reconstruction, albeit unsatisfactory to Deane, because the critic seems to presume that the novel is primarily a historical one. Secondly, it betrays a critical view which serves only to outline its own criteria for a satisfactory novel without attempting to explicate the real impetus of the fiction. Francis C. Molloy also misinterprets the self-reflexive nature of the novel: 'By devoting his talents to studying attempts of historical figures at coping with reality, he has launched himself along a literary road which promises to be rewarding' (Molloy 1981, 51). Although this evaluation contains a level of accuracy, Molloy does not articulate any extra-historical motive behind the novel. *Doctor Copernicus* and *Kepler* are not primarily about how two scientists cope with reality, although this is an aspect of both novels. Instead the novels question how man-made systems of knowledge operate. In *Birchwood*, Gabriel utters the legacy of Modernism at the close of his account: 'Whereof I cannot speak, thereof I must be silent' (Banville *BW* 1984, 175). The two historical novels do not simply repeat this utterance, they explore the meaning of Gabriel's silence and express ways of showing life. Communication itself is the issue, not how to deal with reality. Joseph McMinn offers a more enlightened critique of the historical novels: '*Doctor Copernicus* and *Kepler* present the enterprise of writing in a radically different and more objective way' (McMinn 1988, 18). Banville's historical figures ultimately represent Banville's literary difficulties. Like Copernicus's, his 'book is not about the world but about itself' (Banville *DC* 1984, 128).

The complex parables of Banville's literary imagination are meticulously constructed by the author building multi-layered associative fictions. These layers pertain directly to writing and the act of creativity. On a superficial level, the author offers a multitude of subtle hints and allusions. For example, *Kepler* refers many times to its astronomer's struggle to discover the orbit of Mars: 'And seventeen months were to become seven years before the thing was done' (Banville 1985, 74). The reference to seven years, which recurs several times, is a playful reminder that Banville spent seven years writing the historical novels. That Kepler loses interest in his work parallels Banville's rejection of the genre. *The Newton Letter* again refers to this: 'Seven years I gave to it – seven years...shall I say I lost faith in the primacy of the text' (Banville *NL* 1984, 9). Such intertextual threads render the historicity of the novel secondary. They act as a guide to the reader in that they suggest that the central emphasis of Banville's novels is a documentation of the process of their own formation. He builds a series of correlative elements into the historical narratives and succeeds in not unbalancing the basic historical fiction. Johannes Kepler, frustrated by the demands of domesticity, is ambiguously depicted by Banville:

> So he sat clenched at his jumbled desk, moaning and muttering, and scribbling wild calculations that were not so much mathematics as a kind of code expressing in their violent irrationality, his otherwise mute fury and exasperation. (Banville 1985, 18)

The author blurs the distinction between mathematics and writing. Firstly, there is the word 'scribbling' and the scene itself is evocative of a stylised writer at work. Furthermore, Banville offers a furtive indication of his own system of codes which operate through the historical medium. The image also helps to maintain the comparison between scientist and artist. This comparison not only reinforces the metaphorical power of Banville's fictional figures, it also indicates his view that science, like literature, creates fictions and does not provide absolute truth. The symbolic power of Banville's fiction raises literary issues which have serious implications for science, and all other human epistemological systems.

Doctor Copernicus commences abruptly, launching into a rigorous examination of the problematic issue of the gulf between words and things. The pre-linguistic Copernicus struggles to apply a signifying agent to an object:

> Tree. That was its name. And also: the linden. They were nice words. He had known them for a long time before he knew what they meant. They did not mean themselves, they were nothing in themselves, they meant the dancing singing thing outside. In wind, in silence, at night, in the changing air, it changed and yet was changelessly the tree, the linden tree. That was strange. (Banville *DC* 1984, 13)

As with most of Banville's fictions the central concerns are declared in the opening page. Recalling Gabriel Godkin, the young Copernicus evokes Banville's acceptance of the fundamental chasm between things and the words humanity uses to designate such things. It also acknowledges the endlessly changing world of appearance with which people are forced to contend. Copernicus, at an early age, finds it strange that such an exacting system, words, is used to label life. This whole issue anticipates his tireless attempts to impose a strict code of mathematics on an unyielding cosmos whilst continually turning away from a life he had once recognised as a distinct thing.

The opening to *Doctor Copernicus* contains more than a direct interrogation of language. There is a subtle reminder of Joyce's *A Portrait of the Artist as a Young Man* which begins with the young Dedalus experiencing a sense of youthful, linguistic wonder similar to that of the young Copernicus. The likeness between the two works is limited but Banville's introduction does create a comparison in the mind of the reader. Stephen becomes an artist at the close of Joyce's novel and sets out on his literary quest. Thus a revealing literary parallel is initiated. Copernicus learns a mathematical language, and proceeds to write a fiction of the stars using his exacting language. This has no bearing on the stars themselves but merely describes his own closed observations. Banville's linguistic difficulty is thus reinforced and elaborated upon. Later in the novel Copernicus reflects on this issue: 'The universe of the dancing planets was out there, and he was here, and between the two spheres mere words and figures on paper could not mediate' (Banville *DC* 1984, 105). Copernicus's difficulty parallels Banville's linguistic one and echoes the presence of Gabriel Godkin's closing silence. The novel is being written whilst simultaneously admitting the problematic nature of its own medium. Banville avoids being repetitive because this is given new expression with *Doctor Copernicus* and *Kepler*.

The epigraph to *Doctor Copernicus* is taken from Wallace Stevens's *Notes Toward a Supreme Fiction*.[21] Stevens's self-referential analytical poetics suggests the need to revert to a kind of intellectual ignorance or pre-linguistic vision, in order to rediscover the essence of life. By doing this, one might be able to create what Stevens calls a supreme fiction. The American poet objects to poetry being a system of hidden signs, the result of which is that 'the first idea becomes the hermit in a poet's metaphor' (Stevens 1984, 381). For Stevens it is that first idea which constitutes truth before it is distorted by our acquired knowledge. The first truth, Stevens suggested, can be presented through a fiction, a fiction which should salvage the 'inconceivable idea of the sun' (Stevens 1984, 380). Banville has expressed his admiration for the American poet and believes his poetic ideas to be a part of the solution to his artistic dilemma. Stevens's poetics, coupled with the poetic appeal of Rainer Maria Rilke, from whose *Duino Elegies* Banville takes his epigraph to *Kepler*,[22] provides a synthesised answer for the author. 'The Ninth Elegy' powerfully expresses Rilke's poetic faith:

> Praise this world to the Angel, not the untellable: you
> cannot impress him with the splendour you've felt; in the cosmos
> where he more feelingly feels you're only a novice. So show him
> some simple thing, refashioned by age after age,
> till it lives in our hands and eyes as a part of ourselves.
> Tell him *things*. He will stand more astonished: as you did
> beside the roper in Rome or the potter in Egypt. (Rilke 1978, 65)

Banville has interpreted a fusion of Rilke and Stevens as follows:

> Together the Rilke and Stevens quotations create a synthesis which is the very core of art...of the tension between the desire to take things into ourselves by saying them, by praising them to the Angels and the impossibility finally of making the world our own, that poetry springs, and that other poetry which some of us disguise by not justifying the right hand margin of our books. Hence the note of solitude, of stoic despair which great art always sounds. (Banville 1981, 16)

Like his two frustrated astronomers, Banville cannot capture the essence of life by imposing his form upon it. He applies the Rilkean poetic of praising the world to the angels whilst realising that the world remains stubbornly aloof. Such artistic failure recalls Beckett's artistic silence. The effects generated are not necessarily negative. *Birchwood* confirms Banville's difficulties but also represents his willingness to explore the creative silence he has discovered in the act of writing. The two historical novels record the process of exploration which extends from Gabriel's silence. Banville's writing turns back upon itself, through the medium of his Copernicus:

> You imagine my book is a kind of mirror in which the real world is reflected; but you are mistaken, you must realise that. In order to build such a mirror, I should need to be able to perceive the whole world, in its entirety and its essence. (Banville *DC* 1984, 219)

Realism, with its expansive ambitions, is categorically dismissed. Because of the precise designating systems which man avails of, he creates fictions which do not reflect a real image of a chaotic world, but distortions of it. Thus, Banville's Copernicus is unable to discover truth but his failure is positive because he recognises his work to be a 'process of progressive failing' (Banville *DC* 1984, 105). The parallel is complete; Copernicus, like his creator, suffers from 'redemptive despair' (Banville *DC* 1984, 251). This artistic integrity is aimed at undermining the bloated self-assurance of systems of inquiry like mathematics and language. If such strict defining agents are eroded, then the possibility for creativity is at least progressive because all values are re-examined.

Banville sees the historical Copernicus as the 'initiator of the philosophy of despair' (Banville in Imhof 1981, 72), in that he affirms the failure of systematic definitions of life and the universe. Banville's redemption is that, like Beckett, he will go on attempting to discover truth whilst realising the impossibility of such an absolute. Andreas expresses his brother's failure whilst implying Banville's faith in the non-representational power of words: 'Unable to discern the thing in itself, you would settle for nothing else; in your pride you preferred heroic failure to prosaic success' (Banville *DC* 1984, 250). To accept failure is not the same as progressive failure. Andreas's words illustrate Banville's artistic growth because, whereas *Birchwood* focuses on the negative aspects of creating fiction, *Doctor Copernicus* charts the emergence of a specific direction in Banville's work. Heroic failure speaks of cessation but prosaic success suggests liberty from the repressive nature of strict definitions and the demand to record reality. The books are about themselves but, by an alternate route, they carry a positive message.

Banville's two scientists are each representative of Banville's evolution as an artist. Copernicus's retreat from reality is symbolised most frequently by Andreas. The author forges a powerful portrait of tension by juxtaposing the two brothers. Copernicus is of the world of the intellect and his brother is a representation of life. At the close of the novel these two are brought together in order to reveal Banville's artistic aim, which is to resolve the gap between interior and exterior reality. The tension created by bringing the brothers together is crucial to Banville's aesthetic of failure: 'And so, lashed together by thongs of hatred and frightful love, they set out for Italy' (Banville *DC* 1984, 51). *Doctor Copernicus* emphasises the discrepancy between art and life by virtue of Copernicus's frenzied retreat from life. There is an implication inherent in the novel that Copernicus sacrifices life to pursue austere matters. Kepler, alternatively, is depicted as a man forced to mingle with the very reality that vexes him. Nevertheless, he too grows detached. That he is embroiled in many normal human affairs only serves to embellish his difficulty. Despite the fact that he marries twice, fathers children and races around Banville's fictional Europe, he is no less deluded than Copernicus. Kepler dismisses the Faustian myth that warns that intellectual pursuits inevitably lead to a sacrifice. Kepler is not prevented from living and yet he cannot understand that life. Referring to Weilderstadt, where he lived as a child, the narrator informs us that he was unaware 'that his memory had long ago reduced it all to a waxwork model' (Banville 1985, 89). Kepler creates fictions of the skies but also of life. Man, Banville implies, is unable to apprehend planetary motion and instead records his own observations. Similarly, he cannot force life to expose its meanings. Rather, man creates phantom extensions of himself. In this Kepler predicts *The Newton Letter*'s narrator's rejection of his historical science, a rejection which results in his subsequent failure to comprehend life.

Kepler's misconstruing of his life suggests the author's belief in the impossibility of reconstructing the world in the novel. If the world will not yield to one's individual interpretations then how does one record an exterior reality. This implied solipsism is both the condition and the origin of Banville's fictional endeavours. Copernicus, in a hallucinatory episode inform us:

> ...they were real enough, as real as anything can be that is not of oneself, that is of the outside, for had he not always believed that others are not known but invented, that the world consists solely of oneself while all else is phantom, necessarily. Therefore they had a right to berate him, for who, if not he, was to blame for what they were, poor frail vainglorious creatures, tenants of the mind, whom he was taking with him unto death? (Banville *DC* 1984, 241)

The ramifications for the novel are clear. The artist is God and the narrative is his constructed world, populated by aspects of his own creative consciousness. Also suggested is that the world in which we live is projected solely from ourselves, or as Imhof suggests, that 'the mind of man stamps his own interpretation on the world' (Imhof 1981, 70–71). Thus, all versions of reality simply constitute phantom, solipsistic metaphors of the discoverer's mind. This, wedded to the narrator's linguistic problems:

> Word!
> O word!
> Thou word that I lack! (Banville *DC* 1984, 241)

defines the status of Banville's literary journey. All versions of living and knowledge evade the strict confines of language and are detached extensions of the individual. Nothing else is possible but to invent a 'kind of superreality' (Banville in Sheehan 1979, 84). This superreality is one generated from the solipsistic mind of the author and expounded through the medium of language. Banville's work thus fails in its efforts to capture the essence of life but it dismantles the confines hitherto placed upon it in efforts to signify life.

This optimistic conclusion suggests that art can succeed, albeit a success of progressive failure. The author arrives at this deduction by constructing a historical framework appropriately coloured by his internalised artistic vision. Banville chose the two astronomers because a fictional retelling of their creative processes allowed him a comparative structure upon which he could elegantly impose his own insights. This operates upon a basic system of symbols within which he outlines his literary views in a covert manner, which corresponds to and artistically satisfies his overt narrative. However, this explicit parallel suggests much more. It implies certain elements which are far more enterprising than a kind of internal literary criticism. As Kepler ponders: 'Is not the symbol something holy, being at once itself and something other, greater?' (Banville 1985, 164) Banville avails of the historical novel to superficially discuss the lives of two astronomers. He also builds into the narrative a form of literary theory. However, the act of writing such an elaborate fiction in order to outline certain artistic beliefs, creates many reverberations. Banville's use of the 'divided self'[23] is one which consistently resurfaces in his fiction. Copernicus's alter-ego, Andreas, corresponds to Kepler's Felix, who in turn echoes Hermann's doppelgänger, Felix, in Nabokov's *Despair*. They act as metaphors for the duality of Banville's art in that they represent the yearning the author feels for a life he senses outside his artificial one, a life he can never speak. Andreas tells Copernicus: 'Just so. I was the one absolutely necessary thing, for I was there always to remind you of what you must transcend. I was the bent bow from which you propelled yourself beyond the filthy world' (Banville *DC* 1984, 253). The distinction between life and art is articulated, confirming the intellectual solution which the author presents. The internalised self-probing of the artist's consciousness transcends the detailed literary ramifications of the historical novels. The two novels are not simply metaphors for literary theory. They are metaphors for the artistic self that is Banville.

David Lodge expresses the opinion that: 'total alienation from history leads to solipsism and, in literary terms the abandonment of history' (Lodge 1970, 41). Banville has extended the limitations of such criticism in that his historical narratives, while operating on the level of factual reconstruction, serve to posit the belief that all knowledge is, and must be, solipsistic. In Banville's history novels, this solipsism is kept at an implicit level. Joseph McMinn, evaluating Banville's fiction, claims his 'characters…seem like aspects of one brooding consciousness which reappears in different crises in different situations' (McMinn 1988, 26). This 'brooding consciousness' is an artistic one, obsessed primarily with how the mind creates and weaves patterns. The desire for order is central to Banville's art but life, it is consistently implied, cannot accommodate such an exacting desire. McMinn's commentary continues: 'Banville's major theme is to harmonise – nature with perception, intellect with feeling, self with others' (McMinn 1988, 23). The only way Banville's various incarnations can actually attempt to harmonise such things is by elevating the power of the imagination. By calling up Rilke and Stevens, those champions of the imagination, Banville tries to effect such a challenging venture. Faced with the impossibility of making the world his own, one must infuse life with a poetic intensity, to make a superreality and in doing so praise the world to Rilke's Angels.

On a basic narrative level Banville exposes the self-reflexive nature of his work quite willingly: 'I am no good at stories. It is a new science of the sky I have invented' (Banville 1985, 94). In a more clandestine way he reveals the nature of his literary struggle by virtue of an elaborate, symbolic correspondence with his historical astronomers. However, of major import in the historical novels is evidence of the author's artistic consciousness at work, albeit through an oblique lens. This vindicates the meticulous artistic and philosophical positions which the author takes in the novels, that all systems of interpreting the world offer up only reflections of the mind which uses them. Therefore, Banville's novels, by virtue of their own narrative content, are metaphors for the author himself. Intrinsic in this is the suggestion that the creative mind is the dominant thematic concern. Thus, the question of his own impulsive and relentless creativity is, finally, at the core of the novel. As Banville's Kepler indicates:

> And why had this annunciation been made to him, what heaven hurled angel had whispered in his ear? He marvelled at the process, how a part of his mind had worked away in secret and in silence while the rest of him swilled and capered and lusted after poxed whores. (Banville 1985, 73)

This oblique level is subtly revealed in order to coalesce the literary position taken in the fiction itself. In this *Doctor Copernicus* and *Kepler* are formal successes. Banville's various heroes always question the meaning of their own creation. Ben White does not want to stop writing in *Nightspawn*[24] and Gabriel Godkin stops because he is perplexed by his own voice. *Kepler* emphasises the depth of Banville's intention to discover a way to restore communication when, at the end of the novel, the author's voice rings out, somewhat melodramatically, above the fictional narration: 'Never die, never die' (Banville 1985, 185).

Banville's self-conscious probing evolves in one crucial way with the two historical novels. At the close of *Birchwood* the author's difficulty is firmly established, his narrator must be silent. In a sense both *Kepler* and *Doctor Copernicus* deconstruct themselves because they intrinsically accept that language, among other things, is an inadequate medium. In a more positive light they bask in the inglorious nature of their own inadequacy and thus posit an alternate route to creation, that of creativity itself. This creativity extends beyond the pages of literary activity into all aspect of life, including science and any methods man assumes will reveal truth. Banville's Andreas answers these questions and in doing so evokes the author's idea of perfection, which, of course, cannot be achieved. This means acceptance of the limitations of our systems of inquiry:

> We know the meaning of the singular thing only so long as we content ourselves with knowing it in the midst of other meanings: isolate it, and all meaning drains away. It is not the thing that counts, you see, only the interaction of things; and, of course, the names...It may not be spoken brother, but perhaps it may be...shown...By accepting what there is. (Banville *DC* 1984, 251–2)

Andreas's advice is the key to Banville's enterprise. In the concluding parts to the tetralogy, the act of isolating anything for scrutiny is exposed as utterly unwise. The intricate web that is the cosmos will yield only pictures dictated by the method used to inquire.

Do Banville's historical heroes merely register an academic, theoretical discussion or do they achieve worthy artistic status in their own right? The author flamboyantly expounds his creative perplexity but also illustrates a persistent urge to escape from the limitations imposed upon him by realist fiction. The lessons learnt from Modernism cannot be ignored. But is it the stuff of art or literary theory? In Banville's terms there cannot be a difference because all systems of interpreting the world create fictions. The imaginative sensibility in all life is therefore established. Is this art? Banville's fictions say yes, they argue that they have a bearing on life because in specifying the nature of man's signifying systems they offer an alternative vision. Ultimately, Banville's two historical novels have value because, although affirming the artificial and paradoxical nature of their own existence, they claim a level of power in life. They designate a 'reality' and thus establish a correspondence with life. The meaning of this correspondence is elaborated upon in each respective fiction which Banville creates.

3.4 Intertextual Ontologies

The concluding novels to the tetralogy refrain from using the historical novel genre and the overt scientific content is submerged beneath narratives reminiscent of the invented landscapes of *Birchwood* and *Nightspawn*. Although science remains germane to *The Newton Letter* and *Mefisto* both novels are nominally set in near-contemporary Ireland. However, the two novels are also elaborate pastiches woven from a variety of literary, scientific and mythological sources. The web of intertextual references is crucial to the thematic impetus of the novels in that, like the other distinctive elements in the novels, it is not used simply for virtuoso cleverness. More extensively than in Banville's previous novels, *The Newton Letter*'s and *Mefisto*'s literary derivations combine and reinforce the other strains of craftsmanship to create dense, multi-layered fictions.

The basic plot of *The Newton Letter* relates the plight of a historian who has been writing a history of Sir Isaac Newton. He has retired to a lodge adjacent to 'Fern House', a dilapidated big house. In this familiar Banvillean setting he tries to complete his work but quickly discovers that the extreme vividness of commonplace things encroaches upon him, distracting him from his work. He also becomes fascinated by various human dramas unfolding about him. This is the initial cause of his problems. Believing he has discovered reality, he conjures up an elaborate subjective fiction from the complex network of relationships at Fern House, a fiction which is never wholly resolved with actuality. His ordering mind continually misconstrues the events about him and the short novel serves to record his tentative path to understanding his errors of perception. He entangles himself with two women, Ottilie and Charlotte, but his sexual relationship with Ottilie is in contrast to that with Charlotte, his 'passion of the mind' (Banville *NL* 1984, 53). He persistently misunderstands both relationships, weaving new imaginings about them whenever possible, until he slowly grows to comprehend the bewildering nature of his misconceptions. By the close of the novel he has developed a new way of perceiving life. When informed that Ottilie is pregnant he believes he can isolate the time of conception but now he knows there is a possibility that his version might be flawed: 'God forgive me. I believe that was when she conceived; she thinks so too. More sentimentality, more self-delusion? Probably. But at least this delusion has a basis in fact, The child is there' (sic)

(Banville *NL* 1984, 90). The historian realises that his comprehension of the events of his life might be wrong but this does not alter the actuality of Ottilie's pregnancy and this fact justifies his inquiring mind. Our perception might be flawed, he implies, but reality most certainly exists and thus demands that we continue to engage human knowledge.

The unnamed historian, though not a creative scientist like Copernicus or Kepler, is continually presented as a creator in *The Newton Letter*. Quizzically, the novel is addressed to Clio, who does not participate in the plot. In Greek mythology, Clio was mother to Hyacinthus, Banville's symbol of beauty and life in *Nightspawn*, and she is also the muse of history. *The Newton Letter* acts as Banville's, and his historian's, letter of resignation to the muse of history. The period of seven years, to which he refers at the outset, is the length of time Banville spent writing *Doctor Copernicus* and *Kepler*. Banville's narrator offers the following excuse for his retirement: 'Shall I say, I've lost faith in the primacy of the text? Real people keep getting in the way now, objects, landscapes even. Everything ramifies' (Banville *NL* 1984, 9). It is ironic that the narrator assumes he has discovered reality outside the world of the text and is about to inform us of the minutiae of his experience because he subsequently rattles off a confused mess of misconceived incidents.

Banville's science tetralogy is based upon the classical Greek tetralogy of three tragedies and a satire. *The Newton Letter* is Banville's satire, what he calls an exercise in 'sending myself up' (Banville in Carty 1989, 18). Hence the self-reflexive mode is maintained. Throughout the text the historian is portrayed as a stifled academic who is astounded and hypnotised by his confrontation with what he believes to be reality. He is depicted as one who has sacrificed his life in favour of historical abstracts and it is precisely this concept that Banville exposes as myth in *The Newton Letter*:

> ...of Canon Koppernigk at Frauenberg, of Nietzsche in the Engadine, of Newton himself, all these high cold heroes who renounced the world and human happiness

to pursue the big game of the intellect. A pretty picture – but hardly a true one. (Banville *NL* 1984, 58)

This is precisely the kind of clichéd picture that Banville paints in his historical novels, particularly *Doctor Copernicus*. *Kepler* does indicate the fallacy of such a view because Johannes Kepler, like the Newton historian, also misconstrues human action. The fictions of the skies are no different to the fictions every person weaves in daily life in that all are dependent on man-made systems of communication, which fail to capture reality in its essence. Like that of the two astronomers, the historian's truth is based on personal perceptions and the nature of his tool of inquiry, his language. In *The Newton Letter* Banville shifts his emphasis away from the ambitious heavenly designs of the great scientists and suggests that the designs which his historian imprints on life are equally flawed.

Banville also directs his attention at contemporary Ireland in *Mefisto*, or Gabriel Swan's perception of it. *Mefisto* is an ambitious rewriting of *Birchwood* in that it avails of the big house genre, retains the name Gabriel and returns to the highly invented worlds of his earlier fiction. In addition, both *Birchwood* and *Mefisto* are self-reflexive novels but *Mefisto*'s refinement shows Banville's technical maturity because it absorbs a plethora of influences skilfully and it is far more ambitious than the earlier text. Gabriel Godkin's perplexed artistic silence is also explored by his partial namesake, indicating the author's continued engagement with the Postmodern debate.

Gabriel Swan is a mathematical child prodigy who is befriended by the Mephistophelian tempter Felix and his shadowy followers Dr. Kasperl and Sophie. Gabriel begins to frequent their house, a leased Ancestral home, prophetically named *Ashburn* – and burn it does. After being trapped in a fire at Ashburn, Gabriel is physically deformed and wanders the streets of a city, probably Dublin, and relates a hypnotic, somnambulist tale, closer to Kafka's Prague than Joyce's Dublin. That Gabriel is a mathematician, and therefore a creator, is again central to Banville's enterprise. Gabriel accommodates the author by offering an accessible metaphorical system within which he evokes his own creative vision: 'A number for me was never just itself, but a bristling mass of other numbers, complex and volatile' (Banville 1987, 31–2). In order to decipher Banville's code it is necessary to translate Gabriel's mathematical language. Mathematics and science, like language and literature, are simply signifying systems which we use to describe and order life. Gabriel's difficulty, though not actually linguistic, is synonymous with Banville's in that the world refuses to accommodate his signifying system: '...if a sum had solid things in it I balked, like a hamfisted juggler' (Banville 1987, 21). Like Banville's novels, which struggle with the solid things, Gabriel prefers the ordered security offered by numbers. Life complicates our systems. On one level the novel maps Gabriel's evolving vision, a vision dependent on his mathematical lens. Also the distinction between mathematics and artistic activity is gradually rendered insignificant as the novel progresses. The parallel between the novelist's activity and that of the mathematician is established by their mutual obsession with order, apparent in the self-referential closure to the text:

> Have I tied up all the ends? Even an invented world has its rules, tedious, absurd perhaps, but not to be gainsaid...More than once I have turned in the street at the sight of a flash of red hair, a face slyly smiling among the faceless ones. Is it my imagination? Was it ever anything else? (Banville 1987, 234)

Even an invented world has its rules, like language or mathematics. What Gabriel comes to realise is that these rules are simply necessary regulatory elements, and not life itself, and then accepts their role.

In both *The Newton Letter* and *Mefisto*, Banville blurs the distinction between himself as omnipotent creator and his principal characters in order to establish the fact that his primary interest is the process of creativity, or how the imagining mind orders things. As always, he does not merely present a record of certain incidents but an ordered critique of how one's mind apprehends a possible life. With *Mefisto* the author attempts to discern the meaning of perception and questions the possibility of defining reality. This is one of the fundamental areas where Postmodernism differs from Modernism. David Lodge expresses this particular divergence in terms of Postmodern writing's refusal to designate a reality: 'A lot of Postmodernist writing implies that experience is just carpet and that whatever patterns we discover in it are wholly illusory, comforting fictions' (Lodge 1977, 24). For Banville, acceptance of the fictional nature of perceived experience, is, by *Mefisto*, instinctive. He simply allows this aspect to be an inevitable part of the narrative. It simply must be acknowledged. Unlike the frequently clumsy efforts to state this in the derivative *Nightspawn*, *Mefisto* incorporates the illusory nature of human perception as a constituent part of its narrative but not as its sole, all-consuming emphasis. Albert Cook pinpoints a major drawback with self-reflexive fiction:

> ...artifices would be in vain if they could be purely artificial; they cannot because they must in some way designate the reality from which they spring. When a novel uses reflexivity it must discover a reality. Otherwise we feel it to be gratuitously artificial. (Cook 1960, 25)

Just as a parody cannot justify itself by merely providing belly-laughs, a self-reflexive novel is indeed gratuitous if it only spins off into a self-indulgent fictional void. Banville accepts the fictional nature of art and creates flagrantly fictional worlds but his reasons for doing so are located in life and are dictated by the author's vision of humanity's imperfect perceptive powers. They are imperfect in that they cannot provide exact replicas of a world in motion, a world which refuses to be itemised by our systems. This view is elucidated in all of Banville's mature works and hinted at in the earlier ones. The author does designate a reality but it is a reality which is in constant, evasive motion. Banville's stance against fiction which claims to document reality is not nihilistic or gratuitously artificial. On the contrary, it aims to create an alternative way to say the world while using our epistemological systems. His difficulty is not with reality, it is with the invalid assumptions that we bring to bear on our systems of inquiry.

The confused narrator of *The Newton Letter* temporarily resigns from the science of history because he claims that life is distracting him. Words fail him, as they must. He is unable to continue using an intangible system to describe or know life. Joseph McMinn interprets his confusion: 'The very system which man has developed in order to explain and duplicate reality, ends up making him feel like a total stranger to that reality' (McMinn 1988, 23). The narrator grows to understand that the systems of communication he believed were sufficient, and indeed were in the closed world of his intellect, are not capable of unifying life's essences into an accurate, ordered theory. He had embarked on a journey into the intricacies of other people's lives while failing to grasp the meaning of their existences. According to Imhof, his 'unifying system breaks down' (Imhof 1987, 127). He is thus left without any mode of comprehension. Such is the uncertainty of his position at the close of the novel.

Like Banville's historical scientists, the historian aims to discover truth in his world, a design continually frustrated by the mutable nature of external reality and by his inability to apply significance to real objects by means of his defining systems: 'I had bought guide books to trees and birds, but I couldn't get the hang of them. The illustrations would not match up with the real specimens before me' (Banville *NL* 1984, 13). The essences of life, or Kant's thing-in-itself, will not accommodate such exacting signifying agents. Realising that his methods fail, like those of Kepler and Copernicus, he evaluates his life: 'I was like a man living underground who, coming up for air is dazzled by the light and cannot find the way back into his bolthole. I trudge back and forth over the familiar ground, muttering. I am lost' (Banville *NL* 1984, 90). This is the author's artistic dilemma just as it is the historian's. When one emerges from a purely intellectual vision of existence the intensity of real life dazzles, and raises the question of how to speak of life with a kind of legitimacy. Writing history is an ordered business dictated by its own conventions and methods but locating meaning in a world seething with possibility is a more difficult proposition.

The Newton Letter does not simply display the process of its own creation and its associated problems. It arrives at a conclusion which is of immense significance in its own right. As David McCormack suggests: 'He [the Newton historian] accepts that order and clarity now co-exist with the reality of ambiguity and confusion' (McCormack 1987, 96). Obviously this conclusion is nothing in itself but it does introduce a more informative artistic debate. Compare the Newton historian's words: 'Tell her something, tell her a fact, a fragment from the big world, a coloured stone, a bit of clouded green glass', with these lines from Rilke's 'Ninth Elegy:'

> So
> show him
> some simple thing, refashioned by age after age,
> till it lives in our hands and eyes as a part of ourselves.
> Tell him things. (Rilke 1978, 64)

Banville's absorption of this Rilkean language neatly exposes his artistic alignment. It does not alter or disturb the narrative and yet it contains reverberations which echo a distinct Germanic tradition including Goethe, Mann, Hofmannstahl, Rilke, Nietzsche and Kafka. The implications of his association with this tradition, especially Rilke, are profound.

Rilke's art is obsessive about the gulf between literature and life and his work constantly seeks to discover a poetics which will speak the world. According to John Pilling, this element was a major source of anxiety for Rilke:

> ...we may say that the one conflict which dominated Rilke's life was between the raw material of experience and the shaped artifice of art. 'I do not want', he told his life-time confidante Lou Andreas Salome in 1903, 'to sunder art from life: I want them, somehow or somewhere to be of one meaning'. (Pilling 1982, 98)

Although Banville, the Postmodernist, affirms the artificiality of art through his fictions, he too is driven by the same dissatisfaction with his medium as the Modernist Rilke. Art cannot imitate life but it can be responsive to it in such a way that certain levels of significance can be preserved. Literature is constructed from a language system which is disconnected from life because its signifying powers cannot apprehend the things signified, the essence. Added to this, the perceptive eye of man is highly subjective.

And yet Banville, like Rilke, still retains a belief in the power of art to signify something for life. And the historian informs us of Newton's second letter to John Locke:[25] '...if not in the lines themselves then in the spaces between, where an extraordinary and pitiful tension throbs' (Banville *NL* 1984, 59). This is uncertain ground indeed. Obviously, the tension is generated from a purely linguistic base but it acknowledges that whilst literature cannot provide us with a replica of life it can provide another kind of reality, Rilke's 'Supernumerous existence' (Rilke 1978, 65), quoted by the historian: 'I am pregnant myself in a way. Supernumerous existence wells up in my heart' (Banville *NL* 1984, 90).[26] The self-reflexive condition of the novel again emerges. The author creates a fictional world intending not to mirror life but to recreate it in his own mind. This is his superreality: 'It was a notion of a time out of time, of this summer as a self-contained unit separate from the time of the ordinary world' (Banville *NL* 1984, 58). *The Newton Letter* is a self-reflexive novel which confirms the impossibility of recording the events of life but it does offer, by virtue of its alignment with Rilke and its faith in language, an attempt to merge life and art into that 'one meaning' pursued by Rilke. The historian's acceptance of the mutable nature of his experience registers Banville's growing acceptance of the value of volatile appearance. A strict, absolute reality is not expressly doubted but man's ability to interrogate it with any precision is dismissed.

The historian's acceptance that his ordering systems co-exist with ambiguity and uncertainty forms the basis from which *Mefisto* is born. 'Chance was in the beginning' (Banville 1987, 9), Gabriel informs us at the outset. As the concluding part to the tetralogy it contains many of the ideas expounded in the previous parts but, as Banville claims, 'reformulates them' (Banville in Imhof 1987, 13). Like his previous fictions, *Mefisto* implicitly accepts its own synthetic nature and the omnipotence of the author is openly displayed: 'I could go on. I shall go on. I too have my equations, my symmetries, and will insist on them' (Banville 1987, 3–4). Aside from the playful allusion to the closing line of Beckett's *The Unnamable*, Banville clouds the distinction between mathematics and his narratorial intent from the outset. Within the resultant system of symbolic, mathematical language there is an emphatic thematic concern expressed; beneath the chaotic appearance of life there exists a hidden order. The efforts that man makes to discover such an order represents a harmonising instinct and the power which creates this instinct is the power of art, or the imagination. Banville again turns to Rilke for endorsement of this perspective. Gabriel informs us that when he meets Sophie after a period of separation he discovers something disturbing: '...she had so throbbed in my imagination that now when I confronted the real she, it was as if I had just parted from her more dazzling self' (Banville 1987, 68). Rilke asks, 'Is not the secret purpose of this sly earth, in urging a pair of lovers, just to make everything leap with ecstasy in them?' (Rilke 1978, 64). Banville differentiates between the reality of man's ordering mind and reality itself. For Rilke the mind of man must consciously create in an ecstatic way from the fragments of reality it touches upon. These alternative ontological states are reflected in *Mefisto* which is built around a series of symmetrical images, references and narrative structures. Part One of *Mefisto*, 'Marionettes', is a reflection of Part Two, 'Angels'. The key to the code of Banville's symmetry is Heinrich von Kleist's[27] *On the Marionette Theatre*, which Erich Heller clarifies in the following passage:

> ...to which Kleist has devoted his beautiful philosophical dialogue *On the Marionette Theatre*, where a dancer, a ballet master, is seeking out the perfect model of graceful movement, goes back beyond the child, even beyond the sphere of organic nature, to the mechanical contraption of the marionette; for in its absolute and unconscious obedience to natural laws, the laws of weight and counterweight, the marionette displays in its motions a grace that is wholly unaffected – unaffected, that is, by even the slightest trace of self-consciousness, a grace that is not obtainable by any man or woman: 'Only a god could, in this respect, be its equal'...But the ultimate and at last real show will be enacted only when the Angel – Rilke's embodiment of 'the fullness of being' – will hold in his hands the wires of the puppet. (Heller 1976, 47–8)

Kleist's unaffected puppet movement is dependent on the laws of nature. Such graceful movement is artificial and pure. Yet it is distinct from life and man. 'Only a god could, in this respect, be its equal', and is not the omnipotent author a god, a generator of pure artificiality? The laws of weight and counterweight correspond to Banville's symmetrical patterns in *Mefisto*. In addition, the title of Part Two, 'Angels', implies Banville's ambition to have the second part of his novel attain the status of Rilke's Angels, or 'fullness of being', and to somehow condition the movement of the puppet characters of Part One. How successful such an ambition might be is questionable but the two sections are drawn into a close structural relationship due to the Rilke and von Kleist terminology.

Indeed Banville's deep admiration for Kleist's drama has led the author to pen a translation/adaptation of the German dramatist's *Der Zerbrochene Krug*, or *The Broken Jug* which was first produced in the Peacock Theatre, Dublin on 1 June 1994. Though the play retains much of the original, Banville relocates the play in famine-stricken 'Ballybog', and adds a character, Ball. Interestingly, according to Eileen Battersby, the author 'strengthens the central theme of the play, which is that preserving the system is far more important than justice' (Battersby 1994, 10). The connections with Banville's fiction are clear.

The two sections of *Mefisto* are reflections of each other in other ways, most emphatically with the motif of the lost self. Gabriel often senses the absence of an other, disconnected self:

> ...but a momentous absence. From it there was no escape. A connecting cord remained, which parturition and even death had not broken, along which by subtle tugs and thrums I sensed what was not there. No living double could have been so tenacious as this dead one. Emptiness weighed on me. It seemed to me I was not all my own, that I was being shared. (Banville 1987, 17–18)

Banville constructs this sense of duality in other ways too. The names of the Gemini twins, Castor and Pollux, are used to name Gabriel in the two sections. In Greek myth, the twins were allowed to live on alternate days. Also the two sections both feature Gabriel and Felix and it is suggested that Gabriel evolves into his other self: 'This was the place I had never been before, which I had not known existed. I was inside me' (Banville 1987, 124). The other characters too have symmetrical reflections in Part Two. Kasperl and Sophie are replaced by the appropriately palindromic Kosok, and Adele. Many of the lesser figures also have counterparts in the second half, the mirror into which Gabriel steps. Felix is the one constant, as he has always been in Banville's fiction, under different guises. The Faustus figures, Kasperl and Kosok, are his obvious victims in their seemingly futile search for knowledge. Gabriel, however, does not submit to Felix's offer of knowledge. He rejects systematic knowledge and so chronicles Banville's artistic quest:

> From the start the world had been for me an immense formula. Press hard enough upon anything, a cloud...and it would unfurl its secret, intricate equations. But what was different now was that it was no longer numbers that lay at the heart of things. Numbers, I saw at last, were only a method, a way of doing. The thing itself would be more subtle, more certain, even, than the manner of its finding. (Banville 1987, 185)

Gabriel's mathematical method is similar to Banville's linguistic system. The truth or essence remains aloof. The insistent questioning, in Banville's work, of the systems which we use to order and clarify is one of its most characteristic qualities. However, as Banville and his protagonist realise, there is no order in life and even if there is, it is beyond our comprehension.

Banville is not unique in such thinking. George Lukacs addresses Goethe's similar difficulty:

> ...he is forced to posit a purely individual experience, which may, postulatively, have universal validity as the existent and constitutive meaning of reality. But reality refuses to be forced up to such a level of meaning, and as with all the decisive problems of great literary forms, no artist's skill is great and masterly enough to bridge the abyss. (Lukacs 1971, 143)

Lukacs correctly distinguishes between individual experience which may have universal validity, and reality itself. But Banville and Gabriel know this well, as do Banville's other creations. So what then is the outcome of such a realisation? Gabriel still believes in a way that is 'more subtle, more certain' (Banville 1987, 185). Banville, rejecting Sir Arthur Eddington's vision of science as a construct 'which shall be symbolic of the world of commonplace experience', tells us:

Inside us, however, somewhere in our head or heart, there exists another version, a separate reality which has shape and significance, which we think of as some sort of truth, and which is endowed with a beginning, a middle and an end. It is the desire to see this inward reality made manifest in the world that gives rise to what Wallace Stevens calls our 'rage for order!' Amid disintegration we yearn for synthesis. Religion used to attempt the task. Now in a secular age we must look elsewhere for a 'supreme fiction'. (Banville 1985, 41)

Banville's inexact vocabulary, 'somewhere...version...desire', indicates the fragile nature of his theorising. But uncertainty and fragility must necessarily prevail in an argument which fundamentally questions exactitude, or exact signifying agents. Banville's explanation for Stevens's 'rage for order' is that it is generated from the mind of man, suggesting it to be an intrinsic human need. Thus, as with Copernicus and Kepler, the mind of man stamps his own interpretation on the world. Banville's search for a supreme fiction which will somehow reflect man's desire for synthesis does not deny the possibility of an absolute outer reality, or harmonious order, but neither does it affirm it. He does suggest that man can replace his quest to capture and record external reality by accepting the fictional dimensions of human perception and systems of knowledge and concentrate instead on exploring such matters.

Banville believes that 'a certain seepage' (Banville 1985, 42) between science and art is inevitable because he views scientific endeavour as another misguided attempt to know reality whilst ultimately creating fictions. As *Mefisto* ends, Gabriel completes the circular motion of the novel: 'No. In future, I will leave things, I will try to leave things, to chance' (Banville 1987, 234). Once again the uncertain terminology appropriately acknowledges faith in chance. J.G. Hibben informs us that chance: '...may be defined as a complex of casual elements, in which indefinitely many combinations are possible, and each combination yields a different result' (Hibben in Imhof 1989, 157–8). Can a world of an indefinite number of combinations be comprehended, interrogated or apprehended? Heisenberg's principle in indeterminacy says no. It asserts that science cannot investigate exterior reality because the investigative method damages the essence of that reality. Thus, for Heisenberg and Banville, a certain exterior order may exist but it cannot be isolated or defined. It simply exists without meaning, without utterance, to be known but not said, as Copernicus's brother assures him at the end of *Doctor Copernicus*. Gabriel too touches upon this in *Mefisto*:

> And it seemed to me that somehow I had always been here, and somehow would remain here always, among Mammy's things, with her little unrelenting eyes fixed on me. She signified something, no, she signified nothing. She had no meaning. She was simply there...And would be there, waiting in that fetid little room, forever. (Banville 1987, 230)

Banville recalls Gabriel Godkin's 'blind white doors' shutting him away from understanding his past life. Mammy, the mute essence, is untouchable and meaningless to our interrogative rationality. She simply is. Our systems of analysis are confounded. As Gabriel later complains: 'One drop of water plus one drop of water will not make two drops but one' (Banville 1987, 233). When a man-made system is imposed on the untouchable essences of life it transforms them. The world cannot comply with such a precise system since it was not created by the same mind that dreamt up human reason. The ultimate significance of *Mefisto* is to be found here. Whilst the novel is itself an elaborate, harmonious, symmetrical work it disavows human systems of analysis in their ability to investigate life. Banville simply invents his order.

The issue of narrative structure is crucial to an understanding of *Mefisto*. Joseph McMinn faults the novel for being: '...just a bit too studied, a bit tired, especially in the novel's second half. It loses what *Birchwood* always retained – a story – and becomes a victim of its own self-consciousness' (McMinn 1986, 24). There is a level of accuracy to McMinn's criticism but perhaps the irony of Banville's extremely methodical novel is its inherent refutation of such methodology. Certainly the density of ideas in *Mefisto* supersedes that of any of Banville's previous fictions and the complexity of reference demands much of the reader. The plot is not self-contained in that it depends on the intertextual presences and references to attain full significance. Therefore, *Mefisto* is relatively inaccessible to the uninformed reader. This is a problem which Banville recognises: 'I have a fatal attraction towards ideas…and it really is damaging for a novelist to be attracted to ideas' (Banville in McKenna 1986, 16). In this Banville is his own best critic. However, *Mefisto* remains a remarkable work because it achieves significance from the various levels of depth built into the narrative, each complementing each other and finally merging to register the author's most dramatic artistic comment to date: that the interrogative nature of man's rational systems of definition signify nothing but their own reality. The extension of this is the author's faith in the world of surface appearance, and this is the realm into which his next sceptic is born in *The Book of Evidence*.

Mefisto, as I have previously stated, is composed of an intricate intertextual web, derived from science and literature. One of my primary reasons for evaluating *The Newton Letter* and *Mefisto* together is because both attain a resonance by assimilating many layers of tradition into their narratives. The purpose of such a practice is not simply to honour tradition, as Banville has somewhat coyly stated (Banville in Imhof 1987, 16). The novels borrow heavily from other works and frequently reinterpret the original emphasis in order to complement Banville's own designs. Although this is yet another method of establishing a basic structure from which to build, the particular derivations are crucial to the texts.

Prior to these two novels, Banville habitually observes tradition in his fiction for a variety of reasons. In *Long Lankin* he avails of an old English ballad as a unifying agent in an effort to knit together numerous thematic and artistic issues.[28] He also takes his epigraph to Part Two, *The Possessed*, from Gide's *The Immoralist* in an attempt to dignify the flawed novella.[29] This also aims, like the Dostoyevskian ritual of guilt and atonement, to lend to the fiction what the author has termed an 'international flavour',[30] revealing his desire to be consciously non-Irish from an early stage. Most of all, though, *Long Lankin*'s derivations attempt to bind a work that continually threatens to disintegrate. In *Birchwood* and *Nightspawn*, Banville parodies other genres in his efforts to document his early flirtation with Postmodern fiction. The author has stated that prior to *Copernicus*, all his characters were made for him (Banville in Sheehan 1979, 83). The practice of availing of stereotypical characters from literature means that the presence of tradition tends not to be as obtrusive as direct quotation. Nevertheless, in both *Doctor Copernicus* and *Kepler*, Banville takes his epigraphs from Wallace Stevens and Rilke and also spikes the text with quotations from influences as varied as Kierkegaard and Sir Arthur Eddington. Banville has commented that he feels these quotations add a resonance to his fictions (Banville in Imhof 1987, 13), and accounts for the Stevens references as follows:

> The reason for the shadowy presence of Stevens is that Copernicus, like that poet, was obsessed with the breakdown of the great beliefs that sustained man up to the Renaissance, I mean beliefs in religion as central to life, and confidence in man's place in the universe, etc. Now all of Stevens's work could be said to be notes toward a supreme fiction by which he meant an all-embracing and sustaining, and yet admittedly synthetic, touchstone created by men for mankind. (Banville in Imhof 1987, 7-8)

The flagrant use of Stevens's sentiments acts as a reinforcing agent for Banville's fiction in that they complement the issues with which the author is dealing. They also act as indicators of the process of the novel itself and display Banville's artistic affiliation to Stevens, and to Rilke. This kind of blatant literary intertextuality, similar to Eliot's belief in the value of a 'historical sense' (Eliot 1976, 14), does indeed add a density to the novel. Seamus Deane's conflicting view partly blames the 'literariness' of *Doctor Copernicus* on the extensive use of Stevens's 'quotes and gestures' (Deane 1977, 120). Banville's fictions do exude a literariness but, as I have shown, his use of tradition which spans such vast areas as English ballads, Irish and Greek myth, painting, sculpture, history and a rich selection of literary sources, does not amount to gratuitous pedantry and immature attempts to assign significance, especially in the later works. Furthermore, the use of artistic and scientific precursors whose work engaged with similar issues to those of Banville, and Postmodernism, is a useful reminder of the fact that literary Postmodernism is not actually as new as its given title seems to suggest. Banville's works suggests that contemporary scepticism is at least as old as the Renaissance.

Both *The Newton Letter* and *Mefisto* signal Banville's debt to tradition on a far more extensive scale than previously and the consequences of the extravagant literary derivations in the two novels are many. *The Newton Letter* is reminiscent of Banville's earlier *Birchwood* simply because of the use of the generic conventions of the big house. The narrator avails of the parodic tone of the earlier novel, judging the house to be:'...the kind of place where you picture a mad stepdaughter locked up in the attic' (Banville *NL* 1984, 11). Instantly, the narrator weaves his associative fictions, significantly derived from literature. He tells us of Ottilie's romantic vision of her parents: 'In her fantasy they were a kind of Scott and Zelda, beautiful and doomed' (Banville *NL* 1984, 36). Again he scrounges from literary history to construct his metaphors. This indicates that he has a literary imagination, by which I mean he searches for comparative images in literature rather than in life. This kind of fleeting, respectful nod to tradition is also effected in less obvious ways by many clandestine allusions to literature in order to direct the reader to more important referential layers. It also confirms Eliot's belief that all important literary works are composed from tradition. The narrator's physical love for Ottilie merges with his love of Charlotte to create a third being in his imagination, whom he names Charlottilie, echoing the word-play of Nabokov's Humbert Humbert in *Lolita*.[31] Similarly, the narrator's unassured decision to complete his work at the close of the novel reminds one of Sartre's Roquentin's uncertainty at the close of *La Nausee*.[32] These, and a number of other simple references, although vibrant textual elements, do not contribute anything essential to the novel. However, they act as veiled signals of other more important literary derivations at work in the text because they emphasise the narrator's literary imagination.

In a note at the end of the novel the author informs us that the text of Newton's second letter is actually borrowed from Hugo Von Hofmannstahl's *Ein Brief*, or *The Letter of Lord Chandos*. Hofmannstahl's *Ein Brief*, too, is a confessional letter and relates its author's plight in trying to designate a reality from the words which man has created, expressly in order to know or describe life. Familiar plight indeed! Like Banville's historian, the narrator is isolated from life because his systems fail. John Pilling evaluates Hofmannstahl's *Ein Brief*: 'His letter...is not just a crisis document but the record of a crisis conquered' (Pilling 1982, 90). Such an evaluation can also be directed at *The Newton Letter*. Banville's historian is not confident at the close of the novel, there is no certainty but he does grasp the meaning of his chaotic life, that there is a presence outside of his systematic understanding. He understands that there must be a way of viewing life other than from the strict confines of definite signifying agents. In this way, he too conquers his crisis. Imhof sees *Ein Brief* in the following light: 'Hugo Von Hofmannstahl's Ein Brief, or Lord Chandos's letter to Francis Bacon, which probably for the first time, expresses the artistic predicament of the twentieth century artist' (Imhof 1989, 145). Thus Banville's use of Hofmannstahl's work lends weight to his own continued artistic questioning. The notion of artistic crisis, which is in evidence in all of Banville's fictions, may not be neatly solved in *The Newton Letter* but the narrator is reconciled to accepting that while the traditional systems cannot assess life, another way is possible.

Imhof has also recognised possible similarities between *The Newton Letter* and Henry James's *The Sacred Fount*, in which the problematic issue of appearance and human misreading of social reality is raised (Imhof 1989, 141).[33] More relevant still is Imhof's isolation of Goethe's *Elective Affinities* as bearing resemblance to *The Newton Letter*. Imhof claims that the parallels are 'worked out through what the narrator imagines' (Imhof 1989, 145). Thus, the very fiction that the narrator creates is already a fiction. The implications of this are threefold. Firstly, it reinforces the notion of the narrator possessing a literary imagination. Secondly, it ironically reminds us of the narrator's fictional status. Like Beckett's Unnamable, who also has authorship claims, we are reminded that the narrator is fictional and exists in a fictional world, with Banville at the ontological zenith. Thus, by implication, we are asked who is the creator of the narrator? Such ponderances recall the essential discrepancy between Banville's 'real' world, and that of a possible divinity or ontological absolute. Thirdly, Imhof's isolation of

Goethe is crucial because, in doing so he establishes a link with Newton. Goethe believed that there were two kinds of scientists. Newton was of the first kind that created out of conflict with themselves. They created a world 'out of themselves without any real correspondence to the real world' (Imhof 1983, 165). Herein lies the true relationship between Newton and Banville's historian. The context of the relationship is creative. Banville also establishes a connection between his own artistic resolutions and those of Newton. Like his fictional protagonist, Banville too creates a world, which extends from himself.

By virtue of the author's dependence on a synthetic system of rearranging experience, one can discern yet again Banville's artistic stance, that life cannot be accurately represented in art. The pastiche, which Banville forges, is an intricate collage of illusion and implication born from his peculiar imagination. His memory, he implies, is dependent on literature, at least as much as it is on life itself. This element has continually resurfaced in Banville's fictions, but in *The Newton Letter* the statement is more extreme. Tradition, synonymous with memory for the Newton historian, is the source from which we build our worlds, our fictions. It is here, however, that Rilke's Malte Laurids Brigge's utterance is more potent and ambitious than Banville's:

> For the memories themselves are not important. Only when they have changed into our very blood, into glance and gesture, and are nameless, no longer to be distinguished from ourselves – only then can it happen that in some very rare hour the first word of a poem arises in their midst and goes forth from them. (Rilke 1988, 20)

It is only when memories, or in Banville's case, literary tradition, dissolve into one entity, synonymous with the author's vision, that one can create out of one's self as opposed to from tradition as a distinct and occasionally obtrusive entity. This remains Banville's most unrefined feature. The derivations have not, even in *Ghosts* and *Athena*, changed into glance and gesture. The danger is that Banville's personal utterance might be distorted or cluttered, that is, if he wishes it to be uncluttered.

Banville's *Mefisto*, based loosely on the Faust myth, again raises similar issues regarding the merits of literary pastiche. The direct comparisons between Goethe's *Faust* and *Mefisto* are numerous. *Mefisto*'s basic structure echoes that of *Faust Part One* and *Faust Part Two*, in that Part One of Banville's novel is closely related to the realism of *Faust Part One* while Part Two echoes the surreal quality of *Faust Part Two*. The most striking comparison is the Faustian temptation with Banville's Kasperl and mirror image Kosok corresponding to Goethe's tragic hero. Kasperl and Kosok both sell their souls in the pursuit of knowledge. In *Mefisto* there are many other superficial links to Goethe's work but, as Banville has claimed, the Faustian analogy is only of limited significance: 'one has to have a scaffolding, a base, so that one can then go on and do things more interesting' (Banville in Imhof 1987, 13). Felix, the Mephistophelian schemer of *Mefisto*, like the Newton historian, frequently relies on literary terminology. He continually refers to Dickens, Milton, Shakespeare, Yeats, Greek mythology, Nietzsche, fables, the Bible, and many other sources. As with *The Newton Letter*, this practice endorses the author's stated belief in recognising tradition. Also, Banville's parodic tendencies recur with Gabriel coyly echoing Molly Bloom's solemnity at the close of *Ulysses*: 'Yes, I said yes' (Banville 1987, 210). Furthermore, Rilke's presence is again evident in the skeletal Faustian narrative. *Mefisto* employs many Rilkean motifs including the titles of its two sections, 'Marionettes', and 'Angels'. In addition, Banville uses concepts and ideas from many other writers, effectively forging the text into a dense synthesis of intertextual influences. Gabriel hints at this when he refers to the 'secret depths of things' (Banville 1987, 211). Beneath the random and seemingly dislocated plot there is a binding force which is derived from literary tradition, particularly a Germanic one. Banville inverts Goethe's plot, uses Rilkean motifs and relies on Nietzsche's '*Die ewige Wiederkunft*' (Banville 1987, 223), or eternal recurrence, to justify the novel's philosophical positing. All of this is aimed at infusing *Mefisto* with its own secret order in its attempt to somehow describe life. By this I mean that *Mefisto* ultimately implies that beneath the apparent chaos of life, there exists a complex, interconnected web of order. Unfortunately, just as tugging at the minutiae of Banville's derivations yields no definite significance, the secret order which Banville implies exists in life is not susceptible to human interrogation. Goethe's Faust was aware of this evasive order in life:

> For nature keeps her veil inviolate,
> Mysterious still in open light of day,
> And where the spirit cannot penetrate, your screws
> And irons will never make a way. (Goethe 1967, 53)

All of Banville's work relies to some extent on literary tradition. The extent of this varies but there has always been an effort to acknowledge tradition, at the very least. With *The Newton Letter* and *Mefisto*, the project expands. In these novels, the author appropriates his plots, characters and ideas from other fictions. It is significant that with *The Newton Letter* and *Mefisto*, a particular tradition emerges which itself endorses the use of tradition. The prominence of Nietzsche's thought in Banville's work gains momentum with *Mefisto* and is explored further with *The Book of Evidence*. Both Goethe and Nietzsche, according to Harold Bloom, had positive attitudes regarding the use of tradition:

> Nietzsche, as he always insisted, was the heir to Goethe in his strangely optimistic refusal to regard the poetical past as primarily an obstacle to fresh creation. Goethe, like Milton, absorbed precursors with a gusto evidently precluding anxiety. (Bloom 1975, 50)

For Nietzsche, influence held a promise of revitalisation and for Goethe, it was a practice in which one needed to be immersed. Goethe argued that it did not mean contamination: 'It must be that human nature is endowed with a peculiar tenacity and versatility enabling it to overcome everything that it contacts or takes into oneself, or, if the thing defies assimilation, at least to render it innocuous' (Goethe in Bloom 1975, 52). The ability to naturally assimilate, which Goethe assumes to be part of human nature, is obviously a positive thing and it is to this tradition that both Nietzsche and Rilke belong. There is no real evidence of an 'anxiety of influence' among these writers and Banville has, tellingly, aligned himself with such a tradition. He avails of tradition to pursue similar attempts at gaining universal significance. However, the alternative view is forcefully expressed by Oscar Wilde: 'Because to influence a person is to give him one's own soul. He does not think his natural thoughts, or burn with his natural passions. His virtues are not real to him' (Wilde in Bloom 1975, 6). Such a romantic vision discards the value of the poetical past, denying any possibility for Goethe's assimilation, or indeed Eliot's value of tradition.

More importantly it implies that one can possess one's own soul or nature as a distinct and separate entity. To presume that an author's creativity or persona can exist in a 'natural' vacuum is naïve. That an author's work may be compounded of various influences does not necessitate a lack of originality. In a sense, Wilde's argument is irrelevant to the Postmodern novelist, especially if one accepts Roland Barthes's argument that the 'text is a tissue of quotations' (Barthes 1989, 116). Thus the question arises whether pastiche can be a function of personality or simply a function of the juxtaposition, conscious or otherwise, of inherited texts. In Banville's fictions, the presence of various influences can be construed as disruptive and, more seriously, excessively reliant. However, as with all successful parodies and pastiches, Banville's fictions attempt to justify their high levels of absorption by virtue of their innovative advances from the original texts. He does not simply rewrite other fictions but alters their original perspective in an effort to create an original utterance. In his earlier work he relies gratuitously on Beckett, Nabokov and Gide, among others and it is not until *Birchwood* that his use of tradition begins to discover a distinct voice. Whether a uniquely Banvillean voice manages to assert itself in the way that some of his precursors did is a crucial issue, one which will be considered in the conclusion to this chapter, because Banville's status as an artist greatly depends on his ability to articulate a specifically Banvillean voice within his overt intertextual fictions.

The Newton Letter portrays its narrator as one who invents a world from various inherited influences, echoing Goethe's vision of Newton. Banville sees Newton, who was aware that the absolutes of time and space do not exist, as the creator of a system which was functional but was nevertheless a fiction. He claims that Newton allowed the absolutes to rest with God (Banville in Imhof 1981, 8). In this sense Newton represents the presence of the chaotic in science and also admits to the merely regulatory role of science. Like Banville's historian he too lacked absolutes of judgement. The author does not involve himself directly with the minutiae of Newton's scientific pursuits, choosing instead to establish a connection by virtue of the implications of Newton's mechanistic functional system. Banville's linguistic medium is also confounded by reality but it has a regulatory role. More crucial is that the historian's system of perception is curtailed by pre-conceived, associative ideas. This obscures his ability to define the essence of his surroundings. Similarly, that the mental fiction he creates has already occurred in other fictions registers the notion that the past too is fictional and everything is generated from other inherited fictions. Therefore, Banville's commentary on life is that it is an illusion dreamt up over countless ages of fiction makers. The scientific corollary is that we build layers of scientific fictions upon one another and thus, despite the discovery of little usable truths, the 'smoother pebble or...prettier shell...the great ocean of truth [lay] all undiscovered before me' (Banville *NL* 1984, 14).

The conclusion to *The Newton Letter*, with its anarchic implications, is one with which twentieth century scientific thought has many similarities. The author expands upon this issue with *Mefisto*. Banville informs us that 'Gabriel Swan is more of an 'artist', whatever that may be, than a 'scientist' ,whatever that may be' (Banville in Imhof 1987, 13). Gabriel is initially presented as a mathematical child prodigy, and thereafter the distinction is progressively blurred. *Mefisto* does not reconstruct a historical narrative based on the life of a particular scientist. The scientific aspect is created by Gabriel's fascination with numbers, in particular the number ten. He is therefore a Pythagorean. More significant is that he represents the Greek atomist position, that of Leucippus and Democritus. Imhof enlightens us to the particulars of the atomist world view, as follows:

> The Greek atomists held that behind the bewildering, complex appearance of the forms of matter there lay a structure of atoms – indivisible particles – obeying

simple laws which enable us to explain and correlate the experience of our senses. Chance is the completion and manifestation of necessity, of order of a specific kind. This is to say that beneath the surface of apparently contingent, or chance, events there always is hidden a deeper necessity. (Imhof 1989, 157)

Banville evokes this duality of existence by his literary derivations and by his use of complex symmetrical imagery, some of which I have already illustrated. Gabriel is the primary focus of the dual imagery. In Part Two of *Mefisto* he steps forward into another form of existence: 'But I was different. I was someone else, someone I knew and didn't know. I had stepped into the mirror' (Banville 1987, 132). In addition to the atomists' perspective, Nietzsche's eternal recurrence accounts for Gabriel's rebirth into a world whose inhabitants reflect those in his previous life. What really alters Gabriel is his changed vision. All appearance takes on new meaning for him. In Part One his belief in harmony perseveres, however tentatively. In Part Two the erratic world crowds in on his systems and he realises that the strict defining methodology he once used will no longer suffice: 'A panic of disconnected numbers buzzed in my head. Grass, trees, railings, the road' (Banville 1987, 139).

Gabriel's new and astonished view of life characterises Part Two. In Part One, Gabriel, although confused when a sum has solid things in it, does view the world primarily in terms of numbers. In Part Two the things themselves are of most importance to Gabriel and they shake away from their signifying agents, or systems of numbers:

> Things crowded in, the mere things themselves. One drop of water plus one drop of water will not make two drops, but one. Two oranges and two apples do not make four of some new synthesis but remain stubbornly themselves. (Banville 1987, 233)

Gabriel's sentiments stem from Heisenberg's indeterminacy principle [34] which fundamentally states that all methods of scientific investigation are doomed to failure, due to the altering effect they have on the object investigated. Banville explains his fascination with Heisenberg's principle in the following way:

> Heisenberg's principle in indeterminacy which, put simply, says that we cannot investigate darkness by bathing it in light – a seemingly innocent observation, but one which, in the world of atomic physics has enormous consequences. (Banville 1986, 42)

The obvious extension of this is that signifying systems of all kinds disturb the essence of the object investigated to such an extent that we gain a distorted version of truth, conditioned by the particular method, be it language or mathematics. The parallel which Banville makes throughout his science tetralogy is complete. This does not mean that Banville's primary objective is to reveal the limitations of scientific investigation. Rather, he uses science as a suitable metaphorical structure within which he exposes the meaning of man's quest for truth. Banville's conclusion, dependent as it is on Heisenberg's principle, is not actually a despairing one. Order does exist but, as Gabriel informs us, it is governed by 'chance' (Banville 1987, 234).

Banville's interpretation of chance is of critical importance to *Mefisto* and to *The Book of Evidence*. Chance does not mean random in Banville's fiction. As I have already stated, J.G. Hibben tells us that chance 'may be defined as a complex of casual elements, in which indefinitely many combinations are possible, and each combination yields a distinct result'. Banville's Nietzsche-charged version reads:

> Now, as we know very well if we think about it for a moment, there is no such thing as a cause; there is only, as Nietzsche points out, a continuum. Causation, then is no more and no less than what physicists would call a thought experiment...A thing invented by men to explain and therefore make habitable a chaotic, hostile and impassive world. I foresee a time, not at all far off, when physics will produce a new theory of relativity. In the new schema, chance will play a large, perhaps central part. (Banville in Imhof 1987, 13)

The Banvillean questioning of knowledge continues. There are no events and no causes, at least none that are tangible. This position is not a conclusion by Banville. It is yet another step in the author's perpetual interrogative journey. To accept chance as a valid vision, one obviously touches on a kind of negativity which threatens to undermine man's ontological position. However, as with

Banville's earlier Gabriel Godkin and various other perplexed heirs, the protagonist of *The Book of Evidence*, Freddie Montgomery, attempts to discover a way to justify his and all existence, guided by the light of Nietzsche's teachings and displays that chance does not mean nihilism, nor does it demand, finally, that one drifts into inactive sloth.

Banville's discourse continues. He strips away various systems of knowledge and communication but still justifies his use of a linguistic medium because he is contributing to what might be described as a new kind of novel. Banville does not write realistic fictions. Both *Mefisto* and *The Newton Letter* read like surreal accounts of the flesh and blood reality we all know but cannot speak. Banville does not simply prove that nothing can be proven. These two novels are inextricably linked to human life and its institutions because the exposure of the limitations of our systems of knowledge is not the end, rather it inaugurates a new form of discourse. Banville's fictions are not reflections of reality, they are about reality. They do not mimic the minute details of life, rather they establish a connection by virtue of their attempts to comprehend communication, that strange and valuable gift upon which humanity so depends.

3.5 Nietzsche and the Reformulation of Reality

As I have indicated previously, the emergence of Nietzsche's philosophy gains momentum in *Mefisto*. However, *The Book of Evidence* is more specifically Banville's 'Nietzsche's book' (Banville in Ní Bhrian 1989). It is primarily a product of the author's imagination but its annexation of the German writer's vision becomes almost all-consuming, not simply in terms of how it dictates the actions and inactions of the main protagonist, Freddie Montgomery, but in relation to its dependence on Nietzsche's unique interpretation of language. Still more significant are the ultimate artistic implications which an alignment with Nietzsche generate. The extent of this alignment in itself acts as a commentary on Banville's evolving art.

Until now my brief treatment of Nietzsche's influence is due to the need for the Nietzschean elements in *Mefisto* to be analysed beside those in *The Book of Evidence* in order to map a coherent examination of this particular strain in the author's work. I have already referred to the resemblance between Democritus's atomistic world-view and Nietzsche's Zarathustrian principle of eternal recurrence. Zarathustra's eternally recurring reality is dependent on dualities and symmetries which occur beneath chaotic appearance. Imhof also suggests a possible connection between Banville's *Mefisto* and the work of the physicist, Martin Gardner, who claims that the world largely conforms to symmetrical and mirror-symmetrical patterns (Imhof 1989, 56). A combination of these elements account for the symmetrical relationship between the two parts of *Mefisto*. Banville openly refers to the Zarathustrian principle several times in the novel:

Die ewige Wiederkunft eh? (Banville 1987, 223)
Blind energy spinning in the void! All turns, returns. Thus spake the prophet. (Banville 1987, 226)

Nietzsche's eternal recurrence largely accounts for the structural relationship between the two.parts of *Mefisto*. The characters remain strikingly similar except for the names, but the appearance of the landscape alters, suggesting that all lives recur whilst remaining essentially unchanged. Banville, the artist, recreates the appearance of such a repetitive world.

Banville's *Mefisto* attempts to bridge the traditional disparity between the disciplines of science and art. Heisenberg's indeterminacy principle undermines Newtonian methods of scientific inquiry and so too does Nietzsche's rejection of mathematics and numbers: 'Mathematics, which would certainly have not come into existence if one had known from the beginning that there was in nature no exactly straight line, no real circle, no absolute magnitude' (Nietzsche *ANR* 1977, 56). Such a proposition denies faith in mathematical interpretations of the natural world. In effect, it acts as a deflating agent for the ability of all man-made systems to discern reality. Gabriel Swan grows confused when he attempts to affix numbers to life: '...if a sum had solid things in it I balked, like a hamfisted juggler' (Banville 1987, 21). And yet this kind of objection does not represent a nihilistic perspective. Rather it proposes that appearance is the only reality. This doctrine is central to Nietzschean thinking:

> It is no more than a moral prejudice that truth is worth more than appearance; it is even the worst proved assumption that exists. Let us concede at least this much: there would be no life at all if not on the basis of perspective evaluations and appearances. (Nietzsche 1974, 56)

This correlates with Banville's repeated efforts to interrogate the bloated value we place on man-made systems which dismiss appearances as a kind of camouflage hindering the discovery of truth, rather than an integral facet of it. Nietzsche's objection to mathematics is actually a localised attack on a much larger framework. The delusion of mathematics, he views to be symptomatic of a more fundamental ailment. All logical thinking is suspect and the cause of many other delusory systems such as morality, language and religion. In Gabriel Swan's Nietzschean world of faltering scientific systems, there is no God and no morality. It is a world populated by powerless marionettes and merciless action, the only redeeming aspect being that a fiction is created. And for Nietzsche, the creative act is an expression of gratitude for existence. As Gabriel's reshuffling of Nietzsche's concept of causation informs us: 'However the cause is no matter, only the effect' (Banville 1987, 2).

Banville has commented that *Mefisto* was his pact with the devil and that *The Book of Evidence* is hell (Banville in Ní Bhrian 1989). Gabriel evolves into Freddie Montgomery who is serving time for the gratuitous murder of an innocent girl. Camus's Meursault, an obvious literary relative, seems almost benign beside Freddie. If Gabriel's world was a Faustian one, albeit with a Zarathustrian shape, then Freddie is the spawn of Nietzschean philosophy in the best, and worst, possible way. He assimilates Nietzsche's concepts of sloth and shame and eventually his growth to a kind of self-understanding is dictated by Dionysian principles. That Freddie's view of life at one time revealed nothing but the 'ceaseless, slow, demented drift of things' (Banville 1989, 135), is relevant because it echoes Nietzsche's 'continuum'. Prior to a more elaborate evaluation of these factors, it is necessary to introduce the character of Freddie whose memorable qualities range from the sociopathic to an occasional clarity of expression, a quality which finally redeems him.

The Book of Evidence contains all the familiar Banvillean traits. The novel corresponds to his previous works in that it frequently betrays Postmodern self-consciousness and flaunts its own artificiality: 'I thought of trying to publish this, my testimony. But no. I have asked Inspector Haslet to put it into my file, with the other, official fictions' (Banville 1989, 219–20). Furthermore, the narrator frequently toys with words and jokes at the need for him to obtain a dictionary. By doing so he slyly jibes at the reader's frustration at trying to understand his obscure vocabulary: 'I must see if I can get a catamite, or do I mean a Neophyte' (Banville 1989, 4). Also, Banville's, and Postmodernism's, obsession with an evasive past is reiterated through Freddie:

> In my mind there are places, moments, events, which are so still, so isolated, that I am not sure they can be real, but which if I had recalled them that nothing would strike me with more vividness and force than the real things surrounding me. (Banville 1989, 55)

This recalls Banville's appropriation of Proust's madeleines in *Birchwood*. The big house theme again surfaces, acting, predictably, as a shadowy metaphor for greater things. On this occasion the big house motif is employed as an indicator of the sloth which festers within the crumbling ruins of a mind reliant on the security of an empty ideal. Freddie's consciousness rarely manages to elude the tendency to drift from one self-vision to another. These usually originate in various clichés from the silver screen or literature: 'And there I am, striking an elegant pose, my ascetic profile lifted to the light in the barred window, fingering a scented handkerchief and faintly smirking, Jean-Jacques the cultured killer' (Banville 1989, 5). Freddie contents himself to play with these roles for much of his life. If there is no truth one can only pretend. But this playful, meaningless life is ultimately of no value just as fiction which utterly denies or negates its own power is valueless. Freddie relates his tale of drift as follows: '...a kind of slow subsidence, my shoulders bowing down under the gradual accumulation of all the things I had not done' (Banville 1989, 37–8). Such a history of inaction is the key to his fate. He had floated into a marriage with a woman whose reticence was, appropriately, her most alluring quality. By his own admission, she is possessed of a moral laziness and is thus a fitting companion. She had accompanied him during his years of aimless existence, culminating in the events which forced him to return to Ireland. He had, almost casually, abandoned his wife and child to the custody of Señor Aguirre, a stylised, silver-haired bandit, in order to seek financial aid to repay a debt. The repayment in question had arisen out of a flippant blackmail incident into which Freddie had blundered. His half-hearted efforts to raise funding in order to resolve the Mediterranean crisis lead directly, via his alcohol-sodden and amoral logic, to the murder of an innocent girl. His subsequent capture and imprisonment form the base from which he tells his tale.

Against this framework of events we are exposed to Freddie's mind which repeatedly refuses to make decisions. His only definite reactions are those that refute decisiveness and all strong opinions:

> They knew what they thought about things, they had opinions. They took the broad view as if they did not realise that everything is infinitely divisible. They talked of cause and effect, as if they believed it possible to isolate an event and hold it up to scrutiny in a pure, timeless space, outside the mad swirl of things...(Banville 1989, 17)

Freddie is a cynic *par excellence* but, like all of Banville's heroes, Freddie's real importance is located within a mesh of allusion, the novel being primarily regulated by Nietzschean thought. Prior to *The Book of Evidence* all of Banville's heroes depict a mistrust of various forms of human knowledge and expose their inadequacies. With Freddie, Banville enters a new arena of his interrogative fiction. Nietzsche's philosophy is unlike all the other systems of knowledge that Banville seeks to dismantle because its central impetus is a disbelief in the concept of all closed systems. Nietzschean thought, too, urges the re-evaluation of all set values: 'Behold the good and the just! Whom do they hate most? Him who smashes their tables of values, the breaker, the law-breaker – but he is the creator' (Nietzsche 1986, 51).

Freddie murders the girl because he 'meant to kill her' (Banville 1989, 210), and claims that he 'would do it again, not because I would want to but because I would have no choice' (Banville 1989, 151). This is the nucleus of his *acte gratuit*. He disbelieves in the validity of causes for any given action or isolated act and consequently questions, 'whether it is feasible to hold on to the principle of moral culpability once the notion of freewill is abandoned' (Banville 1989, 16). Within the continual flux, or continuum, of Freddie's life none of the events can be viewed separately and defined in terms of free will. Everything that occurs is dictated by the movement or non-movement of one's life in its totality. Thus morality is exposed by Freddie to be a system of laws created by a regulatory force by man, a force which does not have universal meaning:

> Evil, wickedness, mischief, these words imply an agency, the conscious or at least active doing of wrong. They do not signify the bad in its inert, neutral, self-sustaining state...It makes me wonder. I ask myself if perhaps the thing itself – badness – does not exist at all, if these strangely vague and imprecise words are an attempt to make it be there? Or again, perhaps there is something, but the words invented it. (Banville 1989, 55)

Banville's amoralist does not attempt to excuse his deed, nor does he try to absolve himself through speculations on the nature of morality. Indeed what he sees to be the real crime is outlined towards the close of the fiction. Freddie constantly struggles to clarify the actual crime he has committed. However, while his self-probing account of the events preceding the murder is told, he transforms into a mouthpiece for the Nietzschean philosophy of morality. The German writer's presence in Freddie reveals far more than the plot. Nietzsche argues against morality in a way similar to Freddie:

> ...today, when among us immoralists at least the suspicion has arisen that the decisive value of an action resides in precisely that which is not intentional in it, and that all that in it which is intentional, all of it that can be seen, known, conscious, still belongs to the surface and skin – which, like every skin, betrays something but conceals still more?...we believe the intention is only a sign and symptom that needs interpreting. (Nietzsche 1974, 45)

Obviously, moral culpability is, as Freddie tells us, questionable within such a world. For Nietzsche, morality is only a system of language which can vary for each person and the 'will to a system is a lack of integrity' (Nietzsche 1990, 35).

The philosophical debate which arises out of Freddie's self-indulgent rendition of his experiences is rooted in Nietzsche's beliefs and helps him to understand his sloth, or 'accidie' (Banville 1989, 44). There are no rules in his life. Freddie is a fictional representation of Nietzsche's philosophy of the 'extra-moral' (Nietzsche 1974, 45)[35] and yet the consequences that this has for the actuality of life are nullifying sloth, casual murder and imprisonment. Nietzsche tells us: 'There is no pre-established harmony between the furtherance of truth and the well-being of mankind' (Nietzsche 1977, 198). And yet, even in Nietzsche's world, Freddie's actions are not acceptable. Later in the novel, when Freddie realises that his real sin is a neglect of the imagination, he completes his evocation of the only Nietzschean ethic. *The Book of Evidence* operates outside Christian morality. God is long deceased and has been supplanted by Nietzsche. The well being of mankind is subservient to integrity and this means a perpetual revaluation of all systems. Nietzsche isolates those who predominantly prevent mankind from slipping into stagnation as the evil beings, or those who, through evil action, create something new and revitalised.

Freddie reflects this in that he is reborn after the murder and the dull dream of his former life has been comprehended. However, all new systems must, in Nietzsche's view, be continually destroyed and must evolve eternally: 'It is the strongest and most evil spirits who have up till now advanced mankind the most: they have again and again re-ignited the slumbering passions – all ordered society makes passions drowsy' (Nietzsche 1977, 97–8). The value of Freddie's action is that it assists his elevation from slothful probability theoretician to potential artist. He tells us with conviction: 'To do the worst thing, the very worst thing, that's the way to be free. I would never again need to pretend to myself to be what I was not' (Banville 1989, 124–5). The freedom achieved involves a purgation of pretence and false dignity which have been responsible for the life he has led –

that of the exiled vagabond heir to a worthless landed estate. Simultaneously, he ironically learns that his life has been one disposed to a terrible disregard for humanity and failure to sense the vividness of life. That he comprehends his past errors and has managed to perceive, however transiently, 'that simple, ugly, roistering world' (Banville 1989, 217), gives him hope for the future. That he has awoken from a life of intellectual slumber via the catalytic process of a violent deed once again exposes the Nietzschean inheritance in Banville: 'Almost every genius knows as one of the phases of his development the 'Catilinarian existence', a feeling of hatred, revengefulness and revolt against everything which already is, and which is no longer becoming...' (Nietzsche 1990, 110). This precisely mirrors Freddie's fated quest to locate a solution because there can be none in his Nietzschean world. He gains an understanding of his life only to realise that the future, while not the hazardous existence he had previously lead, is nonetheless as uncertain as that of any other Banvillean hero:

> I don't imagine for a second that such incidents [an epiphanic moment with a drunk in the rear of a police van] as this, such forays into the new world, will abate my guilt one whit. But maybe they signify something for the future. (Banville 1989, 217–8)

Freddie's understanding of his true sin, that of failing to imagine enough and failing to feel joy, represents the most tangible development in his erratic consciousness. He has been stunned into awareness by virtue of an act which he has been too irresponsible to prevent. He begins to regard life, albeit behind bars, in a more vivid way than ever in his dreamlike passive life. The source of his difficulties, like Banville's previous protagonists, is his reliance on a theoretical system of living, which ultimately fails to suffice when confronted with life. He had been a self-proclaimed and gifted probability theoretician but one with a strong scepticism from the outset: 'Better say I took up science in order to make the lack of certainty more manageable. Here was a way, I thought, of erecting a solid structure on the very sands that were everywhere, always, shifting under me' (Banville 1989, 18). Subsequently, Freddie had grown to disbelieve in any possible understanding of reality while, more dangerously, he also lost faith in the value of appearance and the power of imagination. This is, as he finally recognises, within a blur of self-deceit and self-examination, his most grave error. His power to imagine the world and its inhabitants is flawed due to his lack of faith in a tangible reality. Appearance had been something secondary, something which was doubtless illusory and thus he evolved into a passionless creature of stilted emotions who neither believed in reality nor appearances: 'Never wholly anywhere, never with anyone either, that was me always' (Banville 1989, 56). Once more the solution to this is located in Nietzsche:

> Reason is the cause of the falsification of the evidence of the senses. In so far as the senses show becoming, passing away, change, they do not lie...But Heraclitus will always be right in this, that being is an empty fiction. The 'apparent' world is the only one: the 'real' world has only been lyingly added! (Nietzsche 1990, 46)

Freddie's salvation is an extension of Nietzsche's and Heraclitus's sentiments. He understands that his crime is not simply a moral one. His inability to realise the worth of appearance had been his true sin. Thus he neglected to value and imagine life vividly enough. If he had done so, he would have felt the living presence of the girl and the slothful *acte gratuit* would not have happened:

> ...that I never imagined her vividly enough, that I did not make her live. Yes, that failure of imagination is my real crime, the one that made the others possible...I killed her because I could kill her, and I could kill her because for me she was not alive. (Banville 1989, 215)

Like Banville's other artist figures, Freddie had been dedicated to a specific vision of life but his beliefs forced him to turn away from the vividness of life. Banville's Copernicus and Gabriel Swan both initially believe that something can be proven but eventually understand the inadequacy of their systems. Freddie's life is lived in a brutish, callous way based loosely on Freddie's interpretation of probability theory. He had turned away from the messiness of life but he eventually finds consolation in art. Freddie informs us how he became intrigued by the anonymous painting *Portrait of a Woman with Gloves,* to such an extent that he dreamt up a complex, touching scenario. He was capable of imagining a vivid vision of the life of a girl who is but a representation. He creates art from art itself. However, within the dreamlike scenario, the power of art is suggested. After the girl has had her portrait completed she looks upon it in wonder for the first time: 'She had expected it would be like looking in a mirror, but this is someone she does not recognise, and yet knows. The words come unbidden into her head: Now I know how to die' (Banville 1989, 108). The fixed world of art prompts Freddie's reverie but, as Terence Brown has suggested, Freddie is 'a kind of artist, perhaps: one who admires the transformative power of art but who pays scant attention to the stuff of life which must be its base material' (Brown 1989, 23). Doubtless he is attracted by the power of art but his creative scenario is constructed exclusively from art and this will not suffice. His own life has been moulded into a kind of art form based upon clichéd images, in particular his own self-indulgent vision of the wayward son of the big house. In prison he pictures himself: 'like the gloomy hero in a Russian novel, brooding in my bolthole...with my story all before me, waiting to be told' (Banville 1989, 90–91).

In this sense Freddie has been an artist, transforming himself into cosy stereotypes, man-made constructs. Imagining a solipsistic, clichéd world for himself, he neglects to see real life all around him. But life, as Nietzsche knew, and as Freddie discovers, does not mean 'reality'. It means learning that appearance, after all of man's fruitless quests for truth, is all that matters. The hope inherent in the closing pages of Freddie's testimony negates the fallacy that both he and Nietzsche are nihilistic. As Nietzsche argues:

> God degenerated to the contradiction of life, instead of being its transfiguration and eternal *Yes!* In God a declaration of hostility towards life, nature, the will to life! God the formula...for every lie about the 'next world!' In God nothingness deified, the will to nothingness deified. (Nietzsche 1990, 138)

To object to flawed systems of knowledge is to strive for integrity. To accept the flawed knowingly shows a lack of integrity. To object is a negative concept but this does not constitute nihilism.

In Nietzsche's anti-schema we find not a refutation of the limits which are necessary to maintain life but a reshuffling of the levels of significance of these limits:

> ...that the definite shall be of greater value than the indefinite, appearance of less value than 'truth': but such valuations as these could, their regulatory importance for us notwithstanding, be no more than foreground valuations, a certain species of naiserie, which may be necessary precisely for the preservation of beings such as us (Nietzsche 1974, 17).

That mankind needs definite regulatory systems is certain but complete faith in the truth of such systems is, Nietzsche argues, misleading. Freddie represents a tangible evocation of such a position. The facts of his case, as he continually struggles to assure us, are mere shadows of the actual mesh of emotions and the 'incidental things, you see, the little things' (Banville 1989, 211). McMinn clarifies Freddie's position in a similar fashion: 'White (sic) remembers emotions and images more clearly than the facts or meaning' (McMinn 1989, 23).

Freddie represents the belief that definite, closed facts are no more than 'foreground valuations'. He can provide only an approximation of truth. This explains his closing, smug statement, when asked by the police inspector how true his account has been: '"True Inspector?" I said. "All of it. None of it. Only the shame"' (Banville 1989, 220). He can communicate only in blurred terms due to his disbelief in exactitudes. Or so it appears. The word *shame* is charged with significance in Nietzsche's intellectual order:

> A man whose shame has depth encounters his destinies and delicate decisions too on paths which very few ever reach and of whose existence his intimates and neighbours may not know: his mortal danger is concealed from their eyes, as is the fact that he has regained his sureness of life. (Nietzsche 1974, 51)

Shame, for Nietzsche, is a kind of purging process. It is necessary to feel shame to grow. And to what end? Nietszche readily provides the answer: 'What is the seal of freedom attained? No longer to be ashamed of oneself' (Nietzsche 1977, 236). Banville's hero achieves this seal of freedom by means of his purgatorial voyage to self-discovery. His perspective eventually shifts from slothful faith in probability theory to an awakening of his understanding of the power of imagination.

There are no truths in Freddie's world, if by truths one means intransigent structures that can teach one how to live. He acknowledges the chaos of appearance but discovers within this the redeeming power of the imaginative mind. Art transforms life into an artificial order and so too does the mind of man during each moment. Freddie learns that he must accept this transformative element in order to live. A search for absolute truth is destructive if one devalues the worth of appearance. Freddie informs us, ironically echoing an earlier artistic stance assumed by the author (Banville 1981, 13):[36] 'I have looked for so long into the abyss, I feel sometimes it is the abyss that is looking into me' (Banville 1989, 219). Freddie's abyss, originally his devotion to scientific methods as a way of living and later his nullifying sloth, had imposed itself so powerfully upon him that he could no longer appreciate the realities of the events unfolding about him. Nietzsche again clarifies Freddie's position in strikingly similar language: 'He who fights with monsters should look to it that he himself does not become a monster. And when you gaze long enough into an abyss the abyss also gazes into you' (Nietzsche 1974, 84).

Aidan Higgins's Dan Ruttle, in *Balcony of Europe*, too, echoes these sentiments and, in doing so, firmly establishes the Nietzschean inheritance in the Irish critical tradition: 'Gape not into the abyss, lest the abyss gape back into thee, dreamer. The unheard-of depths lure me into them; I experience vertigo' (Higgins 1972, 236). Banville's unlikely hero surfaces from the abyss of the author's endeavours to strip away the systems by which man lives and acknowledges that life, replete with its limitless contradictions and volatile appearances, must be the base from which all understanding stems and consequently, from which art must emerge. *The Book of Evidence* celebrates life although its conclusion is arrived at only after Banville's repeated depictions of various creators' immersions in intellectual rumination. Freddie's allegiance to probability theory was necessary in order for him to discover the worth of appearances. Banville's attempts to dismember systems of knowledge are necessary because through his persistent discourse on these very systems, he finally acknowledges life and appearances. His acceptance that all art must stem from the chaotic appearance that is life verifies his past efforts to demonstrate the value of fiction. Seamus Deane correctly isolates the focus of Banville's intentions when he claims that the author 'is writing about the problem of art...and the worth of being an artist' (Deane in Ní Bhrian, 1989). However, though this assessment is accurate, it is more accurate to say that Banville has, by *The Book of Evidence*, taken his enterprise into a direct interrogation of the imaginative impulse that lies behind artistic activity. As the first part of his trilogy of the artistic imagination *The Book of Evidence* initiates a dialogue which extends throughout *Ghosts* and *Athena*. It is a dialogue which seeks to inquire into the nature of the imagination, after other systems of human knowledge have been deconstructed. In doing so Banville's work seeks to display how the imagination engages life.

Banville locates his resolution in Nietzsche's eternally recurring universe. There is no truth other than an eternal, godless universe which must be accepted, even rejoiced at. Nietzsche realises the full, daunting prospect of such a world: 'Let us consider this idea in its most terrible form: existence as it is, without meaning or god, but inescapably recurrent, without a finale into nothingness' (Nietzsche in Heller 1976, 39). Man has created a complex structure of regulatory systems: science, reason, psychology, morality and, perhaps most desperately, religion and Gods. These are necessary fictions so that one is not forced to confront a void of nothingness. For Banville and Nietzsche, the imagination and the process of creation act as instruments of consolation in an eternally recurring void. And yet, this notion of consolation detracts somewhat from Nietzsche's conception of the world of art: 'The world itself is nothing but art...' (Nietzsche in Stambaugh 1972, 85). Joan Stambaugh elucidates Nietzsche's absolute faith in the essential part art must play in life:

> Art is for Nietzsche the highest form of human activity. In order to understand his treatment of the will to power as art, one must remember for him art is not

restricted to a particular sphere of human life, is not a collection of aesthetic objects and works; rather it is the innermost nature of the world itself: 'The world as a work of art that gives birth to itself'. Nietzsche's aesthetic is based on the artist himself, not on the observer. It thus illuminates the nature of the aesthetic activity rather than that of the aesthetic product. Art is understood in the broadest possible sense as a transfiguration and an affirmation of human existence. (Stambaugh 1972, 82)

For Nietzsche, then, the evolution or 'becoming' of the artist is the embodiment of art and life rather than the achievement of an aim or the creation of a product. The documentation of the transformation is art. Life is reshaped into art and so too is the artist. The artist shapes himself/herself into a living work of art, the ultimate aim being a limitless state of becoming. This is what man must seek; a state of gratitude through the process of artistic creation in a boundless, godless, eternally recurring existence. With *The Book of Evidence* Banville absorbs such ideas in the making of Freddie, whose transformation is even more mesmerising than the poetic articulation of his terrible crime. The self-reflexive nature of Banville's novel too absorbs much of Nietzsche's thought especially with regard to the author's concept of the work of art as an object which is a continuous state of evolution. Ultimately, the novel is about the act of creation and Freddie's representative value holds many implications for the state of Banville's art.

Freddie Montgomery is another emanation from Banville's artistic and sceptical consciousness. Like all of the author's previous creations, his singular most essential value is as an expression of Banville's evolving art. That he is spawned from Nietzschean philosophy is thus appropriate. Banville's most characteristic aspect throughout his oeuvre is an obsessive questioning of the meaning of art, and thus communication, which necessarily implies much for the human condition. Banville dismembers the tangible aspects of creativity, science, philosophy and language and ceaselessly strips away the cushions man has placed between himself and the chaos of living. What is of central importance, aside from the minutiae of Nietzsche's philosophy, is Banville's arrival at a point where he apparently understands, or at least affirms, that art and life are inseparable. We each transform the world each day into our own likeness, whether it is Kavanagh's Monaghan or Dedalus's Dublin. Freddie discovers his failure to be a refusal to see, a denial of the value of appearance and thus a neglect of the imagination which is the only god in the artist's universe. The artist is the most crucial instrument in creating reality. He must salvage life, be it past or present, from the misguided belief in a reality which might not be anything more than a complex arrangement of appearances from which we have no adequate defining system. All of Banville's texts document a mutating, purifying process and *The Book of Evidence* firmly registers that Banville, like Nietzsche, has fully accepted the chaos of life. Any artistic product of integrity must somehow echo this truism. This does not necessitate a refusal to accept man-made regulatory systems which enable life to continue, albeit imperfectly, it simply suggests the need to be aware of their inadequacies while working with them. Banville's novels all contain such a belief because while working with the imperfect strictures of language, Banville's narrators positively rejoice in expressing themselves.

The presence of Nietzsche's philosophy weighs heavily on *The Book of Evidence* and the quality of Banville's fiction in terms of such indulgence must be addressed. Nietzsche's attitude to immersing oneself in tradition was similar to Goethe's in its affirmation of such a practice. As I have already indicated, Freddie Montgomery becomes a kind of fictional ambassador for much of Nietzsche's philosophy. The important question is whether Banville's narrator registers a specifically Banvillean voice within the Nietzschean framework of ideas, which is something both Goethe and Nietzsche certainly achieved. Freddie is a powerful narrative creation and the novel itself is undoubtedly Banville's most accessible primarily because of its vivid and interesting plot, something with which Banville is not always unduly concerned. Furthermore, that this is Banville's most popular novel offers a true but accurate indication of how well the author disguises the presence of Nietzsche. Banville assimilates Nietzsche's ideas with great skill and this, in itself, is commendable. However, the high concentration of the German writer's philosophy is unsettling. Banville's novels always flaunt their high levels of intertextuality but with *The Book of Evidence* there is a sense that the author has exceeded acceptable levels of derivation, to the point where the novel ceases to be exclusively Banvillean. Certainly, Banville's work confirms Roland Barthes' vision of literature as intertextual tissue. Perhaps all literature is inevitably intertextual whether the author wishes it to be so or not but, nevertheless, one feels that any artist of value must also discover a unique voice. The canonical writers of western literature have always managed to do so despite conscious and unconscious assimilation of other ideas and literature in their works. Banville treads a very fine line in this respect. It is a consideration that proves even more consequential in the novels that emerge out of *The Book of Evidence*.

3.6 Reconstructing Artistic Reality

The second part to Banville's trilogy, *Ghosts*, is a surrealistic pastiche in which imagination is the only meaningful power. The landscape is comprised of various art objects and literary allusions, and of the group of marionettes who congregate at the beginning of the text, many are reincarnated from Banville's other fictions. The novel opens with the characters being marooned on an island, an island which recalls all literary islands, most obviously that of *The Tempest*, and the siren voices which sound throughout, recall all siren songs in literature and legend. 'The artist', says Banville, echoing Beckett and Kafka, 'is the man who has nothing to say' (Banville in Bragg 1993), by which he acknowledges his own refusal to write either overtly politicised work or writing directly derived from his own life experiences. *Ghosts* reflects this artistic position. *Ghosts* is a work of the imagination and its debt to other sources is gleefully paid in its extended intertextual play. In short, it is a typical Banville novel, one which resumes the process of inquiry into the meaning of that strangest of human qualities, the imagination, and how it apprehends life.

The rich tapestry of *Ghosts*'s narrative is woven by a narrator who has just recently been released from prison. His crime? The gratuitous murder of a girl. Although unnamed, our narrator is clearly Freddie Montgomery, reborn from the debris into which his *acte gratuit* had allowed him slip in *The Book of Evidence*. But this is no sequel. Freddie Montgomery of *The Book of Evidence* lived in a relatively solid world in which actions seemed possible. Not so on the Arcadian island in *Ghosts*. Here, the little acts in life – eating, sleeping, lovemaking – are all problematic, unfinished, frustrated and anxiety-ridden. This is a world hovering on the brink of disappearing, a world dependent on Freddie's keen eye and imaginative verve to tease it into life. Even the ontological status of the island is highly uncertain. Perhaps it is a figment of Freddie's yearning whilst still locked securely behind bars. Perhaps he is free and is an inhabitant of the island with his companions Licht and Kreutznaer, lost in an intertextual existence. Perhaps the familiar figures led by Felix, the devilish interloper in *Mefisto*, actually land on the island. It matters little, in effect. Such ontological possibilities serve only to contribute to the unavoidably fictional status of the text, a status which Banville accepts more completely than many of his peers. *Ghosts* is a highly self-reflexive pastiche whose primary end is to approach how the mind creates images of itself from the life in which it dwells. Freddie assumes that he must make amends for his sociopathic deed in *The Book of Evidence*, in which he killed a girl 'because I could kill her, and I could kill her because for me she was not alive' (Banville 1989, 216). She was not alive because of a failure of his imagination to conceive her. The lesson is not wasted on Freddie in *Ghosts* in which he experiences 'the hunger only to have her live and to live in her, to conjugate in her the verb of being' (Banville 1993, 70). By somehow quickening his imagination he hopes to imagine her into existence. This monumental task overtly (if anything can be overt in *Ghosts*) forms the basis of Freddie's narrative, a narrative which ponders Freddie's own ontological status as much as any of the other ghosts in the novel.

Freddie's apparent residence on the island, occasionally referred to as Cythera, Venus's love island, is accounted for due to his position as assistant to Professor Kreutznaer whose life's work is the work of the artist, Vaublin. Vaublin, we are told, is the painter of *Le monde d'or*, which receives much attention in the novel. There is, of course, no painter called Vaublin (a near anagram of Banville) or painting called *Le monde d'or*. The artist to whom Freddie refers is strikingly similar in style and content to Jean-Antoine Watteau whose *fêtes galantes*, or theatrical figures in pastoral settings, are among his most famous paintings. In fact it is Watteau's paintings which stand behind the most powerful imagery of the novel, *L'embarquement pour Cythère* and *Gilles*, in particular. Watteau's *L'embarquement pour Cythère* depicts a gathering of theatrical figures about to travel to Venus's love island, Cythera. Watteau used actors from the *Comédie Française* to pose for his theatrical painting and it is this sense of theatricality which extends to the figures who wash ashore on Banville's island. *Gilles* portrays a harlequin and a pierrot, two figures who compare with Freddie and Felix in Ghosts. Freddie himself is very taken with the surface texture of 'Vaublin's' *Le monde d'or*:

> This is the golden world. The painter has gathered his little group and set them down in this wind-tossed glade, in this delicate, artificial light, and painted them as angels and clowns. It is a world where nothing is lost, where all is accounted for while yet the mystery of things is preserved; a world where they may live, however briefly, however tenuously, in the failing evening of the self...in a luminous, unending instant. (Banville 1993, 231)

Banville has availed of the narrative structure of Watteau's *L'embarquement pour Cythère* for *Ghosts* and populated his island with angels and clowns and, as with all his mature fictions, the 'mystery of things is preserved', the thing-in-itself remains hidden, as it must be. The landscape of the novel thus appropriately avails of Watteau's theatrical vision and upon such an unreal, mythical island Banville's characters attempt to act out their own quasi lot. Such intertextual trickery reveals Banville's intentions. It is not the actuality of life which the author pursues but the ambiguities of art and Watteau's canvasses provide a suitable backdrop for Banville's fiction. The paintings of Watteau act as the central images in the novel from which the artistic commentary is delivered. In some of his previous fictions the discoveries of great scientists were used for similar reasons. *Ghosts* utilises a more immediate source; art itself.

Freddie derives much significance from the paintings by 'Vaublin'. They condition the way in which he sees life. Art is crucial to Freddie's method of apprehending the world. It helps him to see. In this Vaublin is not his only inspiration. Freddie is drawn to Diderot's ideas on sculpture and predictably he considers these ideas in relation to his own life:

> Diderot developed a theory of ethics based on the idea of the statue: if we would be good, he said, we must become sculptors of the self. Virtue is not natural to us; we achieve it, if at all, through a kind of artistic striving, cutting and shaping the material of which we are made, the intransigent store of selfhood, and erecting an idealised effigy of ourselves in our own minds and in the minds of those around us and living as best we can according to its sublime example. (Banville 1993, 196)

Freddie likes this notion because he too is a sculpted creature. He believes he is reborn and somehow improved, and yet he remains a ghost, half-alive, a shadow. His real admiration for Diderot, however, stems from the philosopher's reverence for statues:

> ...he thought of them as living, somehow: strange, solitary beings, exemplary, aloof, closed on themselves and at the same time yearning in their mute and helpless way to step down into our world, to laugh or weep, know happiness and pain, to be mortal. (Banville 1993, 196–7)

Freddie's attention is derived from his own questionable ontological status. He too is an artefact, a statue sculpted by a being on a higher state of existence than Banville himself. Freddie is aware of his own fictional status, he knows he is a 'character' and he appeals to his creator to give him life: 'Oh, if you are really there, bright brother, in your more real reality, think of me, turn all your stern attentions on me, even for an instant, and make *me* real, too' (Banville 1993, 181). At the core of the novel lies Freddie's dilemma; if he himself is not real then how does he make his peace and imagine the girl into existence. He grows to understand this and thus begins to understand himself. His fascination with Vaublin and Diderot stems from his attempt to comprehend the nature of the imagined thing. What is the meaning of a Vaublin landscape populated with fakes? What is the nature of the statue? These are the questions he ponders in order to know himself. Echoes of Beckett resound. Banville has his Freddie ponder such things in order to investigate the imaginative mind in apprehension.

As I have already stated, *Ghosts* uses Watteau's *L'embarquement pour Cythère* as a basic structure upon which events are enacted but apart from the novel's heavy reliance on the visual arts, the reader is constantly reminded of literature. The island recalls Prospero's tempestuous isle, the sinister mystique of *Lord of the Flies* and Freddie's attempts to create himself, during his more macabre moments, owes something to Mary Shelley's birthing myth in *Frankenstein*. Aside from these allusions there are direct quotations from Wallace Stevens, Kafka, Goethe and Nietzsche, references to Rimbaud's *bateau ivre*, Pygmalion and Greek mythology, as well as constant overt intertextual reminders of almost all of Banville's fiction. More elaborate a pastiche than any of Banville's previous fictions, *Ghosts* is a dreamlike tale woven from bits and pieces of other works which strive to discover the meaning of the creative process. Freddie is another incarnation of Banville's artistic consciousness, a consciousness which chooses art, not above life, but as a means of understanding life. The title of the novel is entirely appropriate because everything and every character that we encounter has had a previous existence. They are brought to Freddie's island which hums with literary resonance in order to show what the apprehended object is really like, what the bits of life are transformed into by the imagination. Banville litters the text with reminders of his characters' previous existences: '*I have an habitual feeling of my real life having passed, and that I am leading a posthumous existence!*' (Banville 1993, 25) The Mephisphelean Felix too is there to remind the troupe of puzzled day-trippers that they have been here before: '"Yes yes", he said impatiently. "Everyone feels they have been here before"' (Banville 1993, 48). The narrator takes much delight in such gimmickry, opening his account with self-deprecating arrogance: 'A little world is coming into being. Who speaks? I do. Little god' (Banville 1993, 4). The act of pushing disparate characters and worlds together seems to fascinate Freddie: 'Worlds within worlds. They bleed into each other. I am at once here and there, then and now, as if by magic' (Banville 1993, 55). Banville's use of Wallace Stevens's quotation as his epigraph grows clearer: 'There were ghosts that returned to earth to hear his phrases'. The ghosts here are the literary and artistic relics that wash up on Banville's shore to be charged with Freddie's, the Prospero figure, phrases.

Reflecting Banville's artistic intent, Freddie spends much of his account puzzling over how he can imagine a girl into life. He quickly realises how problematic such a task is and learns that he himself is the one that really matters: 'How then was I to be expected to know what others are, to imagine them so vividly as to make them quicken into a sort of life? Others? Other: they are all one. The only one' (Banville 1993, 27). Freddie, echoing Diderot's ideas on statues, learns that he must first create himself before tackling the more difficult task of imagining others. Although he ponders this concept early in his narrative he only fully realises it near the end. However, the girl Flora, both subject and object of Freddie's imaginative intent, does momentarily breathe for him, and lives – not as a result of his attempts to give life but simply by herself:

> She was simply there, an incarnation of herself, no longer a nexus of adjectives but pure and present noun...And somehow by being suddenly herself like this she made the things around her be there too. In her, and in what she spoke, the world, the little world in which she sat, found its grounding and was realised. (Banville 1993, 147)

Flora, the object of Ben White's attentions in *The Possessed*, is finally realised by dint of the power of imagination. She is no longer simply a construct of language, she has somehow risen above it and the effect which such a momentous event has on the world around it is also essential. Is this what fully realised things or people do? Do they make life more real, more vivid? Is this what the power of the imagination can do? Freddie affirms as much.

The momentary vision which Freddie experiences is swiftly replaced by tortured self-doubt and he retreats to the 'realm of art' (Banville 1993, 239). He understands that he has only begun to understand the meaning of the god of imagination which he has placed at the centre of his world: 'I still had, still have, much to learn. I am, I realise, only at the beginning of this birthing business' (Banville 1993, 239). The birthing business of which he speaks is really his own birth. In this he is both Caliban and Frankenstein's monster, confused and questioning the meaning of his own existence, pasted together as he is out of remnants of literature and art. He has even managed, admittedly briefly, to imagine a girl into a kind of existence. Freddie has lost his family, his life, his home, his amoral beliefs. He wanders the island of his mind charging everything with his longings and imaginings, like the Wandering Jew destined forever to make amends for his past sin. The cruel irony is that Freddie cannot imagine himself into life. No matter how he tries, he remains somewhere between death and life, himself a frail ghost of the imagination.

The intertextual world which Freddie inhabits is characteristically Banvillean with its borrowed props and familiar characters, and all serve to raise the resonance of the novel to a fine pitch. The presence of Stevens, who Banville calls 'a great champion of the imagination' (Banville in Bragg 1993), *The Tempest*, *Frankenstein*, Kafka, Goethe and Nietzsche all add to the texture of Freddie's dream, his dream of imagination and creation. All these presences also reflect the relentless pursuit of the meaning of the creative mind and, with Watteau and Diderot, assist in creating a novel which is a shrine to the power of the imagination. Ultimately though, it is upon Freddie's persona that all of it comes to bear. Although he initially believes his role is to charge the girl with life, to make her live, he eventually understands that he must first 'imagine myself into existence' (Banville 1993, 195–6). This is no easy thing for Freddie, existing as he does in the shadows of this already invented world. Ultimately, Freddie, like everything else in the novel, is an emblem of Banville's highly self-reflexive endeavour, even if he is a mesmeric character. Freddie is just another named incarnation of the author's inquiry into how the mind of man apprehends life, a point not wasted on Freddie who avails of the language of those former champions of creativity: 'There they were, the old man in the tower with his books, the damsel under lock and key, and the dark one, my dark brother, waiting for me, the knight of the rosy cross, to throw down my challenge to him' (Banville 1993, 240). Freddie simply represents the author's unwavering engagement with the meaning of man's interpretative systems. Banville's pursuit of this meaning remains constant but it is a progressive journey because his perspective alters with each successive fiction. *Ghosts*, unlike many of the previous novels, is freed of the scientific, historical or philosophical baggage which gave their plots substance. Even the moral questioning inherent in *The Book of Evidence* is absent and in this regard Banville's focus seems to have shifted significantly.

The self-reflexive condition of Banville's fictions has long been a constituent part of their motivation but it nevertheless remains a dominant aspect in all the author does. Freddie, in *Ghosts*, via Banville's self-reflexive play, recalls the author's science tetralogy by mentioning his own prison term:

> Freedom! What a thought! The very word gave me the shivers. Freedom, formless and ungraspable, yes, that was the true nature of my sentence. For ten terrible years I had yearned to be free, I had eaten, slept, drunk the thought of it, lay in my bunk at night...I am free, I told myself, but what does it signify? This objectless liberty is a burden to me. (Banville 1993, 195)

Banville's science tetralogy too took ten years and the author's self-reflexive reminder also alludes to Gide's Immoralist's 'objectless liberty', used as an epigraph to *The Possessed*. Although the epigraph was in essence a bravura attempt to assign significance and coherence to the flawed novella, Banville's retrospective eye avails of the ironic contrast between the two works. The search continues but it yields far more sublime results. More important, though, is Banville's allusion to his ten years in the prison of the tetralogy, during which time he stripped away the concept of science as an arbitrator of truth. Actually, from *Birchwood* onwards, Banville's novels have sought to expose man-made systematic thinking to be providers of version of truth rather than the thing itself. His science tetralogy interprets science as an imaginative pursuit. Mathematics, like language, is merely a system with which we classify life. In *The Book of Evidence* Freddie Montgomery, a failed scientist, experiences a life which has been stripped of morality. What remains, when this final social ordering system is peeled away, he learns, is imagination. *Ghosts*, introduced as it is by Wallace Stevens, tells a tale of a man who has lost everything. Like Gide's immoralist, he lives without the old certainties, science and morality, and it is the 'liberty' he intends to explore.

By *Ghosts*, there is little left for the author to strip away. All those systems with which we designate reality have been exposed as consolatory ordering systems. Freddie lives in a world dominated by imaginative pursuits and, of course, art itself. In his previous novels Banville has used science and mathematics as the central images from which the significance of the works emanates. In *The Book of Evidence* he builds his fiction around a lattice of Nietzschean thinking in order to expose the social illusions of moral systems, and avails of the rich complexity which such a lattice offers. In *Ghosts* there is, appropriately, a concentration on art, in particular visual art. Banville's reasons are unsurprising:

> I suppose because the language of science is too systematised – I couldn't incorporate any actual scientific discourse in my book because it stood out too much. And I am fascinated by the surface of things, and painting deals with these. Painting is the triumph of looking, of obsessed scrutiny. (Banville in Meany 1993, 12)

Banville again recalls Nietzsche's celebration of the surface as the only way we can know life. Perception is all. Freddie too utters such a sentiment in *Ghosts* in that he realises that he is the one who matters, he learns that it is the perceiving mind that creates one's vision of life. When Banville wrote historical novels their intentions were misconstrued due to the thematic baggage, with which Banville is not unduly concerned. With *Ghosts* he has reached out to the core issues, which exist in all his work.

The surface texture of Banville's fictions, in particular *The Book of Evidence*, *Ghosts* and *Athena*, redolent as they are with lyrical description, attempt to suggest the qualities of painted art. The linguistic brush-strokes are at least as important as the scenes they evoke because the way something is expressed is, for Banville, indicative of the way that the mind formulates images of the real. Thus, the visual and the linguistic somehow preserve life. Banville's fictions unashamedly aestheticise life and it is this intention that lies at the heart of the endeavour:

> But style is always aware and style is everything. It is unawareness that is the real sin. I am trying to aestheticise reality in order to redeem it. The world will always reassert itself in a work of art when it has found a fixed style. (Banville in Meany 1993, 12)

Without awareness, or imaginative intensity, and style or the articulate voice, reality is adrift, prosaic. It must be apprehended and aestheticised in order for it to make sense; it must be taken into oneself and said. Banville's argument is one of immense significance for his art. Despite layers of aestheticising images and literary and artistic gestures he feels the world can somehow reassert itself. By imprinting a style or voice upon the world it is plucked from the ceaseless flow of the inarticulate and realised in the art object. Freddie too is privy to such thoughts:

> I am the pretext of things, though I sport no thick gold wing or pale halo. Without me there would be no moment, no separable event, only the brute, blind drift of things. That seems true; important too. (Yes, it would appear that after all I am indeed required.) (Banville 1993, 40)

Such is the philosophical position which Banville's journey reaches with *Ghosts*, to be resumed in *Athena*. Of course, it is not in opposition to his previous positions but *Ghosts* is closer to the realm of pure imagination than any of his preceding fictions and the reasons why Freddie is the pretext of things are more exquisitely expressed than before. *Ghosts* is not about life, it is about how the imaginative mind can respond to life and expresses why this response must be explored and valued because then, perhaps, life itself can be made more lucid. Banville's *Ghosts* is an intertextual dream whose central character dreams of one day understanding what it means to be alive. Freddie's ontological position is thus questioned but also redeemed in the novel's hope-filled message. It is an optimistic novel because, unlike the anxiety-ridden dilemmas of many Postmodern novels (some of Banville's early work included), it justifies itself by discovering life in the unlikeliest of places.

The closing words to *Ghosts*, 'No: no riddance' (Banville 1993, 245), confirm that Banville's expedition is far from complete, if it ever can be. His fictions are as much about transience and the past as they are about how we approach such complexities and they continue to assert that life is chaotic and that we can achieve only versions but this assertion is ultimately liberating and truly constructive in a world where, quite often, dogma is more powerful than dialogue and truth is still yearned for amid a complexity which derides such a crude concept.

With *Ghosts*, Banville has altered his approach to plot in a fundamental way. It is reminiscent of *Nightspawn* and *Birchwood* in its overt Postmodern fictional setting. There is little attempt to place the novel in a realistic Irish landscape, apart from a brief trip from Dublin into the Irish countryside, which is quickly transformed into Freddie's haunted island. Even in *Mefisto*, that surreal fiction, one can recognise a faint outline of Dublin behind the glittering prose. The novel's ontological status is dictated more by dreams, absences, half-formed characters and paintings which are about as real as the characters who gaze at them, than it is by the real world. Banville's use of science, mathematics and morality for comparative purposes had begun to have a repetitive ring to them even though they are essentially optimistic. *Ghosts* is about the imagination itself and this profoundly conditions the narrative. Freddie tells us that we not only create ourselves but the world itself. Reality is, of course, out there somewhere but if we want to make it coherent we must transform it, imagine it and articulate it, and who better to display such a practice than Freddie whose delight in words recalls that other great creative criminal, Humbert Humbert.

To say that nothing is real in *Athena* is fatuous, considering the radical reordering of this very concept in Banville's work, and yet this novel confirms and extends the stylised ontology of Banville's fictional landscape so unremittingly that it has profound implications for the significance of the work. As the third part of Freddie Montgomery's (now renamed Morrow) testimony, *Athena* continues Banville's direct inquiry into the nature of the creative imagination. In *The Book of Evidence* Freddie killed a girl because he failed to imagine her. In *Ghosts*, the newly released Freddie attempts a prolonged effort at effecting an imaginative parturition. With *Athena* that birth, we are led to believe, occurs. But, then, nothing is as it seems in *Athena*.

Art is made out of art. This is the artistic assumption upon which Banville's vibrantly intertextual trilogy rests, and this is the key to *Athena*'s endless series of textual tricks. Everything in the novel is self-consciously fake. Aunt Corky (not an aunt to Freddie at all) has perpetually invented her entire life and, appropriately, has her life history invented by Freddie after her grotesque death, because the attendant doctor is too lazy to discover the 'truth'. The Da, that 'Master of disguise' (Banville 1995, 70), switches identities with each brief appearance while A., Morrow's love interest, is hardly there at all and everyone in the text is rendered textual by virtue of Freddie's artistic consciousness. Even the afternoon light has a 'Hellenic radiance' (Banville 1995, 35). Banville has again constructed a landscape composed out of fragments of art, literature and comics. There is nothing new in this. More intriguing is the author's use of a Greek mythological structure to underpin the work, revolving around the title of the work. Athena, daughter of Zeus, was born fully formed emerging from the forehead of her father after Hephaestus split open Zeus's head to cure him of his headaches. She is, variously, the Goddess of wisdom and civilisation, war, artisans, or, in Homer's *Odyssey*, she is an arch deceiver and liar. Her emblem, the owl, associates her with wisdom, death and the night. In all of these aspects, her relevance to a Banville fiction is obvious.

However, Banville has never simply availed of a mythical structure to order his work. If A. is Athena then her father, The Da, is Zeus, the Master of disguises. In this reading, the squalid underbelly of gangland Dublin is thus being structured by the Godly. Fortunately, this does not quite add up because the mythical narrative does not bear fruit upon analysis. A. is no virgin, as Athena was reputed to be, and the Da's cross-dressing is but a parodic rendering of Zeus's disguises. Furthermore, A.'s mother is called 'that Parsiphae of the Plains' (Banville 1995, 124). Parsiphae is the mother of the Minotaur, who, in this text, is Freddie. Thus, through Banville's frequently sordid reinvention of Greek myth, A. becomes Freddie's sister, and their love affair recalls Ben White's and Flora's incest in *The Possessed*, and also echoes the recurrence of the motif of the lost twin in Banville's work, from *Birchwood* onwards. As such Banville's own myth supersedes the Greek. The apparent mythical structure is really just a game which the author uses to disguise his own myth, the same myth that he has persistently endeavoured to construct.

The highly stylised landscape into which we accompany Morrow is derived from a plethora of artistic and literary works, many of which are entirely appropriate to the kind of endeavour in which the author is engaged. By *Athena*, Morrow's consciousness adopts and dispenses with literary and artistic reflections with ease and thus he is, variously, Zeus having given birth to Athena, Actaeon, Marsyas and Pygmalion. In addition he wonders how could he be Theseus, 'left weeping on this desolate shore?' (Banville 1995, 174) He is finally, of course, the Minotaur, who too has a history of violence. The point is that Freddie has many precursors, reinvented or otherwise. In a textual universe, anything is possible because the intention is not to mirror anything fixed. Everything is the same, and yet different.

The novelist, Patrick McGrath, makes much of the 'mechanistic world' which he finds in *Athena* (McGrath 1995, W9), and certainly the reader is perpetually reminded of the non-realistic nature of the world in which these characters are assembled. Morrow's world is, after all, a world of art in which everything is driven by the artificial. In fact, those moments which are especially fake are the most seductive to Morrow. Recalling Kleist's marionettes, Morrow marvels at A.'s movements:

> She would take a deep breath, drawing back her shoulders and lifting her head, carefully keeping her glance from straying in the direction of the spyhole; her movements were at once stiff and graceful, and touched with a strange unhuman pathos, like those of a skillfully manipulated marionette. (Banville 1995, 156)

The world of the consciously invented is where Morrow lives, the world of careful artistic gestures and intentions. Morrow has no interest in replicating the real, whatever that may be. Rather, he wishes to imagine a thing of beauty into existence. In order to say his world, he borrows from the world of art. In order to create A. he must recall all her predecessors, many of whom he has previously invented. And in turn, he might just manage to compose himself.

The secret to Banville's *Athena* lies in his other work because all the primary figures appear in the earlier novels. When Morrow dreams of youthful summer days, he is remembering the story, 'Summer Voices', from *Long Lankin*. When the reader feels the tremor of violence in Morrow, he/she should remember that it too stretches back to the residual terror of *Long Lankin*, and is not exclusive to the Art trilogy. Most importantly, Morrow himself, self-reflexive counterpoint to Banville the artist, has always existed in various incarnations in the work. So too has A., as the constant unsayable mystery, or absence, after which Morrow trails. A. is Flora (from *The Possessed* and *Ghosts*), Sophie/Adele (*Mefisto*), Daphne (*The Book of Evidence*), Rose (the imagined sister in *Birchwood*) and all other evocations of the mystery of art who appear and vanish throughout the author's work. Similarly, Morrow, or Freddie, is all of Banville's artist-figures, reborn anew, still engaged on the same journey. Furthermore, the house on Rue Street is a fictional counterpart to the house in which Banville's heroes have always lived, the same house in which Gabriel Godkin ensured us that he would remain at the close of *Birchwood*. Morrow reveals the significance of this quite openly when he quotes Adorno: 'She is the perfect illustration of Adorno's dictum that "In their relation to empirical reality works of art recall the theologumenon that in a state of redemption everything will be just as it is and yet wholly different"' (Banville 1995, 105).

Banville's fictions have always been the same, and yet different. Morrow's proximity to his subject seems closer now than ever and yet everything too seems the same. But that is precisely Banville's point. The almost overwhelming echoes of other textual models confirm that the activity of artistic creation is, and always has been, a ubiquitous human fascination. In *Athena*, references to birthing myths abound, including Athena's own mythical birth, A.'s birth, Dr. Frankenstein's imagined misery at the loss of his monster (Banville 1995, 223), H.G. Wells's *The Island of Dr. Moreau* (from which Morrow's name is partly derived) and Jekyll and Hyde. As a self-consciously fictional rendition of artistic parturition, *Athena* probes the precise nature of that very process, just like Banville's heroes have always done. The difference with *Athena*, is not necessarily that Morrow manages to create a woman, but that in the process of trying to imagine her into existence he manages to realise himself. That is what it has always been about, the novel implies. Morrow is then both Dr. Frankenstein and the monster simultaneously, self-reflexively composed, as he is, of shreds of other fictional creations. Banville implicitly suggests that all creative enterprises fundamentally aim to replicate the creator, consciously or otherwise. However, in the process, the artist too is transformed by the ineffable mystery of art, by that silent room which recurs over and over in Banville's work.

In *Ghosts*, Freddie realises that this is the crucial issue: 'Was that it, that I must imagine myself into existence before tackling the harder task of conjuring another?' (Banville 1995, 196). In *Athena*, this realisation takes more defined shape: '…and from the start that was supposed to be my task: to give her life. Come live in me, I had said, and be my love. Intending, of course, whether I knew it or not, that I in turn would live in her' (Banville 1995, 223). Ultimately, that is what Banville's enterprise has been about; the incessant journeying towards the creative act and all that it entails. In the process, he self-consciously reveals the various stages of his process. With *Athena*, the destination is by no means reached, because it can never be. The essence of art remains forever just out of sight, forever disappearing, just as A. has disappeared. What remains is the record of the imagination interrogating itself, or, as Imhof has it: '*Athena* is concerned with imagination imagining itself' (Imhof 1995, 27).

Athena extends Banville's fictional exercise because never before has the self-reflexivity reached such proportions. By building Morrow's artistic commentaries on the paintings into the text Banville directly comments on his own work. All the paintings are by artists whose names are anagrams, or near-anagrams of John Banville or J. Banville (all too are Banville's age at the time of writing the novel) and all correspond to various aspects of *The Book of Evidence*, *Ghosts* and, in particular, *Athena*. The paintings are, of course, inventions, both on the plotted level and in real terms, just as Banville's novels are. Thus the fictional Morrow comments on fictional paintings which turn out to be inventions of his own creator, and as such occupy the same ontological status as Morrow himself. Art talks about itself in an endless commentary about its own workings and qualities. Surely this is the point. As has been emphasised in the science tetralogy, man's systems reflect only themselves and what appeared to be a stripping away of the authority of science actually becomes a vindication of the metaphorical power of science, and art. All synthetic systems talk about themselves, using their own frames of reference, and thus designate their own textual realities. However, *Athena*, as the final statement of the trilogy of art, emphasises that the system, the textual actuality of the work of art, far from being its undoing, is closer to the truth. The stylised world of *Athena* facilitates Morrow's enterprise precisely because it is stylised. In this art contains truth. Reality is a shabby relation. Morrow does not like the real: 'Real people: I am never at ease in the presence of real people' (Banville 1995, 113).

Ultimately, *Athena* confirms what Banville's work has been saying for a long time: that we each imagine our existences. But the quality of those imaginings are all important. Morrow forges himself into a different creature by virtue of his attempts to create another, and that, it is implied, is the meaning of art. Late in the novel Morrow reflects on life:

> What we see up there are not these tawdry scenes made to divert and pacify just such as we: it is ourselves reflected that we behold, the mad dream of ourselves, of what we might have been as well as what we have become, the familiar story that has gone strange, the plot that at first seemed so promising and now has fascinatingly unravelled. Out of these images we manufacture selves wholly improbable that yet sustain us for an hour or two, then we stumble out blinking into the light and are again what we always were, and weep inwardly for all that we never had yet feel convinced we have lost. (Banville 1995, 227)

Art then, after all, is about life. The self-reflexive metafictional conventions employed by Banville throughout his career may have exposed the limitations of realism as a style but that does not mean that he has rejected the real, rather he has reconstructed what is considered real. It is all a matter of style, of finding ways to see and say the world which has 'unravelled'. Ironically for all his metafictional antics, Banville has never strayed too far from traditional narrative forms. They have always remained as loose literary shapes within which the author has played his games. They are, and have always been, very serious games which have tried to enunciate, not reality, but art. However, the real is already art for Banville's heroes of the imagination. Their difficulty has always been finding a way to say that truism without disturbing the essence of truth. What *Athena* suggests, via its macabre yet vibrant narrative, is that the truth is only there in the saying and responding to Rilke's command to: 'Praise this world to the Angel', Morrow manages to locate a sense of himself, however tentative that may be. To be tentative, it would seem, is the way to be real.

3.7 Conclusion

Banville's novels are dominated by ontological issues. Having acknowledged the impact of Modernism's epistemological investigations, he propels his creative heroes in pursuit of ways to designate a reality which might respond to the impasse unearthed by his predecessors. Banville's metafictional work uses many of the stylistic devices of literary Postmodernism and certainly corresponds to Brian McHale's identification of Postmodern fiction with a poetics dominated by ontological issues. In addition, his work corresponds to Richard Kearney's claim that the second generation of his counter tradition 'interpreted the stalemate as a surrender of memory to the order of the creative imagination' (Kearney 1982, 396). Furthermore, Banville's work continually echoes that of Nabokov, Beckett, Calvino and a host of other Postmodern novelists. In general, in its bleakest moments, Postmodernism implies that experience is just a matter of style and that reality is a system of signs within which we remain trapped, babbling out our empty messages. However, Banville has sought to reach beyond this cul-de-sac which Gabriel Godkin recognises to be a 'collapsible kingdom' (Banville *BW* 1984, 108), as far back as *Birchwood*. Even though the self-reflexive voice has become a constituent part of Banville's artistic voice, he has striven to discover a way to escape the limits of the Postmodern novel, as he found it.

He does this by retaining many of the narrative conventions of the realist novel while he constructs his own mythical universe. Although parody is never absent from the various narrative voices, from *Birchwood* onwards, Banville generally uses tradition to greater effect than simply parodying all that he inhabits. The reason for this is that Banville's work has never fully relinquished the idea that literature has a direct relevance for life, unlike many other Postmodern novelists. Literature may not be able to represent life as realist fiction purported to do, but this in no way means that literature cannot have a relationship with life. Thus Banville has sought, throughout his work, to construct an extended metaphor which might speak of life. However, responding to Modernism, Banville's work must simultaneously accept the imposition of man's epistemological methods in the communicative act. This is why the self-conscious voice continually analyses itself in the act of forging its extended myth of creation. Such a literature of process must lead somewhere. Taken as one interconnected journey, the novels are uncanny in their emphatic sense of direction. Tracing contemporary scepticism back to the great astronomers of the

Renaissance, Banville pursues the idea of the active creative mind in the process of self-analysis, as with all reductive systems of knowledge. Moving from Renaissance science and history to mathematics and modern physics in the tetralogy, the work establishes the defining nature of man's systems of knowledge. Truth is the elusive quality for his various scientists and scientist-figures because they cannot encode it in their systems. With the trilogy of art this interrogation is directly applied, first to morality, and then to art itself. Freddie Montgomery, or Morrow, finally establishes that the purpose of it all has been to discover the nature of the impulse that drives the creative mind, to discover the self in the act of creation.

Banville writes himself out of the theoretical abyss of Postmodernism because he ultimately suggests that by talking about art one talks about the world, by talking about metaphorical systems one reveals the urge that creates the systems. In Banville's universe of absences, mirror images and lost twins it is impossible to represent reality but it is possible to reveal the meaning of man's searches. Gabriel Godkin's search is Freddie's search, as it is most certainly Banville's search. Just as enlightenment analysis has sought to discover the truth beneath the appearance of things. As such Banville's journey becomes a metaphor for all similar searches and failures. In *Athena*, Morrow expresses this fact near the close when he acknowledges that all we see is a: 'mad dream of ourselves', when we behold a work of art, or any other complex system for that matter.

Thus, Banville's fiction confirms the fictional nature of our systems and our lives. We 'manufacture selves' (Banville 1995, 227), invent scientific, religious, moral and artistic systems which in no way reflect reality, only ourselves. By a process of self-revelation, his fictions attempt to eke out a correspondence for life. It is grossly simplistic to suggest that Banville's fictions are not about reality, they are about nothing but reality. Our confusion arises when we imagine that reality to resemble the stylised versions we have grown accustomed to in realist fictions, replete with unswerving belief in systems of morality, causation, temporal sequence and personality. Banville has always refused to respond to that particular style of representation, preferring instead to immerse himself in a body of tradition, not only confined to literature, from which he might derive a way of saying. This is one of the primary reasons for the high levels of intentional intertextuality in his work.

Belonging to that tradition of writing which emphasises the text rather than the author, or what Barthes calls 'eternal copyists' (Barthes 1989, 116; Morden insists on the word copies as opposed to fakes in *Athena*), Banville embraces tradition like few other writers of his generation, Rushdie included. In doing so he selectively assimilates, in particular, that sceptical tradition which has been engaged in similar concerns to his own. Language is an intensely complex way of designating reality and Banville has embraced a body of tradition which offers him archetypal models with which he assembles his tales of creation. The whole enterprise, especially in *Ghosts* and *Athena* has an intensely familiar feel to it precisely because it is familiar, as familiar as the whole weight of the Western intellectual tradition. The author's technical brilliance is this respect is astonishing.

Art is made from art in Banville's fictions. Its intertextual resonance is a crucial part of its artistic ethos and Banville's use of tradition is employed effectively on a technical level. However, despite the artistic justification of tradition in Banville's work the question of acceptable limits of derivation must certainly arise. Works of the literary canon distinguish themselves by virtue of, among other things, establishing unique voices. Banville's extensive use of tradition is a peripheral concern if it establishes a distinct Banvillean voice in the process. By consciously weaving so many allusions into his work one wonders is this possible. All stories may well represent the same human urges somehow to realise ourselves, but not all stories are the same and even Shakespeare, that great coloniser of other literary models, clearly managed to say what no one else had quite said. Can the same ultimately be said about Banville? Every reader of Nabokov will recognise the immense debt Banville owes to that source and I have indicated some of the Nietzschean references and echoes in *Mefisto* and *The Book of Evidence*. Admittedly, Banville has forged a distinctive landscape in the process of his literary endeavours and the very enterprise he is engaged upon necessitates drawing his work close to that branch of Western intellectual thought which he clearly feels to be so relevant for the contemporary moment. Banville's work is derivative but he would, I am sure, argue that all literature is. However, it must also be acknowledged that what makes great writers unique is that they create a body of work which has the immense power of myth, the memorable ability to linger in the minds of generations of readers and writers. Banville's work, engaged on an elaborate game of pastiche, despite his theoretical justifications, sometimes risks getting lost in the clamour of voices he has built into his work. And yet perhaps the risks are worth taking, because Freddie Montgomery in his various incarnations manages to register his own peculiar ontological status in a universe of literary relatives and ghostly presences. In the Irish context, Banville has certainly responded to the problematic inheritance of Joyce and Beckett in an immensely significant way, though the influence of the Germanic tradition – Nietzsche, Goethe, Kleist and Rilke especially – is at least as important to his work, and most likely more important. However, Banville's work represents an enormous contribution to the Irish critical novel by virtue of his efforts to establish art itself as an artistic subject that merits attention, because of the profoundly human implications it entails.

CHAPTER 4

Neil Jordan: Dissolving Selves

'My selves dissolving, old whore petticoats' Sylvia Plath, 'Fever 103°'

4.1 Prelude

The inclusion of Neil Jordan's fiction in this study demands some brief explanatory comment, primarily because Jordan's body of literary fiction is by no means as substantial as that of either Banville or Higgins, but also because, as I will illustrate, his fiction amounts to a limited achievement beside that of my two other primary subjects. The foremost value that Jordan's work offers to this study is, firstly, harsh as it sounds, a clear comparative indication of the immense worth of both Banville's and Higgins's extended inquiry into the Modernist and Postmodernist novel when viewed beside the relatively marginal achievement of Jordan's work, and secondly, because Jordan offers an alternative approach to the complex formal dilemmas faced by novelists since the 1960s. The latter reason is the more important one, of course, because the primary purpose of this book is not essentially to evaluate the worth of these writers. Rather, it is an analysis of how they confront both the legacy of Modernism and contemporary Postmodernism. Thus I include a study of Jordan's fictions to illustrate the alternative methods that he employs to confront issues similar to those engaged by Banville and Higgins. No doubt Jordan begins from a similar aesthetic basis as Banville, in particular, but the formal conventions he invents to resolve the Modernist communicative *impasse* are quite different to those of either Banville or Higgins.

Night in Tunisia, Jordan's debut collection of short stories, is written in the tradition of Modernist fiction in that its dominant ethos is one of questioning of modes of human knowledge, while his various narrators attempt to articulate their surroundings. Later, with *The Past*, Jordan, like Banville, embraces the formal metafictional properties of the Postmodern novel and attempts to construct a stylised artificial universe composed via the narrator's imagined reconstruction of his parents' past. Reacting against the intense formal difficulties of such an enterprise the author, in *The Dream of a Beast*, effectively rewrites Kafka's *Metamorphosis* by imposing the idea of a creative consciousness on the metaphorical model. The intention remains the same, to discover a form which might express the complex relationship between the imagining mind and the world it inhabits. Most recently, with *Sunrise with Sea-Monster*, Jordan again returns to the problematic nature of human communication and the familiar Postmodern dilemma of how to know and articulate reality. To Jordan's credit he has consistently striven to confront the deconstructed nature of the novel form and has not contented himself with the negativity of much of Postmodern fiction. Like Banville, he has continually attempted to find a way that might restore validity to human communication in its attempt to say the world. However, unlike Banville's endeavours, Jordan's literary journey has rarely achieved a specific philosophical direction, instead returning to the same issues again and again, without ever formulating a sustained body of ideas. Thus, though the author's work, on the whole, does not register a convincing resolution to the problems he seeks to resolve, it does employ a number of interesting, and rewarding strategies in its engagement of the critical debate in Irish fiction.

The dominant focus of this chapter is on Jordan's literary fiction but it also incorporates a brief analysis of one of Jordan's film texts, *The Crying Game*. My foremost reason for including *The Crying Game*, essentially an advanced and highly stylised version of Jordan's first full-length film, *Angel*, rests on the assumption that Jordan's confrontation of the problems associated with representative fiction extends to his filmmaking. As such, *The Crying Game* also bears the traces of the author's innovative artistry particularly in its attempt to reveal stereotypical images to be an aspect of social conventions which rarely hold true upon close scrutiny. Jordan implies that on a social and a personal level, in our often-perverse desire for ordering systems, we conceive of our world and the people who inhabit it, by virtue of inherited fictions which disguise much more than they reveal. *The Crying Game* is an attempt to expose some of those stereotypes in much the same way as *The Dream of a Beast* is an attempt to show that existence can be transformed by changing the fictions we bring to bear on it. While accepting that certain formal difficulties arise in the comparative analysis of different media, my analysis of *The Crying Game* will show that these are peripheral issues which diminish when one acknowledges the vagaries of each medium.

Like Banville and Higgins, Jordan's art is characterised by an obvious interrogation of the formal aspects of the work. Indeed, like Banville's, Jordan's work overtly reveals its own process. Human experience is not presented as an ordered, sequential truism, which is easily translated into verbal or visual images. Instead, Jordan, like Banville and Higgins, questions how one can present experience through art. Like those two authors, Jordan is part of the tradition of critical questioning but, in essence, what these artists share is an understanding that experience is not easily translatable into words or moving pictures. All three, of course, approach this essentially Modernist position in different ways. Higgins never turns away from the primacy of experience and his work, in later years in particular, grows increasingly fragmentary as a consequence. Banville, alternatively, like Beckett, erects a house of fiction inhabited by mannequins and intertextual gestures in an attempt to communicate his highly self-conscious artistic vision. Jordan too forges a distinctive response. Occasionally, he attempts to embrace a life coloured with carnivals, jazz music, and the brooding presence of a troubled Northern Ireland. In addition he debates the meaning of the self, of memory and the deceptive intricacies of language. *The Dream of a Beast* is Jordan's *Metamorphosis* and yet *Sunrise with Sea-Monster* tries to retain some of the mechanisms of realist fiction, while extending Jordan's inquiry. What ultimately places Jordan firmly in Richard Kearney's counter-tradition are his persistent attempts to explore the nature of his media whilst trying to renegotiate the relationship between the eye that sees and reality; ultimately he challenges himself to map a world which refuses to conform to conventional human articulation. Like Banville and Higgins, he sees complexity in the act of living, rather than in easily recognisable ordering systems, and he too refuses to turn away from the challenge of mapping that complexity.

4.2 Spatial Form and the Rejection of Temporal Sequence

Night in Tunisia unveils the striking imagery which has typified Jordan's poetic imagination ever since that work. Seaside towns, American jazz and complicated love are some of the recurrent images which emerge from the highly sensitive minds of Jordan's narrators, images which are refreshingly new in the context of Irish fiction. Instead of using recognisable images of Irish life, Jordan imbues his work with significance by using metaphors like the song, *The Tennessee Waltz*. This is a result of the writer's conscious desire to break away from the specifically Irish images he saw all around him and so he set out to: 'express another reality, everyday facts, ordinary facts, not referring to ideas of national identity, something mundane, contemporary' (Jordan in Pernot-Deschamps 1997, 19). Already Jordan exhibits a belief that there is a difference between the ordinary lives of people and the inherited stories carried forth on the nationalist enthusiasm of independent Ireland and all its attendant mythologies. Instead, Jordan, a youth of the 1960s, is a vessel for other kinds of stories that people were telling themselves about life. Nationalist pride belonged to the imaginations of a different generation:

When I started writing I felt very pressured by the question: How do I cope with the notion of Irishness? It meant almost nothing to me...how was I to write about the experience I knew, as someone born in Sligo and growing up in the suburban streets of Dublin in the sixties? The great books of Anglo-Irish literature had very little to do with this, they had no real resonance at this level. (Jordan in Pernot-Deschamps 1997, 19)

Like the youth of so many new generations, Jordan obviously found little comfort in the language he inherited from his predecessors. He has also expressed his need to avoid the language and mythology of Joyce when writing about urban areas[37] (Jordan in Pernot-Deschamps 1997, 19). While all of this simply reveals a young writer's attempt to discover a language and imagery appropriate to his generation, it also suggests a watershed in Irish literature where all the old emblems had lingered for many years. In Jordan's search for a language and form that might accommodate the world into which he grew, it is easy to recognise early indications of contemporary globalisation in that Jordan's inheritance, while primarily Irish, was one which had already begun to assimilate a diversity of influences, a diversity of stories about what it meant to be young. Thus, Jordan's images are sourced in a wider framework, but they are still images, a realisation which didn't take long to find its way into his work.

Many of the stories in *Night in Tunisia* are of youth with its attendant needs and painful embryonic awareness. The various narrators articulate confusion at a life never adequately explained. Loss of innocence is coupled with a shrewd understanding, earned by intense curiosity, which charges things with life. The innocent tone of many of the stories is tempered by the author's questioning of language and memory. Experience, chillingly authentic experience, is presented as a complexity of fears, joys and sometimes fragmented moments in language, which is gently probed by the author. Memory is accepted, finally, for what it is, a dream of a long vanished past.

The initial charm of Jordan's stories is their use of youthful experiences which tremble with authenticity because of their distinctiveness. Rather than replicate the traditional fictional emblems of much of Irish fiction, Jordan's stories are informed by more inclusive literary images. Charlie Parker and the lilting sounds of jazz are some of the most unique aspects of this collection, as are Jordan's various narrators' attempts to confront their experiences, not simply as conceptual arrangements of ideas but as life in all its strangeness. Such an approach renders the stories unique to Jordan's imagination. Writing of Jordan's originality Sean O'Faolain highlights that the author is: 'responsive to all the things, people, surroundings and influences that have affected him as a youth' (O'Faolain 1993, I). O'Faolain too emphasises the value of the jazz music to the stories in that it raises the stories above, what he terms, 'regionalist' (O'Faolain 1993, I). In some of the stories Jazz acts as a metaphor of release into maturity. Also, however, Jordan's narrators are distinctive in their interrogation of what it means to be young, to grow up and how to make sense of the mass of experience before them. In 'Last Rites', a tale of alienation and suicide, the narrator's pain is an extension of his inability to comprehend the meaning of change. Jordan portrays him as one who ponders his familiar landscape but is unable to accept what his life has become: 'He took in his surroundings with a slow familiar glance. He knew it all, but he wanted to be a stranger to it, to see it again for the first time, always the first time' (Jordan 1993, 10). Many of Jordan's stories probe such matters. The need to feel authentic in a world which refuses to remain static fuels both 'Skin' and 'Outpatient': 'And she discovered to her surprise that she thirsted for pain and reality' (Jordan 1993, 91). This yearning for something more than the lethargy of ordinary life reveals a kind of spiritual malnutrition in some of the narrators. The vacuum is filled with pain or, as in 'Skin', with daydreams which aim to compensate for the lack of vivacious life: 'The odd fantasies we people our days with…' (Jordan 1993, 74). These characters are not presented as outsiders and this is precisely where their strength lies. Because of the ordinariness of their lives they imply a kind of universal social malaise. They remain individuals but become emblematic of humankind's inability to feel close to the essential heart of things.

Human experience itself is thus implicitly questioned. How does one make contact with the primacy of experience? Is the only real life, that 'inner secret life?' (Jordan 1993, 77) Jordan asks such questions, effectively, by virtue of the extreme authenticity of his creations. In this he is no less confused than Marlowe is in his epistemological jungle of brambles and tangled branches in Conrad's *Heart of Darkness*, one of Modernism's first literary texts. Jordan too enters the interrogative realm of Modernist fiction when his narrators fail to accept experience as a given thing. The present is shown to be a complex entity, hidden behind a fine gauze through which his characters peer. To present the past as a dream is a relatively effortless task for the Modernist thinker but to destabilise perceptions of the present has far greater ramifications for the landscape in which Jordan's characters exist. This becomes one of the foremost issues which dominates Jordan's artistic journey thereafter. The past becomes an even more problematic issue lingering as it does in bygone days: 'She had been shrewish, he told himself as her memory grew dimmer, her hair had often remained unwashed for days...Thus he killed the memory of another her neatly' (Jordan 1993, 41). Memories can be discarded as they are not fixed concepts. Jordan alters the past at will and his characters accept the foibles of memory as normal: 'As I remember you I define you, I choose bits of you and like a child with a colouring book, I fill you out' (Jordan 1993, 112). When his characters focus their attention on the past the resultant memories are fluid, the past can be recreated at will. The note of acceptance is revealing in that Jordan inherently questions the exactitude of much of realist fiction which purports to 'tell it as it was'. His confrontation with this fact is implicit, hardly worthy of conflict in the overt confrontational way of Banville's fiction or the frequently tortured position taken up in Higgins's early work. That the past is a complex remote concept is as unquestionable as the transience of life: 'You were different and the same, I was different and the same, I knew that that is how things happen' (Jordan 1993, 109). Such an acceptance is crucial in that it betrays no Modernist epistemological anxiety. Rather it accepts the essential mystery of life and attempts to suggest some of the tone of that very mystery.

Jordan does confront the Modernist legacy of linguistic uncertainty in *Night in Tunisia* by acknowledging the discrepancy between signifiers and the things, or concepts, signified. Once again, the central metaphor, that of jazz, assumes considerable significance in his attempt to establish some alternative to the specificity of language. Initially though, he simply acknowledges the gulf between words and life itself, or Kant's *Ding an sich*. In 'Mr Solomon Wept', the narrator's sense of confusion at the world takes many forms but his intense mental isolation leads to an awareness of the fundamental problems underlying language: '…the words love and hate…those words were like the words school or god, part of a message that was not important any more, a land that was far away' (Jordan 1993, 40). Language grows indistinct, as do the concepts he tries to reach. Jordan's differentiation of language from the actualities they attempt to represent is implicit. Such an awareness of the gulf between words and actual life recurs several times in the collection, nowhere more forcibly than in 'Tree', a harrowing story of barren isolation and unfulfilment:

> The woman answered, speaking the way children do, using words they don't understand. She used phrases to describe the dead inhabitants of those castles that were like litanies, that had filtered through years to her, that must have once had meaning…as her mouth spoke the forgotten phrases. (Jordan 1993, 98–9)

Her 'forgotten phrases' are subsequently pondered in Jordan's effort to suggest a less formal linguistic power: 'She wondered about phrases, how they either retain the ghost of a meaning they once had, or grope towards a meaning they might have' (Jordan 1993, 99). The vague suggestiveness of these lines reveals little except the author's willingness to consider the possibility of another less exact significance to language. In this *Night in Tunisia* is reminiscent of the persistent Modernist attempts to symbolically evoke human communication. In the same story the narrator reveals the significance of Jordan's subtle enterprise: 'The impossible possible she thought. She knew the phrase meant nothing. She remembered an opera where a walking-stick grew flowers' (Jordan 1993, 96). This is the very essence of metaphor and Jordan's collection, at its best, uses images to compensate for the inherent representative deficiencies of literal language. Hardly an original approach but the unobtrusive assurances of Jordan's most powerful images, suggestive of the unutterable forces which govern a life, are expertly employed.

With the fascinating centrepiece to the collection, *Night in Tunisia*, Jordan's formidable achievement is fully realised. Crudity and beauty struggle for supremacy. Communication is minimal but an almost perpetually present narrative alternative conspires to bridge the distance between people – music. A staccato of vignettes resonates, almost with musical precision, to suggest the narrator's consciousness. The reader is not exposed to any direct linguistic interrogation. The meaning must somehow assert itself by virtue of the suggestiveness of the narrator's roaming consciousness. Thus, music acts as the central metaphor and becomes suggestive of human expression: 'He fashioned his mouth round the reed till the sounds he made became like a power of speech, a speech that his mouth was the vehicle for but that sprang from the knot of his stomach, the crook of his legs' (Jordan 1993, 69). Verbal communication is unnecessary, is bypassed, and another kind of language emerges, in communion with music. Liberated from the demands of linguistic communication momentarily, the narrator reaches, and comprehends, his own self for the first time:

> He played later on the piano...all the songs, the trivial mythologies whose significance he had never questioned...as he played he began to forget the melodies of all those goodbyes and heartaches, letting his fingers take him where they wanted to, trying to imitate that sound like a river he had just heard. (Jordan 1993, 62)

The extra-linguistic, the essential part of him, long since named and invented by language, is restored and his frustration, so evident in the story, is somehow momentarily healed.

Night in Tunisia is written against a backdrop of acute awareness of the contemporary writer's linguistic dilemma. Jordan's strength in this early collection is his willingness to forage for a kind of freedom from the seemingly insurmountable problems associated with language. Not for him the lapse into silence and endless play of authors like Brautigan or Robbe-Grillet whose sole purpose often appears to be to diminish their own medium. Jordan strives, in a modest way, to find freedom by accepting the nature of language but by also hinting at the suggestive power of words. In this he aims to redeem language from the simplistic, hyper-rational debate about language's deficiencies. For the contemporary writer the question is what one does with the truism that language is an inaccurate medium. Jordan accepts this but his short fictions have a suggestive power which clearly indicates that language is relevant. It is simply the relationship between words and life that we must renegotiate.

An equally revealing and distinctive aspect of Jordan's *Night in Tunisia* is its author's occasional attempts to avoid traditional sequential narrative forms. Actually, those stories which employ sequential narrative seem quite limiting compared to the more inventive 'Last Rites' and 'Night in Tunisia'. With 'Last Rites' the narrative continually shifts temporal focus so that the reader is repeatedly exposed to the conclusion of events when the suicide victim's/narrator's body is discovered. The effect of such narratorial shifts is harrowing in its stark emphasis of the finality of the death of his consciousness. It also adds a powerful sense of pathos to the present, knowing, as we do, the finale. In addition, the story does not limit itself to the interior monologue of the narrator, offering us glimpses of the minds of the other characters who too are showering, emphasising not just the narrator's alienation but that of all the others. The banality of his act is thus indicated and further enforced by the onlookers' calm, almost numb, comprehension of his act.

Much more inventive is the staccato of vignettes rattled off in 'Night in Tunisia' which conspire to communicate the protagonist's consciousness. The narratorial voice is the only gelling agent for the diffusion of images and impressions as they imply the sheer complexity of experience. Images from the past mingle with those of the present and future, in particular near the close, with the narrator's 'imagined place'. Images are presented and remain unexplained. Only in totality does their suggestiveness reveal itself. Reminiscent of Higgins's later fictions, Jordan's work appears to be trying to position the narrative consciousness in a less formal relationship to life than in realist fictions. In *Night in Tunisia* Jordan, again like Higgins, presents authentic experience without resorting to conventional narrative techniques which, while offering comfortable reassurance, fail to adequately imply the vast complexity of the predominantly adolescent narratorial consciousnesses which try to comprehend their world. There are no certainties here, no formalised fictional solutions for the chaos of experience. Instead Jordan's protagonists map the world without the benefit of sequential narrative, or without unswerving faith in language and memory. Experience is therefore approached in an extremely direct and imaginative way. Herein lies the real success of the collection. Life is not neatly transferred into digestible fiction, rather, Jordan tries to reinvent the rules to accommodate the relationship between his vision of life and the craft he uses.

The hazards of making definitive statements about a collection of stories are obvious but Jordan's *Night in Tunisia*, paradoxically, achieves a unity of purpose, all the more starkly because of the variety of styles employed. The freedom that *Night in Tunisia* promises is great and its gentle probing of the Modernist impasse is refreshing. *Night in Tunisia* operates within a basic Modernist framework because of its treatment of primarily epistemological concerns, reflected most successfully in the author's narrative inventiveness and exploration of the mind in the act of apprehending life. Successful as they are, the stories of *Night in Tunisia* remain a promising debut from Jordan. Though he indicates his awareness of the deep epistemological concerns of the Modernist writer, and offers some interesting responses, a more sustained interrogation of these issues was inevitable. *The Past*, Jordan's first novel, evolves from a

Modernist dominant of questioning the meaning of man's systems of knowledge and engages the Postmodern debate in a highly self-conscious manner.

4.3 The Past as Imagined Ontology

Night in Tunisia is essentially a Modernist text which ponders some elements of artistic crisis and its associated questions: memory, perception and language. Jordan's first work attempts to suggest the possibility of an alternative relationship between the perceiver and experience, in particular in the title story, by virtue of its metaphorical use of music as a non-rational but effective mode of communication. *The Past*, alternatively, takes a leap into an altogether different realm. The narrator's consciousness strikes up a different relationship with reality. The familiar Modernist difficulties are clearly outlined but the narrator's response is no longer simply one of puzzlement and gentle probing. Like Banville, Jordan makes that leap of imagination into the unknown, or more precisely, into that world not directly experienced. Rummaging around in other peoples' past lives, assisted only by textual materials like photography, verbal folklore and gossip, the narrator takes the plunge into the realm of pure fiction. The narrator's imagination dominates the landscape more than the representation of an objective reality. The problems of creative puzzlement, evident in *Night in Tunisia*, are certainly not ignored but Jordan brings the force of his imagination to bear on a world which escapes definition and in doing so implicitly accepts the limitations of human systems of inquiry and offers up the imaginative process as an alternative.

As the title of the novel suggests, the narrator's quest is to somehow recreate, and know, the past lives of his parents and his mother's (Rene's) parents. Using postcards, random information, Lili's account, photography and his own fragmented memories (second-hand or otherwise), he tries to erect a structure which will colour in the uncertain lives of those who came before him, of those who, in a sense, contributed to the making of him. His imaginative journey follows many routes, a result of his predecessors' colourful lives, in particular his mother's acting career with a travelling theatre group. He too makes the same journey made all those years ago by his mother, while she carried him inside her and the dominant suggestion is of recurrent lives somehow shadowing each other through the dusty byways of two Irish summers. Ultimately the journey ends where it begins, in the narrator's mind, but something important has been achieved in the telling, in the imagining. At the close of the novel the narrator's use of language testifies to this: 'Father Beausang tips Lili's cheek and now I in that standing train the steam of which was hissing towards silence through those waters and that musk of generation came' (Jordan 1982, 232). The curious mix of tenses coupled with the absence of punctuation implies a coming together of past and present. Furthermore, the 'silence' is redeemed by the 'musk of generation'. Artistic silence has thus, in Jordan's view, been circumvented. Truth, accuracy, such absolutes, have been abandoned and instead, an approximation of those things, 'the musk of generation', has been achieved because of the imaginative power which he brings to bear on an uncertain past, which is essentially what all people unconsciously do with their pasts but Jordan's narrator eventually does so consciously and delightedly. In his way he makes the past live.

A number of elements in *The Past* allow Jordan to engage in a self-reflexive dialogue and ultimately this renders the novel Postmodern because the representation of reality is subservient to the analysis of the epistemological mechanisms employed in the construction of the account, although both Colbert Kearney and Fintan O'Toole, puzzlingly, offer readings of the text as a kind of realist historical reconstruction (Kearney 1988, 136–7; O'Toole 1988, 19). Jordan is more concerned with perception and communication than he is with the historical world and he foregrounds such issues in a number of ways. The narrator's reliance on postcards and photographs allows Jordan to overtly discuss the nature of the visual media and in turn any medium which attempts to freeze moments of a life. Faced initially with two postcards sent from a holiday town in the south-west of England, the narrator immediately moves beyond the world of represented experience: 'So I extend the picture on the postcard beyond the serrated edge with a line, say, of unobtrusive shrubs, not quite trees, between the esplanade and the road proper' (Jordan 1982, 15). The limitations of the photographic image will not prevent him from creative pursuit. More telling still are his views about his father's, James Vance's, photography: 'I see both of us trying to snatch from the chaos of this world the order of the next' (Jordan 1982, 76). Drawing a distinction between the inherent order of text and the complexity of experience, Jordan's narrator indicates his intention to impose an order, rather than try to locate order in what lies before him. There is a profound difference between these two acts.

In his metaphorical parallel between photography and writing Jordan's narrator's commentary on photography becomes a self-reflexive analysis of his own art:

> Technically, too, this group of prints is an immense improvement. You've forgotten your reticence in the face of objects. I can see it, that you focus with such a clarity on one that all the objects around her fall into place...the intractability of the world you looked at through your shutter seems to have given way, as if a veil has been lifted. (Jordan 1982, 152)

The narrator's journey does not simply follow the faded trails followed by his mother, he too journeys deep into unknown crevices of the imagination in his efforts to apprehend a vision of the past. James Vance, the photographer, also undergoes creative development. Little by little he grows to a point where the shutter is no longer an obstacle to apprehension but an instrument of it. The veil, the gauze which separates the artist's gaze from the objects upon which it is fixed, is thus minimised.

Moving beyond the power of photographic stills, the narrator suggests other more potent forces. When James Vance later loses faith in the power of photography: 'loses his urge to grasp at years, to stick his moments into albums and annotate each one' (Jordan 1982, 178), the narrator offers alternate ways of perceiving the object, or life itself:

> His camera dies, and there is only the spoken word to replace it, and memory, and imagination. And all three are frighteningly elastic, handing us as a gift that freedom that annihilates more than time, the contours of our subjects themselves. (Jordan 1982, 178–9)

Jordan uses the self-reflexive parallel of the photographic still in order to reveal its inadequacy in much the same way that realist fiction is inadequate because it too tended to limit itself by virtue of its close relationship with the visible, known and quantifiable world. The camera dies for Vance because there is too much that it cannot say, too much fluidity that remains outside its frame. When Rene and Luke leave him, his camera is utterly useless to him. Only imagination, memory and language can suffice in tracking them. This is 'frighteningly elastic' weaponry indeed but that freedom, of which he speaks, reveals the hopeless static quality of stills in the face of a world which positively refuses to be frozen and instead swirls in apparently erratic patterns. His solution is to allow the imagination liberty from the static visions with which he has been familiar. In this sense Jordan is not expressing artistic failure, rather he acknowledges the failure of realist methods to accommodate the unpredictability and enormity of life. This freedom, he assumes, can take him anywhere. And it does. It defeats time, distance, logic and even language because for him language is no longer a narrow defining methodology. The words are used to serve imaginative perception and not the concrete world of the quantifiable outer landscape.

The rhythm of Jordan's characters' lives is conditioned by the author's refusal to accept the limitations of synthetic order. Michael O'Shaughnessy's understanding of life is a telling example of Jordan's vision: 'He feels outside time, events pass round him, he is in another time, an older time, his mind, once so energetic, so logical becomes a glaze through which he sees the world scream on a distant opaque horizon' (Jordan 1982, 22). Such an understanding, of course, is actually the narrator's retrospective, imaginative view of how things might have been for his dead grandfather. Thus, it is the narrator's vision that is revealed via his imaginatively constructed grandfather. In fact, all is similarly conditioned by the narrator's vision. And herein lies the central question surrounding *The Past*. Is the novel, however poignant at certain times, merely a prolonged imaginative exercise on the part of the narrator? There is little to suggest that the intensity of his imagination merits acceptance as a substitute for truth. It is here that the success of Banville's endeavours is obvious because the articulate poetic story, which Freddie for example obsessively constructs, far outstrips Jordan's narrator's ontology.

The theoretical argument, constructed primarily via the parallels offered by the photographic medium, does not manage to erect a powerful imagined past and thus the worth of all the narrator's attempts is limited. Everything in the novel conspires towards literary device; the photographs, postcards, Lili as emblem of memory's foibles and Michael as emblem of confusion in the face of an impassive world. Rene's mother, the narrator's grandmother, is ironically quite revealing in this respect because, for her: 'theatrical pose and political history were inseparable' (Jordan 1982, 27). In Jordan's narrator's case, theatrical pose supersedes the past it feigns to capture. Arguably, this, in itself, is not so problematic. By virtue of the narrator's obsessive imaginative journey everything evolves into functional devices through which the author can express his artistic position. Because of this it is rare that anyone is realised in any sensual way. He tells us of the 'musk of generation' but is it really just invented musk? Is it enough to simply discuss the nature of communication and perception? The difference between Banville and Jordan centres on Banville's ability to interrogate the meaning of that musk in a far more profound and convincing way. Ultimately, his heroes of the imagination manage to construct a vision of the world as an expression of powerful fictional models. Jordan's claim at the close of the novel is an unconvincing one. That a novel whose characters and objects continually evolve into literary device should simultaneously claim to have evaded the Wittgensteinian silence which Gabriel Godkin lapses into at the close of Banville's *Birchwood*, is extraordinary. The only musk obvious to this reader is that Jordan's novel is a highly self-conscious and self-reflexive artifact which, for all its theoretical attempts to establish a convincing ontology, fails to do so because the imaginative energy of Banville's later imaginative heroes, for example, is never quite achieved.

On a more positive note, *The Past* does reveal Jordan's discomfort with pure fiction which fails to retain contact with life. Jordan was later to claim that *The Past* is a 'satire on the attempt to write a novel' (Jordan in Hanly 1992). In this he succeeds admirably but he also realised that he had actually failed to achieve that musk, that sense of life as he admits that he had 'written [himself] into a corner within that form' (Jordan in Hanly 1992). It is therefore unsurprising that his second novel *The Dream of a Beast* is altogether different, written more in the shadow of Kafka's *Metamorphosis* than in the Postmodern glitter of self-reflexive reductive analysis.

Although *The Past* is an original novel, especially in terms of subject matter, it does occupy the same metafictional ground as some of Banville's early fiction. Self-conscious comments litter the text: 'But then I could be wrong, we could all be wrong' (Jordan 1982, 13). Jordan's narrator too ploughs backwards in time whilst acknowledging the dangers of such an act. The problematic act of recording the imagined past is foregrounded in the early work of both novelists. Jordan appears to be writing of the actual world with the familiar seaside memorabilia of his youthful imagination, whereas Banville parodies any attempts at temporal or positional locations. Ultimately, though, as previously illustrated, Jordan's esplanades and bathing costumes are kept distinctly subservient to the act of perceiving and are ultimately dominated by the same self-conscious dominant as Banville's fictions. Both write self-referential fictions of the mind and their plots rarely achieve more than the status of the marionette theatre.

Alternatively Jordan's use of historic personalities, like the Archduke Ferdinand and de Valera, has an anchoring, resonant effect on the mass of imaginings with which we are confronted. Aidan Higgins too uses such a technique in *Langrishe, Go Down* and *The Balcony of Europe*, albeit in a far more substantial way. And herein lies the difference. Jordan's anchors to the world of historical reality are not secure enough to keep his fiction in credible dialogue with the world of experience. No doubt this was not his primary intention but his sparse use of such elements suggest authorial uncertainty. His encyclopedic anchors are swamped by the tide of overt literary discourse. His most recent novel, *Sunrise with Sea Monster*, is in many ways, a more accomplished effort at accepting the vagaries of the act of writing and simultaneously accommodating the actual world.

The Past is a Postmodern novel because its dominant characteristic is a metafictional one. In a sense, it compares to Banville's *Nightspawn*, an 'inside-out novel' (Banville in Imhof 1981, 6), but, unfortunately, lacks the partially redeeming parody. In Brian McHale's terminology its dominant is an ontological one rather than an epistemological one. By marginalising a concrete reality and concentrating instead on the artificial, synthetic aspects, Jordan renders the novel Postmodern. He tries to construct an imagined world which might accommodate his vision, rather than accept the given images of conventional reality. Modernist texts like *A Portrait* or Woolf's *To the Lighthouse* never make that leap, while constantly threatening to do so, preferring instead to retain the basic shape of conventional reality while probing the nature of their intellectual discourses. Jordan's second novel *The Dream of a Beast*, maintains Jordan's search for a literary model which will conform to his philosophical ruminations but he completely refrains from the use of authentic historical detail from the outset.

4.4 Reconstructing the Self

The title of Jordan's second novel, *The Dream of a Beast*, contains a promise of the surreal, of a life beyond actual experience. The metamorphosis myth, central to Jordan's short novel, has been frequently used in both fiction and film for its associations with the horrific. Jordan does not retreat from such fertile symbolic ground and, like Kafka's *Metamorphosis*, *The Dream of a Beast* contains such associations within an ambitious structure. Jordan's skilful, gradual evocation of his central character's evolution from man to beast includes the paradoxical notion of the attainment of a freedom of consciousness. The life of the human ultimately seems more ghastly than that into which it evolves. And yet the account is much more than a tale of freedom and release into the consciousness of the beast. The prime characteristic of the narrator's metamorphosis is one of evolution to a new, more enlightened state of mind. His vision expands and Jordan uses the metamorphosis to evoke such a change. Finally, the narrator's change is more intellectual than physical. The novel tells of an awakening of the imagination and the relationship between reality and the narrator's perceptions is radically renegotiated. The conventions of the horror genre are effectively used in this radical reassessment of the meaning of human consciousness and perception.

The narrator's gradual realisation of a change within himself is convincingly enacted: 'Streets I had walked on all my life began to grow strange blooms in the crevices' (Jordan 1983, 1). His relationship with his wife too alters under the intensity of his obsessive gaze: 'I watched her undress and thought of all the words to do with this activity' (Jordan 1983, 9). Gradually, because of his obsession with seeing, and saying, it becomes clear that Jordan's narrator is an artist figure. He attempts to penetrate the reality of both his own existence and the meaning of the natural world of objects. Such attempts lead him on a journey of haunting power, one which absorbs him to the extent that he imagines himself to be a beast, one which, despite his certainty, he cannot visualise clearly: 'I tried to imagine what she must see below her, but no effort on my part could make that leap. Sure of what I felt like, all images of what I looked like were beyond me' (Jordan 1983, 45). It is this failure to fully realise himself in the images that are available to him which leads to his initial exploration. Confronted by a life which refuses to yield up its Kantian essence, the narrator travels darkened confused routes to try to discover a solution.

All the usual twentieth century artistic dilemmas are present. Language is probed, or rather its inadequacies are implied: 'The moods that were between us were almost richer than speech' (Jordan 1983, 13). More significantly, Jordan directly assaults the realist assumption that language, and the concepts that it signifies, can exist in an uncomplicated relationship: 'Anger, pity, love, hate, the names we give to our emotions signify a separateness, a purity that is rarely in fact the case. She had stared with anger, pity, love and hate' (Jordan 1983, 34). The effect of such an awareness is that the narrator rends language from the essences they appear to represent and this firmly places Jordan's endeavour in the Kantian linguistic revolution, which influences both Modernism and Postmodernism. This has far-reaching implications for the narrator. How does one articulate such a problematic plethora of emotion? All attempts seem inadequate. Furthermore, Jordan questions the concept of life as having shape: 'She told me how her life to others seemed to follow no shape, since she never worried or guarded against the diminishing future' (Jordan 1983, 39). Inherent in this is the idea that life, as shape or as story, cannot be comprehended without the possibility of a future, if that future is unable to resolve itself into some pattern then it defies human expectations. Here Jordan goes much further than a basic revaluation of communication. Rather, he touches on the idea that we impose patterns on life which, unlike literary production and artistic form, do not necessarily have a shape. Instead we gratify ourselves with the construction of forms, the imposition of shape on random life. In this way Jordan gravitates towards the kind of investigation that characterises Banville's fictions. In order to comprehend life without the help of human systems, without the established patterns with which one views life, Jordan builds an edifice of fictional horror to try to suggest his intuitive grasp of the meaning of reality:

> I told her about the sounds I had discovered beneath the surface of things, the hum from the girders, the mauve twilight. As the surface of everything becomes more loathsome, I said, thinking of the thing I was, the beauty seems to come from nowhere, a thing-in-itself. (Jordan 1983, 40)

Grasping at the ungraspable, the Kantian *thing-in-itself*, Jordan's narrator attempts to circumvent the theoretical position of much of Postmodern criticism and attempts to give a sense of things, if not to ascribe any specific meaning to them.

In many ways Jordan's novel engages many of the issues engaged by Beckett, Nabokov and Banville. He too inquires into the Wittgensteinian silence which rings soundlessly at the close of *Birchwood* and uses much of the language of silences and doorways familiar to Postmodern fiction:[38]

> I stood on the landing, listening to the new quality of this silence. Slowly it came to me that silence was not what for years I had supposed it to be, the absence of sound. It was the absence, I knew now, of the foreground sounds so the background sounds could be heard. These sounds were like breath – like the breath of this house, of the movement of the air inside it, of the creatures who lived in it. They seemed to wheel around me till I heard a piece of furniture being pulled somewhere, too much in the foreground, and the spell was dispersed. (Jordan 1983, 28–9)

Jordan's appropriation of the linguistic imagery of Postmodernism speaks of silence not as a negative quality. Instead, it represents a presence, one which is part of the actual world but is submerged beneath the noises, the fictions of conventional reality. It is a world lost beneath the age of reason with its unswerving belief in man's systems of knowledge. Ultimately Jordan's narrator is feeling his way towards an attempted realisation of imagination, or towards an acceptance of the imagination, in a Blakean sense (Blake after all provides the epigraph to *Dream*). As Blake insists in *Jerusalem*:

> I must Create a System, or be enslaved by another Man's
> I will not Reason and Compare: my business is to Create. (Blake 1996, 651)

Jordan's association with Blakean ideas reveals his intention to somehow resolve the essentially rational abyss which exists between language and objects, perception and life, and memory and the past. In addition to Jordan's Blakean epigraph, he occasionally uses the poet's imagery in *Dream*, in particular that related to the romantic poet's doctrine of Desire. Nearing the completion of his transformation, and the close of the novel, Jordan's narrator expresses such a doctrine: 'To fly cleanly you must learn pure desire, a desire that has no object. Any attachment to things of the world leaves you earth bound once more' (Jordan 1983, 84). This clearly echoes Blake's *Proverbs of Hell*: 'He who desires but acts not, breeds pestilence'. Furthermore, Jordan's narrator's attempt to flee the fetters of rationality, the rationality which, after all, submerges artistic silence, and is also echoed in Blake's *The Marriage of Heaven and Hell* in which he speaks of the 'abyss of the five senses'.[39]

In essence Jordan is trying to discover a way out of the abyss of Postmodernism wherein language enters into a discourse with itself at the expense of the world of objects which, after all can only be framed in man's systems. How fully he realises such a discovery, availing of Blakean philosophy is questionable. A doctrine of desire coupled with belief in the imagination makes for a powerful assault against contemporary fiction but the difficulty with this is that *Dream*, finally, is a novel of process, intent on exploring its own possibilities. Arguably, life, internal or external, remains floundering in the self-reflexive text. To relocate Seamus Deane's evaluation of Banville: 'Talking about it [Art] is not at all the same as creating it' (Deane 1975, 332). However, the novel, as metaphor, does achieve something that many other Postmodern novels arguably do not. It offers an alternative vision which, while greatly enriched by Blakean ideas, is not fully realised. The essential interrogative nature of the novel prevents a more complete realisation of the possibilities offered by Blake. In that sense, *Dream* seems more a starting point for a more powerful evocation. Talking about the meaning of the human perceptive process, even in the context of Blake's imaginative poetics is only part of the challenge. To establish a powerful fictional ontology is something that the novel fails to do and as such, again, Jordan's achievement is flawed.

However, Jordan's realisation, finally, of a haunting dreamscape, does challenge conventional literary representations of reality. The world of objects still exists. It is not radically transformed into watermelon sugar, or mannequin gestures. Jordan's metaphor of change merely suggests that our perception of life must be radically revised and, in so doing, a fuller understanding of that life may be possible. That he does not offer a comprehensive treatment of the nature of that revision is the primary failing of the novel.

The Dream of a Beast occupies the same metafictional ground as Banville's fiction. It is a novel in search of the meaning of its own process, its own ontological status, and is therefore distinctly Postmodern in the same sense that I outline in Chapter 1. However, Jordan's interesting appropriation of Blakean ideas promises a moving forward, an attempt to go beyond the critical debate which surrounds Postmodernism. With *Dream* there is an attempt, however limited, to integrate the visionary with the intellectual, the imagination with the world. Richard Kearney emphasises the need for such integration: 'We must never cease to keep our mythological images in dialogue with history; because once we do we fossilise' (Kearney 1985, 80). If one accepts Kearney's point, then *Dream* flirts with fossilisation because the quasi-visionary dreamscape achieved at the close of the novel bears little resemblance to the world of actual power and discourse which one associates with a functioning existence. However, the novel, viewed in context as an ambitious metaphor, insists on revaluating perception and language in an effort to re-open the lines of communication which Beckett saw strewn about him (Beckett 1931, 47).[40] In this sense *Dream* conforms to Kearney's view. It also implicitly suggests that starkly obvious demands such as those made by Kearney may not always result in immediately recognisable results. *Dream* exemplifies this.

Dream signalled Jordan's movement away from literary fiction as he chose to engage the visual fictive medium of film. His reasons for doing so include the charm of what he sees as the 'immediacy of the medium', the lack of 'ancestral gods' in Irish film, unlike in literature and, most importantly, the problem of having 'written myself into a corner within that form' (Jordan in Hanly 1992). This final point, made as it was in relation to *The Past*, is revealing. *Dream* was thus written with such a belief in place and its surreal antics display Jordan's discomfort with plot, whilst his narrator's quest for artistic liberty seems to stem from the author's attempt to confront an artistic crisis of form. In *Dream*, Jordan implies the power of imagination over conventional understandings of reality and attempts to discover a way to suggest the chaotic nature of life. The problem with the novel, for all its merits, is that the nature of his metaphorical apparatus does not manage to communicate a powerful sense of the silence about which the narrator speaks. This is the inevitable risk involved with engaging the trap of epistemological uncertainty with which Postmodernism has grappled. Jordan clearly recognises the problematic nature of the novel form which he inherits but, in *Dream*, his attempts to locate a solution are not convincing.

4.5 Mythic Gateways and the Retreat from Realism

Published eleven years after *Dream*, *Sunrise with Sea Monster* does not so much maintain Jordan's dialogue with the Postmodern dilemma as re-engage the actual world in a way reminiscent of his earlier text, *Night in Tunisia*. The surreal landscape of *Dream* is abandoned for what initially seems to be a naturalistic setting, albeit one which is deeply compromised in the final section of the novel. There is, however, no less desire to inquire into the processes of human communication and, finally, into the meaning of imagination, again in an attempt to circumvent the apparent artistic cul-de-sac of Postmodern fiction.

The novel opens with its protagonist, Donal Gore, imprisoned in a Spanish jail during the Spanish civil war. From this setting Donal wades deep into a flood of memories of Ireland and his family home in an attempt to explain his reason for being in such a desolate place. Much of Part One alternates between Donal's remembered world and the nightmarish hours of his incarceration. Both worlds are peppered with different kinds of intrigue, sexual, paternal, political, and an intellectual sparring driven by the German officer, Hans, informed by Heidegger and Heisenberg. In return for undefined political intelligence Donal is freed by his unlikely ally, Hans, and returns to Ireland in order that the past might confront the present in some meaningful way. All is changed, dramatically, irrevocably. His father, having suffered from a stroke, has lost the power of speech and now their lack of communication, in both past and present, becomes the focal point of proceedings. Intrigue, political high jinks, lack of communication and the intensely complicating factor of a woman called Rose all combine to provide Jordan's experimental vision with richly fertile metaphorical material.

Sunrise revisits the familiar literary ground of *The Past*. Language, memory, perception are all once again among the dominant issues for Donal Gore, but unlike in that earlier text these concerns are articulated in a narrative informed by Irish and European history and underpinned by his relationships with Rose and his father. As such it attempts to retain some of the thematic concerns of realism, although not for purely representative purposes. *The Past* at times evolves into a fiction of metafictional self-reflexivity in an attempt to subvert the very problems with which it deals. With *Sunrise*, Jordan tries to fuse Postmodern ontological anxiety with a recognisable plot in an attempt to transfer such issues onto a human stage. This is effected by Donal radically interrogating, and rejecting, various established traditional beliefs, both intellectual and familial. For example, Donal, in an attempt to evade the restrictive constraints of the historical past, willingly invents: 'But what matter, we should be able to choose the pasts of those around us. I would have her...' (Jordan 1994, 39). The past is not an exact entity for Donal. Instead, recalling the narrator's vision in the title story of *Night in Tunisia*, it is presented as a fluid set of possibilities. His father, presented as a fixed creature in this respect greatly troubles him: 'Come father, I should have whispered, talk to me, tell me why you so disapprove, show me the drama of your past, not your stiff present' (Jordan 1994, 14). The fluidity of the past is further emphasised by Donal's view of his life as a: 'series of accidents, beginning with the accident of birth' (Jordan 1994, 59). He is unable to transfix anything and consequently his tale evolves into a series of interconnected vignettes which increasingly grows more diffuse as one moves towards the nightmarish final scenes.

All this relatively overt metafictional commentary strives towards an attempt to comprehend, investigate and finally renegotiate the stratagems of our systems of perception and communication. Having dwelt on Blake's visionary poetics in *Dream*, Jordan once again attempts to not simply subvert realist narrative (although this he does) but he tries to offer an alternative which might make sense of the world his Donal inhabits. *Sunrise* adheres to Brian McHale's Postmodern ontological dominant because past and present realities are presented as unstable ontological fixtures. It is continually stressed that the world inhabited by the characters is not a fixed entity conditioned by an ordered set of principles. The reality principle is radically reinterpreted in the process of the novel. Donal's faith in imagination is the primary way that the effect is achieved: 'It could be only in your imagination, Rose. If it is in mine, she said, it is in yours too' (Jordan 1994, 145). Furthermore, the spectral one-dimensional figure, Hans, champions, as does Banville,[41] Heisenberg's uncertainty principle, and what he sees as the human tendency to generate systems of meaning:

> He had become convinced from an early age that the greatest triumph of the human being was the most useless: the attempt to create meaning from a meaningless world; to create a moral system out of the random chaos of human affairs. The Reich's greatest triumph, he told me, was its recognition of chaos, of the arbitrary maelstrom that raged beneath the veneer of what we term civilisation. (Jordan 1994, 72)

The seductive power of Heisenberg's uncertainty principle with its portrait of a world impenetrable to clumsy human empirical systems is clear and its relevance to Postmodernism is also obvious but so too is the consequence of embracing chaos as an end in itself. Banville's Freddie Montgomery also succumbs to the attraction of this view and his subsequent abandonment of all human systems lead to his sociopathic deed in *The Book of Evidence*. Locating the impossibility of knowing the world is the essence of the most negative aspects of Postmodern thought but it does not, finally, offer a solution. Heisenberg's principle functions, in Jordan's novel, not just as a world-view or scientific position. It echoes much of what we know of Donal's imaginative faith, of his belief in the realm of possibilities. But Donal's vision is also fundamentally different to that of Heisenberg and Hans. Confronted with a fluid world which he readily accepts, and painfully aware of the treachery of memory and the inadequacy of words, Donal strives to do the impossible, to communicate with his speechless father: 'I am imagining things, I thought, making the dumb speak' (Jordan 1994, 159). And, in a way, he succeeds, albeit in an irrational, hallucinatory episode which has more in common with Medieval supernatural literature than Postmodernism. Donal takes an enormous leap of imagination, fuelled by his longing for communication, and for him the impossible becomes possible.

Donal's preoccupation with the communicative act stems from his fixation with the paucity of meaningful discourse which existed between himself and his father. This fixation informs much of the motion of the fiction and the communicative divide occupies the central metaphorical movement in the novel. The silence, which exists between them thus acts as the key to the novel's artistic value: 'We were in the country of silence, I realised, and any speech only serves to remind us of it' (Jordan 1994, 156). Indeed, the entire fiction exists in the country of silence, not simply in the sense that Donal and his father do not communicate until the end, but because the novel itself is Jordan's attempt to locate meaning in a world where man's systems, including language, are impaired and insufficient in any efforts to locate: 'the hidden meanings, the hidden landscapes which lay behind the apparent ones' (Jordan 1994, 75). Like all else in the novel, Donal's relationship with his father is of real significance only in a metaphorical sense. The novel itself is a self-reflexive attempt to discover ways in which the author might communicate. It is no surprise that Rose, Yeats's symbol of truth, is the one character with whom Donal has an almost mesmeric instinctive connection.

The primary intention underlying the fiction is not to tell a tale of familial distress or political intrigue. These are simply convenient plotted strategies which facilitate Jordan's artistic intentions. Jordan is unwilling to accept the abyss of non-communication and tries to supersede the rational epistemological problems he inherits from the Modernist (and Postmodernist) traditions. In *Dream* he veers towards a kind of visionary union with William Blake. *Sunrise*, though at variance with this position, at least in an overt way, does not ostensibly move away from its predecessor's thinking. Instead, it positions the actual world of politics and family life and love beside the haunting moments near the end of the novel in an attempt to make sense of it all. Unlike with *Dream*, Donal accepts the resonant qualities of real events and facts. Thus the use of the actual: 'Some facts draw all other facts into themselves, create a mystical union between disparate things, and the thought of de Valera brought me back once more to him' (Jordan 1994, 171). Positioned beside such a specific historical background Jordan's hero attempts to subvert the rational in the closing sequence to the fiction by merging a meeting with his dead father with the myth of the Salmon of Knowledge. Donal's father appears from out of the sea after Donal catches a strange elemental fish. With an invisible fishing line of longing he has somehow brought his father ashore to the land of communication. On eating the fish, communication, finally, becomes possible:

> If he were to die, he told me, he would rather die in that element which had given voice to all we never said. It was our language, he knew that and suspected I had always known that, and the accidents that had muddied our efforts to be in that language were just that: accidents. (Jordan 1994, 177)

Like Banville and Beckett, Jordan names the unnamable as silence, which is a kind of speech beyond words: 'But began is the wrong word, since from the silence with no speech, there was simply silence and speech' (Jordan 1994, 178). Here, Jordan is occupying the same linguistic ground as Postmodernism in his efforts to move beyond the literal problematic nature of language and perception as valid forms of discourse. These efforts, informed as they are by a collage of myth and magic (Donal's dead mother too makes a brief appearance), can be interpreted as metaphors for the imagination. Jordan's use of the surreal is similar to his willingness to embrace the imagery of magic in *Dream*. But the magic in *Sunrise* serves not only to act as a metaphor for how the imagination creates its own meaning but also facilitates Jordan's attempt to articulate the inaudible, almost mystical, union possible between Donal and his father because of their shared love of the sea. All the losses they both felt are not losses at all: 'And he realised those lost possibilities were not losses, they were always there, intimated by the fabric of what had come to happen: unravel one of them and the infinity of others present themselves' (Jordan 1994, 181). His father advises him that losses are of the past but life is of the present and lost possibilities are forever informed by the present. The past, in itself, is meaningless. It is only when the present conscious mind interacts with images of a former life that meaning occurs. He speaks of a 'perpetual present', implying the true significance of the past, in all its masks, as simply an aspect of the present. One of the fundamental problems of Modernism, with its questioning epistemological spirit, is that of the past and memory. Jordan, through Donal and his father, does more than just accept the indefinite nature of past events, he dissolves them in the pool of the present. In a sense, then, Jordan does not simply acknowledge Modernist uncertainty but attempts to resolve the strictures of such thinking.

The key to Jordan's effort to lead his fictional enterprise out of the potential cul-de-sac of Postmodern negativity lies in his central group of metaphors, the fishing lines, Rose and the adaptation of the Salmon of Knowledge myth, from which the novel takes its curious, optimistic title. The title is revealing in its promise of regeneration mingled with the horrific. The Sea-Monster is Jordan's terrifying fish of knowledge while Donal wears the unlikely garb of Finn macCumaill. The evocation of the pagan Irish myth is made possible though only by virtue of the artist's constant dwelling on the fishing rituals shared by father and son. The metaphor of fishing lines has many dimensions but ultimately the central focus lies in the symbolic possibilities for the communicative act. The ritualistic coming together of father and son always existed beyond normal human discourse but Jordan extends the possibilities of the metaphor to express his conception of language: 'The reaping was never as rich as the sowing, somehow. I knew that then and would connect that paradox with speech' (Jordan 1994, 3). The sowing of the lines, like the utterance of words, is where value lies for Donal and not what they actually signify. As with Winnie's desire to hear Willie's occasional words in Beckett's *Happy Days*, the primary function is a kind of mutual consolation. The expression of words is not akin to some sort of transmission of precise meaning, a kind of linguistic Morse code. Instead everything emanates from the ritual, the mystery of union created by speech and its attendant communicative acts. Jordan's hero grows to realise that and the fiction progressively gravitates away from the intellectual severity of exacting linguistic signification. Beyond such severity lies true communication:

> There was a shocking relief in the silence there, in the knowledge that we could abide together amidst this ritual, and as with the nightlines, not have to blunder towards speech. So I came to think of God as a great mass of quiet, a silence that was happy with itself, a closed mouth. (Jordan 1994, 17)

In accordance with this view the text grows progressively more symbolic, less literal, from the allegorical lover of father and son, *Rose de Vrai* with her crudely suggestive name, to the variation of the Salmon of Knowledge myth.

Jordan appropriates early Irish literature to evoke Donal's symbolic evolution into a seer poet or *filidh*. The prerequisite for a poet was to have discovered *imbus for osnai* or 'great knowledge that lights up' and this acquisition is frequently associated with the eating of hazel nuts or the eating of a salmon which had eaten the nuts (McCone 1990, 168). The symbolic tale of the eating of pure wisdom suggests the elevation of the poet's consciousness and Jordan's use of the myth is an extremely powerful variation, clashing, as it does, with 1950s Ireland. The use of the symbolic is a potent device in early Irish literature in its use of recurring images and archetypes, rather than more prosaic literal fictions, and as *Sunrise* moves towards completion it embraces a way of seeing and saying reminiscent of suggestive form and thus is in confrontation with the vision held by Donal throughout most of the text. He is released from his tortured attempts to grasp reality by conventional rational means, whether simple apprehension of the phenomenological universe or toying with fashionable Heisenbergian principles. Donal, by virtue of Jordan's evocation of an older myth and thus an older way of seeing, attempts to recreate the poetic persona of the hero and thus recreates the world. The eating of the fish heralds the instance of metamorphosis for Donal: 'I ate it in turn and knew why he had smiled as the unfamiliar filled my mouth, flesh that was hardly flesh, fish that was no known fish, taste that was somewhere beyond the bounds of sensation' (Jordan 1994, 176). The subsequent surreal sequence amounts to a kind of revelation and acceptance of all those aspects which seemed incorrect in his previous state. Language is the primary target:

> We are born out of accidence, he told me, and out of accidence we imagine is created the necessary, the indomitable self, which, if we only knew it, could change in a minute with our intervention. But we fill our years, he told me, with the business of that self, with the way it walks down the promenade, takes the black car to work, the way it sits at the green baize table, fills the world with what it thinks is purpose, till the range of possibilities has narrowed to the ones just that self wants. And death, he told me, is the realisation of all those lost possibilities in the life we have left. (Jordan 1994, 180)

As the novel reaches its philosophical climax, what emerges is yet another attempt by Jordan to find a way to articulate what it means to live. That he associates 'accidence', or that part of grammar concerned with changes in the form of words for the expression of tense, person, case etc, with life is a powerful indication of Jordan's view of life as a construct of language and the subsequent fictions created by that language. Self, in turn, is an elaborate construct dreamt up over years of living, of confirming and inhabiting the illusion. However the potential mutability of that self is acknowledged and the result is the possibility of a highly fluid concept of man's self.

Thus, the novel suggests that we enslave ourselves in systems of language and self, all of which are invented by a combination of accidence and apparent volition. The solution to this self-imposed body of limitations, the novel finally implies, is the realisation of the fluidity of self and systems. Effectively the consolatory act of erecting firm ordered fictions of self, and life, paradoxically leads to all our problems of communication and inevitably leads to the isolationism of private distinct selves. In this *Sunrise* engages that concept of self perpetually peddled in Postmodern culture, where one's self-definition is a matter of style and style is dictated by social, political and consumer fashions. The problem with the view expressed at the close of *Sunrise* is that it offers a promise of freedom without establishing what that freedom might actually mean. Of course, a loosening of fixed beliefs in selfhood and social roles holds a promise of tolerance and a hope that past differences become meaningless ritualistic foibles in the present. In that the symbolic coming together of Donal and his father has many ramifications for both private and political squabbles.

4.6 Visual Ontology

In Jordan's *The Crying Game*, similar ideas to those in *Sunrise* are engaged by virtue of the author/director's attempt to reframe the common conception of some of the most residual social stereotypes in contemporary Ireland. The film attempts to redress conventional images of terrorism and homosexuality by evoking a transformation in the central figure, Fergus. Characters who undergo various kinds of illumination are common in Jordan's fiction, depicted primarily, by a process of contrast, in order to suggest that people are not necessarily irredeemably trapped in conceptions of their self. Jordan has spoken about the difficulty of convincingly effecting this metamorphosis in *The Crying Game*:

> Can this character who comes from South Armagh, from a republican background and a Catholic background with all the certainties that that implies…can this character change believably? I knew I could make him change but perhaps the change wouldn't be deserved….Can someone who is used to dispensing with people's lives really become someone who, to put it in a sentimental way, has to actually nurture life. I suppose that was the theme of the movie…It was a movie about people freeing themselves from politics and can they find human beings under political definitions (sic). (Jordan in Dwyer 1997, 9)

Political definitions, like the sexual definitions explored in the film, are shown to be inherited versions of self which do not serve to improve people's lives. Redemption is to be found in the loss of those versions and the discovery of something more instinctive. The implication is that the fundamental definitions, self-imposed or socially inherited, with which we order our lives frequently prevent us from embracing life.

Donal and his father, though linked through love and longing, were separated by definitions of themselves for many years and only when these are shed can they achieve happiness. In *Sunrise* the father and son theme, so familiar to Irish fiction, is given a powerful metaphorical twist to suggest Donal's ability to reach out to life once he abandons his restricting concept of self. In *The Crying Game* the representative value of the dramatic tale of terrorism and homosexuality reaches similar conclusions. Fergus and Dil achieve a coming together which allows human imagination to overcome social stereotypes and preconceptions. The suggestion inherent in Jordan's recurring images of humans asserting themselves and escaping from stereotypical self-definitions is that the complexity of humans cannot be restrained by systematic categories of any kind. This is a provocative suggestion, which challenges many ritualistic forms of human demarcation. Undoubtedly, many of the stereotypes which Jordan effectively targets are in need of humanising but one wonders is it feasible to maintain social relationships and human discourse if all delineating signals are broken down. Friendship and basic human goodness, *The Crying Game* implies, are more powerful agents of human relationships than any concrete socio-political notions of self.

In many ways Jordan's film tries to challenge the idea of life as a series of fixed patterns. As Dil says to Fergus: 'Funny the way things go – never the way you expected'. And this is the essence of the lives his characters live. Systematic belief-systems can never hope to respond effectively to the unexpected. For example, Jody is a homosexual who hails from Antigua, via Tottenham, he plays cricket, gets sent to Northern Ireland and ultimately dies under the wheels of a British Army armoured car. The issues, it is suggested, are so much wider than the Republican cause, which, of course, in turn, is also wider than a political cause. Human systems seem so narrowly foolish in the face of the unexpected nature of human lives.

Richard Kearney has convincingly written of the reinvention of traditional themes in Irish cinema, claiming that *Angel*, Jordan's first film: 'debunks the orthodox portrayal of Irish political violence' (Kearney 1992, 146). The same artistic intent underpins *The Crying Game*, as it does most of Jordan's fiction.

More important is Kearney's suggestion that the stylised unreality of *Angel*: 'interrupts the linear melodrama of the narrative, turning our attention to a deeper level of awareness' (Kearney 1992, 151). This filmic technique, much practised by Jordan, reveals the same impulse that drives his attempts to evade the limitations of realism in his prose fiction. By constructing highly stylised non-representational scenes in the films, he manages to take his viewers beyond the mere depiction of visual and aural events. In *The Crying Game*, this works by virtue of the recurrence of cricket images throughout the narrative. The dead Jody loved playing cricket and the image of him playing cricket returns to Fergus's consciousness, in a series of dream sequences, throughout the text, interrupting temporal sequence with a view to offering us glimpses of Fergus's consciousness. Thus, much like the author disrupts temporal sequence in *Night in Tunisia*, the same innovative desire to test the limits of sequential narrative form is evident in his film texts. Although the visual and aural nature of the filmic medium admittedly differs from that of language-based prose, Jordan clearly attempts to infuse his work in both media with the same issues. The problematic Modernist epistemological legacy is, of course, relevant to all branches of the arts and thus, Jordan's work will inevitably house the same concerns. Despite his acceptance of different processes underlying both forms, he has also acknowledged a similarity: 'For the images became objects in the way that words in a sentence were objects, so one could manipulate these images and again, somehow, end up with a story' (Jordan 1982, 34). Jordan's work, both film and prose, is constructed around similar images (seaside towns, carnival wheels, Northern Ireland violence); it exhibits a recurring desire to expose the destructive and debilitating effect of socially inherited definitions, persistently depicts his characters undergoing profound transformations of self and is always engaged, sometimes self-reflexively, in trying to construct fictional models which will communicate alternative visions. There are problems associated with such experimental activity and Jordan's work does not always succeed in convincing his readers of his solutions to the problems of naming which he tackles, but he is very aware that those problems translate across the fictive media (Jordan 1993, viii).

4.7 Conclusion

In the context of this study, Jordan's work merits consideration beside that of Higgins and Banville because his work too, in both media, is occupied with the dilemma thrown up to the creative artist by developments in contemporary literature. Unlike Higgins and Banville, Jordan's fiction does not offer a sustained engagement of the contemporary fictional debate. However, it does offer an interesting alternative to the work of those two authors in its repeated efforts to construct extended metaphors of transformation of self, parables of illumination. These transformations are driven by an epistemological awareness similar to that of Higgins and Banville, but Jordan's strategy for overcoming the problems of self and communication are quite different. After the overt Modernist interrogation of problems of human knowledge, initially in *Night in Tunisia* and more explicitly in the metafictional *The Past*, Jordan's *The Dream of a Beast* and *Sunrise with Sea-Monster* seek to communicate, via instances of transformation of self, a Postmodern expression of self as systematic social construction. Human consciousness, in these texts, is imprisoned in static models that are derived from social, even tribal, influences and the novels seek to dramatise a process of enlightenment which rejects such fixed notions of self.

Of course the dramatisation of changes in consciousness is as old as literature but they usually amount to a movement from one concept of self to another, as in Shakespearean tragedy. Similarly, there is nothing particularly original in social-constructionist theories of identity. In *The Dream of a Beast* and *Sunrise with Sea-Monster*, in particular, Jordan depicts consciousnesses in the act of freeing themselves from social and familial notions of themselves. Erving Goffman, all too aware of the role of society in the construction of self, claims that one's consciousness is:

> not an organic thing that has a specific location whose fundamental fate is to be born, to mature, and to die; it is a dramatic effect...the means for producing and maintaining selves...are often bolted down in social establishments. (Goffman 1959, 252–3)

Ultimately though, Jordan's conclusion differs from this kind of perspective because the novels represent the lost or social self as something from which one can extract the organic self. Beneath the layers of social and familial narrative self-consciousness, there is an attainable self. Of course, the familiar Postmodern problem of naming, a kind of totalisation, arises in this context. This remains Jordan's most pressing fictional difficulty. Jordan's narrators in *Dream*, *Sunrise*, and even *The Crying Game*, move from fixed senses of self to fluid, more inclusive ones. This is by no means a final solution, and Jordan would be the first to admit that, but his work does suggest by its portrayal of illuminated selves, that all fixed systems enslave far more than they assist. The most powerful central thread that extends throughout this author's work is his desire to test the limits of what he inherits. On a narrative level this desire reveals itself in his temporal interruptions and his metaphors of music and metamorphosis. On a representative level, Jordan's narrators typically, in the act of apprehension of a fragmentary world, are forced to dissolve their belief in themselves in order to find themselves. As such the rituals, the categories with which we order our world, and our selves, are shown to be flawed, if we believe in them too much. Notions of self, like all other systems of definition, are useful only as long as we are aware of their systematic nature.

Like Banville, Jordan identifies self with fiction, although Jordan's fictive models are more specific, more firmly fixed in the social world. Banville's way of confronting the intertextual truth of the human self is to offer complex parables of the imagination which suggest that one must sculpt the self by intensely imagining the world, and thus imagining oneself in the process. This by no means guarantees realisation of self, which forever remains a shifting set of fluid possibilities. Jordan's fiction, especially *Dream*, and his most successful novel, *Sunrise*, endorses Banville's conception of self as a fluid set of possibility rather than a fixed truism but his work lacks the necessary complexity of Banville's because the aftermath of his characters' awareness of the fluidity of their lives usually amounts to a vague romanticised coming-together of characters, or, as in *Dream*, a symbolic suggestion of the fusion of self and world. Part of the reason for this is Jordan's evocation of Blakean mysticism in *Dream* and the Irish myth of poetic transformation in *Sunrise*, implying that, beneath the multitude of selves which dissolve in the process of his fictions, there lies a singular mystical centre in all humans and our challenge is to locate that oneness of being which is cluttered by man-made systems of communication and self-conscious identification.

Though there is nothing specifically objectionable in that age-old credo, Jordan's work seems to stop short of a more elaborate engagement of this essentially un-Postmodernist enterprise. Thus, his works ultimately seem to imply the existence of a true, almost mystical self but retreat from a more complete depiction of this possibility. It is treacherous ground no doubt but, nevertheless, it represents another distinctive alternative possibility to the Postmodern world of signifiers and theatrical human gestures. The imaginative possibilities offered by a fusion of Postmodern reductive analysis and mystical conceptions of the self which lie beneath our systems are many and it certainly seems to be a fruitful point of departure. The intensely sceptical dominant in all Modernist and Postmodernist writing, however, suggests that such a fusion is unlikely precisely because a poetics of rational reductivism does not seem to fit well with one of mystical faith. Nevertheless, finally, Jordan's work is valuable because of its suggestion of freedom in a debate that is perpetually beset by limits rather than imaginative enterprise.

CONCLUSION

'Reality is a question of perspective'. Salman Rushdie, *Midnight's Children*

The intense sceptical scrutiny of epistemological systems which characterises much of Modernism and, to an extent, Postmodernism, resulted in an identification of reality with language, or of experience with human ordering systems. The consequence of this identification means that reality, or at least our comprehension of it, is dependent on the system(s) of thought with which we investigate. The articulation of experience thus becomes an expression of form, rather than a direct communication of reality. Reality, in fact, becomes a construction of form. That there are profound connections between the birth of Modernist investigation and empirical science is undoubted since both derive their impetus from a reductionist impulse, which seeks to analyse the structural qualities of any given system. The inevitable evolution to a dominant self-reflexive mode of expression finds its origins here, and not only in the isolation of literary evolution. Indeed, the birth of sceptical intellectual discourse in the European tradition dates back to the Renaissance, the same time as the re-birth of interest in rational scientific investigation and both Shakespeare and Marlowe directly engaged such issues in *Hamlet* and *Doctor Faustus*, respectively.

Similarly, some of Romanticism's greatest texts were produced not in the fervour of Romantic idealism but in the despair that followed such idealism, as in Coleridge's wail of anguish when faced with an unresponsive world:

> O Lady! We receive but what we give,
> And in our life alone does Nature live:
> Ours is her wedding garment, ours her shroud!
> And would we aught behold, of higher worth,
> Than that inanimate cold world allowed
> To the poor loveless ever-anxious crowd. (Coleridge 1993, 368).

Coleridge associates the meaning of existence with the models imposed on it by human consciousness and thus reality is an aspect of the imagining mind. Such a consensus grows in the Western intellectual tradition, leading to the dominant state of epistemological doubt in late nineteenth and twentieth century thought. If reality is an aspect of the imagining mind, then how does one locate a style, a model, with which that reality can be convincingly engaged, or articulated within a recognisable communicative vehicle?

The erosion of epistemological certainty leads directly to the absence of a master narrative, a fact bemoaned by many critics of Modernism and Postmodernism. And yet the prevailing fantasy of the master narrative also represents nostalgia for totalising narratives. In Modernist and Postmodernist fiction, the loss of epistemological and ontological certainties, respectively, results in a loss of faith in such fixed expressions of human experience. That critics like Eagleton and Hebdige, to name but two, interpret this negatively as an indication of intellectual barbarism is indeed ironic. Lyotard will always be more convincing when he claims that we: 'have paid enough price for the nostalgia of the whole and the one, for the reconciliation of the concept and the sensible, of the transparent and the communicable experience' (Lyotard 1989, 82). The master narratives of religion, truth, morality, cause and effect, chronological time and rationality are themselves fictions generated to suggest an achieved cohesion, a certainty in human experience and knowledge. It seems clear to this writer that the ancients absorbed this fictional truth in their literary works. The oral Greek epic contains no direct mimetic impulse, nor does it confine itself to the apparent precision of fact, sequence or dates. Because in the oral imagination the metaphorical gesture is all, the desire to mythos is dominant and a deep awareness of the centrality of the act of telling in generating meaning is a fundamental part of the shaping of story and meaning, albeit a fluid one.

The intention of this book is to establish how Aidan Higgins, John Banville and Neil Jordan have responded to the destabilisation of epistemological models in their work, and how they have managed to construct fictional models which might meaningfully contribute to a re-engagement of the world of human experience. I believe that they have all succeeded in doing so because they have managed to generate fictions that accept epistemological uncertainty as a constituent part of the process of knowing and telling. Their work, from the outset is beset by a deep awareness of the formal and intellectual difficulties with which the twentieth century artist is faced. All of their early work expresses a fascination with memory, language and human perception and all have sought to investigate such problematic faculties. I have attempted, through an analysis of their fictions, to suggest how they have dealt with the problems of the Modernist inheritance and, in doing so, contributed something of significance to contemporary literature. Again Homer offers insight, because Banville, Higgins and Jordan all ultimately revert to a kind of narrative that rejects the need for realism and instead weave highly imaginative ontological universes that do not gain their significance by mirroring reality.

Dominated by memory and the patterns one weaves on the past, Aidan Higgins's work has consistently attempted to articulate the fluidity of a life, which refuses to be explained by ordering systems. Reacting against the mythic structures of Modernism, Higgins's work is anti-formal in its rejection of any fixed literary model. In Higgins's work, fiction and autobiography merge because he refuses to impose aesthetic form on his life experiences, preferring instead to let the formlessness of it all act as his central statement. The essentially chaotic nature of human experience cannot be articulated in fixed artistic forms and thus his work grows increasingly fragmentary in the years after *Langrishe, Go Down*. What emerges, though, is the suggestion that human lives are already private fictions, albeit of a far more fluid kind than in the stylised worlds of literary art.

The past, life itself, such matters, cannot be recaptured in Higgins's world, but the presumption of accurate representation is replaced by a belief in story. Life is a story in the process of being lived and his work attempts to react to that story, in all of its fragmentary losses. At the heart of Higgins's writing there is a profound mistrust of any method that seeks to name the unnameable, to capture the essence of the often-heartbreaking transience of things, precisely because these aspects *are* the essence of life. All attempts to box them in are a loss of life. So Higgins's work, then, is about nothing but life and in his rejection of epistemological systems, he attempts to eke out a way of speaking by allowing us to glimpse at the frequently harsh, occasionally wondrous moments of a life. That he circumvents formal convention in the process is one of the reasons for the negligible attention which this writer receives. Literary conventions are useful points of recognition in the reading process, but they are limiting when we cannot see beyond them. And this is the essence of Higgins's work. Secure in the fictions with which we order our world, we can evade the messiness of existence, the truth of memory and the reality of loss. It is not always a bad thing and Higgins's unyielding work demands much courage on the part of the writer, especially considering that it is his own life at which he tirelessly gazes.

Alternatively, John Banville's work is a treasure trove of literary conventions. However, the verity of the conventions is no more secure with Banville than with Higgins. Banville's response to the epistemological uncertainty he inherited from Modernism has been a sustained artistic quest which is astonishing in its continuity. His work does not so much investigate the veracity of human systems of knowledge as confirm their invented status. Informed by the literary practices of self-reflexive Postmodernism, Banville has constructed an interconnected series of fictions which offer up their own processes as parallel images of the inventive exercises engaged in by the author's fictional creative heroes. To a far greater degree than Higgins, Banville builds his fictions upon an intertextual framework which appears to be a refutation of the primacy of experience in favour of art. However, Banville sees a correlation between art and experience, not in the realist representational fashion, but in other ways. Banville's intertextual zeal reveals the meaning of this correlation because his combination of Rilke's insistent gaze and Nietzsche's belief in appearances results in his desire to say the objective world, or what he calls the 'polished object itself' (Banville 1996, 119). The answer, for Banville, is not to resolve the tradition of intellectual scepticism. Instead he sees that very tradition not as an expression of failure but as a metaphorical mirror of man's own searches.

Banville's work, in its totality, is a symbolic reflection of man's search for meaning, for order, and implicit in this is that there is no solution, only the perpetual search, the endless construction of images of ourselves which can, in great art, speak of our desires and difficulties. Banville, quoting Adorno, explicitly confirms what his fictions have always been saying: 'The unresolved antagonisms of reality reappear in art in the guise of immanent problems of artistic form. This, and not the deliberate injection of objective moments or social content, defines art's relation to society' (Adorno in Banville 1996, 119). The epistemological 'crisis', then, is not so much a problem of human systems of knowledge but an error in the way we view such systems. All elegant systems of knowledge represent innate human yearning in its essence, and our awareness that these systems do not have universal validity, in a representational manner, has resulted in a rejection of them rather than an acknowledgement of them as artistic, scientific and religious metaphorical records of the human desire to order existence. In this Higgins and Banville differ greatly. Higgins reads the lack of consolation in the primacy of experience as proof of the facile nature of artistic form, while Banville clearly views art as a metaphorical expression of desire for order. In Banville this desire is accepted as a central part of human activity, whereas in Higgins it is not.

Neil Jordan's work, too, confronts the meaning of human ordering systems, most interestingly on the level of self. The self, for Jordan, ultimately means an inherited fiction which can imprison one in the limitations of the conventions of that fiction. Thus, implicit in Jordan's work is the notion of inherited fictions as dangerous. Although Jordan's work does not amount to a sustained interrogation, *The Crying Game, Sunrise with Sea-Monster* and *The Dream of a Beast* all portray the transformations of their protagonists in an attempt to suggest that our personas are invented and as such can be discarded in the name of improvement of political, familial and sexual sensibilities. Like Banville, Jordan sees in human experience a series of systems with which we order the world. Unable to accept the patterns of limitation which he sees, Jordan wilfully transforms his characters. Lacking perhaps, the wider universal vision of Banville's fictions, Jordan simply replaces one self with another and does not suggest the implications of a wider pattern. That Jordan's characters cling to their inherited personas so tenaciously is a vindication of Banville's suggestion that our fictions are an expression of our desire for order. Reality for Jordan, is a series of shifting surfaces which does not have a central motivation, apart from a suggestion that we need to get beyond the fictions of ourselves in order to find the truth of ourselves. In this Jordan's work retains an essentially mysterious, even transcendental dimension. The truth of ourselves, for Banville, is the truth inherent in those very fictions or order:

> Nietzsche, one of the most profound aesthetic thinkers, argues that the 'real presence' that we seem to feel is nothing more that the twitching in us still of a primordial reflex of fear and awe in the face of the natural world. (Banville *IT* 1989, W8)

Herein lies the central difference between Banville and Jordan. Jordan's apparent belief in something beneath the fiction is effectively denied by Banville, who places his faith in the fiction as a document of man's essential needs and desires. In addition, Higgins's work locates mystery only in the almost transcendental nature of love. Thus, in this Godless secular world, the signifiers are not empty. They speak of, in Banville's case, the deep yearning at the heart of man and, in Higgins's case, the brutality of transience and loss. Jordan alternatively, seems to believe that Banville's and Nietzsche's 'primordial reflex' may have hidden depths beneath the symbolic gestures of our systems of order. Those depths remain unspoken.

The act of reading literature as symbolic gesture is ancient. To read other forms of creative human designs as parallel, symbolic expressions of basic human needs is not entirely original. What distinguishes Banville's work is his unyielding inquiry into the nature of obsessional human creative urges. His quest takes him to the heart of creative imaginative activity, replete with its mysterious depths. His work does not end nor does the growing critical reaction to his work. What remains for Banville is to further chart the enigmatic oceans of the creative imagination and discover on his voyage the intricacies of the ceaseless human need to transform its own likeness into artistic, scientific and religious form. Higgins's work too ponders what it means to be human and continues to search for a way to express it. Unlike Banville, he sees artistic form as a turning away from the chaotic, refusing to accept that life can be contained in any symbolic gesture. Jordan too rejects the legitimacy of formal arrangements of human lives but has yet to offer the kind of sustained expression of transience and loss found in Higgins's work.

The validity of their various claims is not in question. What matters is that these writers have consistently sought to contribute to a wider intellectual discourse engaged upon by writers as diverse as Garcia Marquez and Rushdie and, in the process, have revealed that the act of engaging reality, even constructing reality, is but a matter of how one looks at it. In these writers one discovers not a refutation of reality but an overwhelming fascination with the nature of our methods of investigation and self-definition. One discovers not a rejection of reality in this but an acknowledgement of the complexity of human epistemological systems, and an acceptance of the multifarious nature of the relationships between people and the lives they inhabit.

NOTES

Chapter 1

[1] The recent study, *Ireland and Cultural Theory: The Mechanics of Authenticity* (eds Colin Graham and Richard Kirkland, London: MacMillan Press, 1999), is a particularly useful and revealing appraisal of the history of cultural theory and the cultural analysis of the literature of Ireland. Apart from an intriguing array of perspectives, it offers evidence of the sheer weight of cultural analysis in Irish literary academic life, making reference to work by Kiberd, P.F. Sheeran, Seamus Deane, Terry Eagleton, Luke Gibbons, Edward Said and many others.

[2] Imhof's specific interest in what he terms the 'fringes' is evident in a number of articles, the most prominent of which are, Rüdiger Imhof. 'How it is on the Fringes of Irish Fiction'. *Irish University Review* 22.1 (Spring/Summer 1992): 151–167, and Rüdiger Imhof, 'Post-Joycean Experiment in Recent Irish Fiction', *Ireland and France – A bountiful friendship: Literature, History and Ideas*, eds Barbara Hayley and Christopher Murray (Buckinghamshire: Colin Smythe Ltd, 1992). More recently, Imhof's book-length study, *The Modern Irish Novel: Irish Novelists after 1945* (Dublin: Wolfhound Press, 2002), considers the contribution of twelve post-war novelists: Samuel Beckett; Aidan Higgins; John Banville; Edna O'Brien; Jennifer Johnston; Julia O'Faolain; William Trevor; Brian Moore; John McGahern; Roddy Doyle; Dermot Bolger, and Patrick McCabe.

[3] Kearney's work on this aspect of Irish studies is formulated in two articles: Richard Kearney, 'A Crisis of Imagination', *The Crane Bag Book of Irish Studies* (Dublin: Blackwater Press, 1982) 390–402, and Richard Kearney, 'The Nightmare of History', *The Irish Literary Supplement* Vol. 2 No. 2 (1983): 24–25. Kearney's crisis is ultimately a recognition of what he views to be the fundamental epistemological questioning at the heart of a specific tradition in Irish literature.

[4] By 'problematic', Kearney means that the work, written in the spirit of Modernist epistemological doubt, generates a poetics dominated by the problems of knowing and communicating. Thus, the legitimacy of act of writing is questioned, implicitly (Modernist texts) or explicitly (Postmodern texts).

[5] Hassan's desire to locate what he terms a 'unitary sensibility', stems from his awareness of the absence of what Lyotard, among others, refers to as a 'grand narrative' (Lyotard 1979). Despite the integral role of fragmentation in the very concept of Postmodernism, the need for a unitary sensibility, a way of doing and saying, is required, even if it remains provisional and illegitimate.

[6] Responding to Jakobson's suggestion that the shifting dominant is 'not so much a question of the disappearance of certain elements and the emergence of others', (Jakobson 1971, 108) but simply a shift in emphasis, McHale asserts that the relationship between Modernist and Postmodernist fiction can be characterised as follows:

Intractable epistemological uncertainty becomes at a certain point ontological plurality or instability: push epistemological questions far enough and they 'tip over' into ontological questions. By the same token, push ontological questions far enough and they tip over into epistemological questions – the sequence is not linear and unidirectional, but bi-directional and reversible. (McHale 1996, 11)

The validity of McHale's claims is evident in my analysis of Higgins, Banville and Jordan, all of whom vacillate between Modernist and Postmodernist poetics, to varying degrees. The fluidity of McHale's and Jakobson's method helps to prevent one from totalising on the basis of selective evidence.

Chapter 2

[7] What Eliot called the, 'continual extinction of personality' (Eliot 1993, 2173) is also referred to by Joyce, through Stephen. The personality of the Artist, claims Stephen, 'finally refines itself out of existence, impersonalises itself, so to speak' (Joyce 1992, 233). Higgins's autobiographical zeal is deeply compromised, intentionally it appears, by his adherence to this particular aspect of Modernist aesthetics.

[8] Otto Beck's study of Ossian acts as a rebuke to certain continental European tendencies to romanticise Ireland's Celtic heritage. His study of Ossian refers, in reality, to James MacPherson who published translations of two poems that he said had been written by Ossian; scholars subsequently proved that they were actually a combination of traditional Gaelic poems and original verses by MacPherson himself. Otto's intellectual prowess is further eroded by this unfortunate association, and it introduces another level of irony to the novel, especially in the context of Otto's intellectual barbarism.

[9] A foreword by the author indicates that the Sligo town and surrounding geographical detail depicted in the novel is, in fact, Celbridge and its peripheries. A minor authorial liberty no doubt, but one which reveals his willingness to interchange locations. The representation of place, hence, is more of a necessary narrative backdrop, than an end in itself.

[10] *Helsingor Station* and *Ronda Gorge* were published within months of each other. For this reason alone they deserve to be treated together but there are more substantial reasons. Their titles echo each other, the temporal span is the same, almost all of each text has been published previously and, most significantly, when read as an inseparable pair, the texts act as a commentary on Higgins's previous work. Much of the material in these texts is relocated and reformulated from *Felo De Se*, *Balcony of Europe*, *Scenes from a Receding Past* and *Images of Africa*.

[11] An earlier draft of 'Sodden Fields' is entitled 'Imaginary Meadows', published in *The Review of Contemporary Fiction* Vol. III, No. 1, Spring 1983.

[12] It seems to this author that this is a crucial point of distinction between Modernism and Postmodernism – Woolf, Eliot and Joyce all retained recognisable ontologies which acquire stability from encyclopedic geographical entities like London, Dublin, the Hebrides etc, even though these very ontologies are being eroded by the epistemological doubts generated in the texts. This kind of ontological stability gradually ceases to play a significant part in Higgins's work.

[13] This is an observation made by Bernard Share, who knew Higgins when he lived in Spain, and not a declaration by Higgins. On the evidence of Share's account it is apparent that Higgins wrote out of his life as he lived it. Consequentially, the idea that a life can be ontologically stable is challenged.

[14] The epigraphs to *Lions of the Grunewald* read as follows:

I see the Berlin Wall, flowers, graves,
H. speaks of the last days here, the streets on fire, the lions loose, the
World that has outstripped our nightmares,

Our subconscious.
John Cheever, *Journals*

Marriage knots aren't going to slip apart
Painlessly with the pull of distance.
There's got to be some wrenching
And slashing.
Alice Munro, *The Progress of Love*

In the evening there, in little cul de
sacs, the soul seems to dissolve.
Vladimir Nabokov, *Speak, Memory*

[15] Parts Two and Three of Higgins's autobiography have since been published: *Dog Days*, London: Secker and Warburg, 1998 and *The Whole Hog*, London: Secker and Warburg, 2000.

Chapter 3

[16] Banville's unswerving awe of Joyce is nowhere more apparent that in his John Banville, 'Survivors of Joyce', *James Joyce: The Artist and the Labyrinth*, ed. Augustine Martin (London: Ryan, 1990) 73–81.

[17] For an in-depth analysis of Banville's collection of stories, *Long Lankin*, and his first novel, *Nightspawn*, please refer to my doctoral thesis, *The Reconstruction of Reality: A Critique of the Epistemological Crisis in Contemporary Irish Fiction* (National University of Ireland, Dublin, 1999).

[18] In *Nightspawn*, Ben's attempts to comprehend his world are conditioned by his acting out of stock roles; he is an exiled writer, a spy, a gangster and even imagines himself to be a cunning murderer in a landscape which always evades his powers of interpretation. Even a taxi-driver is more informed about the revolution than Ben, and he is supposedly a major participant. Ben's patchwork character is a playful comment on the value of mimetic fiction, with its delusion and stock roles.

[19] According to David Ellison, the madeleine was, for Proust, 'involuntary memory, which unlike the purely conscious, conserves the essence of past events' (Ellison 1984, 101).

[20] Echoing Kant's 'thing in itself', Lily Briscoe's intense epistemological and artistic dilemma is elegantly expressed in Part III of *To The Lighthouse*, reflecting her immense struggle to repair the wound between the multifarious aspects of the chosen material for her painting, and her Art. Powerfully expressive of the point at which McHale's epistemological dominant meets the ontological dominant, Lily's anguish is apparent:

> What was the problem then? She must try to get hold of something that evaded her. It evaded her when she thought of Mrs Ramsay; it evaded her now when she thought of her picture. Phrases came. Vision came. Beautiful phrases. But what she wished to get hold of was that very jar on the nerves, the thing itself before it has been made anything (Woolf 1977, 208).

[21] The epigraph to *Doctor Copernicus*, taken from Stevens's *Notes Toward a Supreme Fiction*, is as follows:

> You must become an ignorant man again
> And see the sun again with an ignorant eye
> And see it clearly in the idea of it.

[22] The epigraph to *Kepler*, taken from Rilke's *Duino Elegies*, is as follows:

> Preise dem Engel die Welt....

(Praise this world to the Angel)

[23] Ciaran Carty, 'Out of Chaos Comes Order', *The Sunday Tribune* (14 Sept. 1989): 18. This is an interview with Banville in which he discusses his interests in the divided self, physics and fiction.

[24] The close to *Nightspawn* reads as follows: 'Come, one more effort to transfix it all, to express it all. Try. I cannot. The world is…Art is…No, no use, I cannot. You must, there must be a conclusion. A word, even. Try. Try now, here. Could I? Try. Chapter one. My story begins at a –' (Banville *NS* 1993).

[25] The second letter from Newton to John Locke is a fiction, much of which is derived from Hugo von Hofmannstahl's *Ein Brief* ('The Letter of Lord Chandos').

[26] Rilke's lines from the *Duino Elegies* (The Ninth Elegy) read as follows:

> Look, I am living. On What? Neither childhood nor future
> are growing less…Supernumerous existence
> wells up in my heart.
> (Rilke 1964, 65)

The direct connection with Banville's historian is clear.

[27] Banville's fascination with Kleist is evident in his 'The Helpless Laughter of a Tragedian', *The Irish Times* (3 Dec. 1988): W9. In addition, Banville has adapted two of Kleist's dramas, *The Broken Jug: After Kleist* (Gallery Press, 1994), and *God's Gift*: a version of Heinrich von Kleist's *Amphitryon* (Gallery Press, 2001).

[28] The title, *Long Lankin*, is appropriated from a traditional Old English ballad, variously known as *Long Lankin* or *Lamkin*, which relates a tale of injustice and revenge. Imhof correctly asserts that although the commentary on the blurb of Banville's fiction refers to the '…old belief that a leper can heal himself by spilling innocent blood…' there is no mention of a leper or a blood-spilling, healing process in the ballad. The leper aspect becomes part of the mythic structure of the work with its associations of alienation, social exclusion and torment. Hence Banville's appropriation of the ballad is not very faithful to the original(s).

[29] The epigraph, from Gide's *L'Immoraliste*, reads as follows: 'Take me away from here and give me some reason for living. I have none left. I have freed myself. That may be. But what does it signify? This objectless is a burden to me' (Gide 1983, 157).

[30] An observation made by Banville to this author at a reading in the Galway Arts Centre, May 1989.

[31] Humbert Humbert, at this point in the novel, variously refers to Lolita as Lotte, Lolita, Lottelita and Lolitchen (Nabokov 1988, 76).

[32] Roquentin's closing lines, redolent with artistic and epistemological insecurity, are as follows:

> I am going, I feel irresolute. I dare not make a decision. If I was sure that I had talent…perhaps one day, thinking about this very moment, about this dismal moment at which I am waiting, round-shouldered, for it to be time to get on the train, perhaps I might feel my heart beat faster…(Sartre 1970, 252–3).

The recurrence of the word *perhaps*, reminiscent of Beckett, engenders a note of uncertainty which indicates Sartre's unwillingness to assign his narrator with narratorial stability.

[33] Imhof has pinpointed a range of incidents/comments from James's *The Sacred Fount* that bear resemblance to the plot of *The Newton Letter*, none more revealing than the narrator's introspective commentary during dinner on the second night: 'I remember feeling seriously warned not to yield further to my idle habit of reading into mere human things an interest so much deeper than mere humans things were in general prepared to supply' (James 1979, 156).

[34] Writing of Heisenberg's uncertainty principle, Fritjof Capra raises an interesting issue:

> It is important to realise…that this limitation is not caused by the imperfection of our measuring techniques, but is a limitation of principle. If we decide to measure the particle's position precisely, the particle simply does not have a well-defined momentum, and vice versa. (Capra 1991, 158).

Capra's comment raises an intriguing possibility, albeit on an atomic level, that the problem is not with our measuring systems. Instead reality (on an atomic level at least), does not behave in a well-defined way and thus it is problematic for us to map it with our systems. It is not, then, evidence of inaccurate tools, rather, it is an indication of the intense complexity of the momentum of matter on a sub-atomic level.

[35] Nietzsche's concept of the extra-moral is generated from his dissatisfaction with the idea that the origin of an action determined its value. Clearly, intention is an implicit part of origin. Nietzsche's extra-moral, alternatively, suggests that the value of an action should be determined by that which is not intentional and that the intention is only 'a sign and a symptom that needs interpreting, and a sign, moreover, that signifies too many things, and which thus taken by itself signifies practically nothing…' (Nietzsche *BGE* 1977, 45).

[36] Banville speaks of the lessons the writer must learn regarding the discrepancy between words and the objects they aspire to signify: 'He must learn, and unlearn. He must leap, executing graceful somersaults as he goes, but look down, always, no matter how vertiginous the view' (Banville 1981, 13).

Chapter 4

[37] Responding to images of Irishness, Jordan seems to view Joyce, and Yeats, very much as part of an Irish inheritance from which he feels a generational distance:

> When I started writing I felt very pressurised by the question: How do I cope with the notion of Irishness? It meant almost nothing to me. I was, of course, profoundly moved by the Irish literature I encountered as a student – Yeats and Joyce. But how was I to write about the experience I knew, as someone born in Sligo and growing up in the suburban streets of Dublin in the sixties? The great books of Anglo-Irish literature had very little to do with this, they had no real resonance at this level. My most acute dilemma was – how to write stories about contemporary urban life in Ireland without being swamped in the language and mythology of Joyce…The only identity, at a cultural level, that I could forge was one that came from the worlds of television, popular music, cinema which I was experiencing daily. (Jordan in Kearney, *Across the Frontiers* 1988, 196–7)

Jordan's response to notions of Irishness is reflective of his generation's inability to identify fully with nationalist ideas and the drama of the independence era. Interestingly, despite Jordan's apparent inability to identify with the specificity of Joyce's images of suburban Dublin, there is little doubt that he has been deeply influenced by Joyce's narrative innovation and this is where Jordan's significance lies, in the context of this study. Escaping from the great master may not have been as easy as it appeared.

[38] A recurring body of images has evolved in Postmodern fiction, predictably endeavouring to express the inexpressible, to allude to hidden depths and absent truths. Beckett, Robbe-Grillet, Banville and Jordan all attempt to eke out significance, using the images of rooms, doorways, corridors, and silence. A number of telling examples are included herewith:

> …the blond strands of seaweed smelling of iodine, the bloodstains, the delicate evening shoes, the cries of the gulls. And I move on, yet again, faced with the row of closed doors, down the endless empty corridor, unalterably neat and clean (Robbe-Grillet 1978, 142).

> And it seemed to me that somehow I had always been here, and somehow would remain here always, among Mammy's things, with her little unrelenting eyes fixed on me. She signified

something, no, she signified nothing. She had no meaning. She was simply there...And would be there, waiting in that fetid little room, forever (Banville 1987, 230).

The Silence, a word on the silence, in the silence, that's the worst, to speak of silence, then lock me up, lock someone up, that is to say, what is that to say, calm, calm, I am calm, I am locked up, I am in something, it is not I, that's all I know, no more about that, that is to say, make a place, a little world, it will be round, this time it will be round, it is not certain, low of ceiling, thick of wall, why low...(Beckett 1976, 373).

[39] Blake's reaction against sensual experience as a means by which one gains wisdom, bears significance for Jordan's attempts to metaphorically transcend empirical reality in both *Dream of a Beast* and *Sunrise with Sea-Monster*. It would appear that he has confronted the limits of human epistemological systems and indicates a desire to at least symbolically extend his search.

[40] In his *Proust*, Beckett had already formulated what was to be a lifelong perspective, that of the essential ineffectiveness of human communication: 'There is no communication because there are no vehicles of communication' (Beckett 1931, 47). Implicitly rejecting human systems of discourse, Beckett sounds a despondent note, which resonates in the work of Higgins, Banville and Jordan.

[41] Banville's interest in Heisenberg is apparent in his 'Physics and Fictions: Order from Chaos', in which he indicates his belief that modern physics reads like philosophy and thus 'a certain seepage' between art and science is inevitable. Banville clearly conceives of Heisenberg's uncertainty principle as similar in significance to Modernist epistemological doubt.

BIBLIOGRAPHY

Primary Works

John Banville

Long Lankin (London: Secker and Warburg, 1970).
Nightspawn (London: Secker and Warburg, 1971).
The Newton Letter (Panther Books, 1984).
Long Lankin (Dublin: Gallery, 1984).
Birchwood (London: Panther Books, 1984).
Doctor Copernicus (London: Panther Books, 1984).
Kepler (London: Panther Books, 1985).
Mefisto (London: Paladin, 1987).
The Book of Evidence (London: Secker and Warburg, 1989).
Ghosts (London: Secker and Warburg, 1993).
Athena (London: Secker andWarburg, 1995).
The Untouchable (London: Picador, 1997).
Eclipse (London: Picador, 2000).

Drama
The Broken Jug (Oldcastle: Gallery, 1994).
Seachange (Radio Telifis Eireann, 1994).
God's Gift: a version of Heinrich von Kleist's *Amphitryon* (Oldcastle: Gallery, 2001).

Aidan Higgins
Felo De Se (London: John Calder, 1960).
Images of Africa (London: Calder and Boyers, 1971).
Balcony of Europe (London: Calder and Boyers, 1972).
Scenes From a Receding Past (London: John Calder, 1977).
Bornholm Night-Ferry (London: Abacus, 1985).
Langrishe, Go Down (London: Paladin, 1987).
Ronda Gorge and Other Precipices (London: Secker and Warburg, 1989).

Helsingor Station and Other Departures (London: Secker and Warburg, 1989).
Lions of the Grunewald (London: Secker and Warburg, 1993).
Donkey's Years (London: Secker and Warburg, 1995).
Flotsam and Jetsam (London: Minerva, 1997).
Dog Days (London: Secker and Warburg, 1998).
The Whole Hog (London: Secker and Warburg, 2000).

Neil Jordan
The Past (London: Abacus, 1982).
The Dream of a Beast (London: Chatto and Windus, 1983).
Night in Tunisia (London: Vintage, 1988).
Sunrise with Sea-Monster (London: Chatto and Windus, 1994).

Film
The Crying Game Director and Script: Neil Jordan. Producer: Stephen Wooley. 1992.

Other works/Secondary sources

Baneham, Sam. 'Aidan Higgins: A Political Dimension', *Review of Contemporary Fiction* (Spring 1983): 168–74.
Banville, John. 'Colony of Expatriates', *Hibernia* (Oct 6, 1972): 18.
Banville, John. 'So Stout a Gentleman', *Hibernia* (10 Sept. 1976): 26.
Banville, John. 'Heavenly Alchemy', *Hibernia* (4 Feb. 1977): 28.
Banville, John. 'A Talk', *Irish University Review*, 11.1 (Spring 1981): 13–17.
Banville, John. 'Physics and Fictions: Order from Chaos', *The New York Times Book Review* (21 April 1985): 41–42.
Banville, John. 'The Helpless Laughter of a Tragedian', *The Irish Times* (3 Dec. 1988): W9.
Banville, John. 'What do we mean by meaning', *The Irish Times* (July 1 1989a): W8.
Banville, Vincent. 'Banville on Banville', *The Sunday Press*, (15 Oct. 1989b): L12.
Banville, John. 'Survivors of Joyce' (Ed.) Augustine Martin. *James Joyce: The Artist and the Labyrinth*. (London: Ryan, 1990): 73–81.
Banville, John. 'Enlightenment's Leading Light', *The Irish Times* (June 13, 1992): W8.
Banville, John. 'Living in the Shadows: Interview with Salman Rushdie', *The Irish Times* (Jan. 16, 1993a): W1 and W3.
Banville, John. 'A Great Tradition', *The Sunday Times* (March 21, 1993b): B 8–9.
Banville, John. 'Making Little Monsters', *The Agony and the Ego. The Art and Strategy of Fiction Writing Explored.* (Ed.) Clare Boylan. (Harmondsworth: Penguin, 1993c): 105–12.

Banville, John. 'The Personae of Summer', *Irish Writers and Their Creative Process: Irish Literary Studies* 48. (Eds) Jacqueline Genet and Wynne Hellegouarc'h (Gerrards Cross: Colin Smythe, 1996): 118–22.
Barnes, Djuna. *Nightwood*. Introduction T.S. Eliot. (London: Faber and Faber, 1985).
Barthes, Roland. *Image–Music–Text*. (Trans.) Stephen Heath. (London: Fontane, 1977).
Battersby, Eileen. 'John Banville', *Books and Bookmen* 365 (March 1986): 20–21.
Battersby, Eileen. 'Comedy in a Time of Famine: Interview with John Banville', *The Irish Times* (May 24, 1994): 10.
Bayley, John. 'The Real Thing', *The New York Review of Books* (17 May 1990): 6.
Beckett, Samuel. *Proust*. (N.Y.: Grove Press, 1931).
Beckett, Samuel. *The Beckett Trilogy* (Molloy, Malone Dies, The Unnamable). (London: Picador, 1979).
Beckett, Samuel. *Ill Seen Ill Said*. (Trans.) Samuel Beckett. (London: John Calder, 1982).
Beckett, Samuel. 'Letter from Samuel Beckett Concerning Manuscript of Story "Killachter Meadow"', *Review of Contemporary Fiction* (Spring 1983): 156–57.
Beckett, Samuel. *The Complete Dramatic Works*. (London: Faber and Faber, 1990).
Beja, Morris. 'Felons of Our Selves: The Fiction of Aidan Higgins', *Irish University Review*, 3.2 (Autumn, 1973): 163–78.
Blake, William. *Complete Poems*. (Ed.) Alicia Ostriker. (London: Penguin, 1977).
Bloom, Harold. *The Anxiety of Influence: A Theory of Poetry*. (New York: Oxford UP, 1975a).
Bloom, Harold. 'Wallace Stevens: The Poems of Our Climate', *Figures of Capable Imagination*. (New York: Seabury Press, 1975b): 103–19.
Borges, Jorge Luis. *A Universal History of Infamy*. (Trans.) Thomas di Giovanni. (Harmondsworth: Penguin, 1985a).
Borges, Jorge Luis. *Fictions*. (Ed.) Anthony Kerrigan. (London: John Calder, 1985b).
Bradbury, Malcom and McFarlane, Jane. *Modernism: A Guide to European Literature 1890–1930*. (London: Penguin, 1991).
Bragg, Melvyn. Special John Banville Episode, *The South Bank Show*. (UTV March 28, 1993).
Brautigan, Richard. *In Watermelon Sugar*. (London: Picador, 1973).
Brown, Terence. 'Paying Attention', *The New Nation* 6 (May–June 1989): 22–23.
Brown, Terence. 'Redeeming the Time: the Novels of John McGahern and John Banville', *The British and Irish Novel Since 1960*. (Ed.) James Acheson. (New York: St. Martin's Press, 1991): 159–73.
Browne, Vincent. 'Neil Jordan Profile', *Film West* (Spring 1995): 32–34.
Buckeye, Robert. 'Form as the Extension of Content: "their existence in my eyes"', *Review of Contemporary Fiction* (Spring 1983): 192–95.

Burgstaller, Susanne. '"This Lawless House" – John Banville's Post-Modernist Treatment of the Big House Motif in Birchwood and The Newton Letter', *Ancestral Voices. The Big House in Anglo-Irish Literature*. (Ed.) Otto Rauchbauer. (Hildesheim, Zurich, New York: Olms, 1992): 239–56

Calvino, Italo. *Invisible Cities*. (Trans.) W.Weaver.(London: Vintage, 1997).

Camus, Albert. *The Outsider*. (Harmondsworth: Penguin, 1971).

Carty, Ciaran. 'Out of Chaos Comes Order', *The Sunday Tribune* (14 Sept. 1989): 18. An Interview with John Banville.

Cashman, Kara. 'The Darkness Within: Identifying a Uniform Macabre Psyche in Contemporary Irish Fiction', *Review of Postgraduate Studies* No.4 (Spring 1995–96): 44–48.

Connolly, Peter. (Ed.) *Literature and the Changing Ireland*. (Buckinghamshire: Colin Smythe Ltd., 1982).

Conrad, Joseph. *Heart of Darkness*. Intro. Paul O'Prey. (London: Penguin, 1989).

Cook, Albert. *The Meaning of Fiction*. (Detroit: Wayne State UP, 1960).

Cronin, Gearoid. 'John Banville and the subversion of the Big House novel', *The Big House in Ireland: Reality and Representation*. (Ed.) Jacqueline Genet. (Dingle: Brandon, 1991): 215–30.

Cumming, Laura. 'Kicks of the old grey bull', *The Guardian* (Feb. 7, 1995): 2:14.

Daly, Ita. 'Trial for Murder', *Irish Independent* (24/25 March 1989): 10.

Donnelly, Brian. 'The Big House in the Recent Novel', *Studies* 254 (Summer 1975): 133–42.

Deane, Seamus. 'Be Assured I am Inventing: The Fiction of John Banville', *The Irish Novel in Our Time*. (Eds) P. Rafroidi and M. Harmon. (Lille: Université de Lille, 1975/6). 329–39.

Deane, Seamus. 'The Literary Myths of the Revival: A Case For Their Abandonment', *Myth and Reality in Irish Literature*. (Ed.) Joseph Ronsley. (Waterloo, Canada: Wilfred Laurier University Press, 1977): 317–29.

Deane, Seamus. 'Review of *Doctor Copernicus*', *Irish University Review* 8.1 (Spring 1981): 120–21.

Deane, Seamus. 'Witness for the Defence', *The Irish Times*, 25 March 1989: W9.

Dostoyevsky, Fyodor. *Notes from Underground/The Double*. (Trans.) Jessie Coulson. (Harmondsworth: Penguin, 1980).

Dunne, Sean. 'Review of *The Crying Game*', *Film Ireland* (Nov/Dec 1992): 2425.

Dwyer, Michael. 'Neil Jordan In Conversation With Michael Dwyer at the Galway Film Fleadh'. (Galway: Film West/The Fleadh Papers, July 1997).

Edgeworth, Maria. *Castle Rackrent/The Absentee*. (New York: Dover, 1966).

Eliot, T.S. *Selected Essays*. (London: Faber and Faber, 1976).

Ellison, David. *The Reading of Proust*. (Oxford: Blackwell, 1984).

Farren, Ronan. ' Fiction Writers on Four: John Banville', *The Fiction Magazine*, 1.3 (1982).

Farren, Ronan. 'Fiction Writers on Four: Neil Jordan', *The Fiction Magazine,* 1.3 (1982).

Farren, Ronan. 'An island of dreams', *Sunday Independent* (April 4, 1993): 8L.

Farren, Ronan. 'Tarnished Goddess', *Sunday Independent* (Feb 19, 1995): 8L.
Freely, Maureen. 'Works of Art', *Literary Review* (June 1989): 7–8.
Garfitt, Roger. 'Constants in Contemporary Irish Fiction', *Two Decades of Irish Writing – A Critical Study*. (Cheshire: Carcanet, 1975): 207–41.
Gass, William H. *The World Within the Word*. (Boston: Non Pareil Books, 1979).
Gefter Wondrich, Roberta. 'A Great, Sinister Performer: John Banville, *The Untouchable*', *The Canadian Journal of Irish Studies*, 23.2 (Dec. 1997a): 123–29.
Gefter Wondrich, Roberta. 'The Familiar Otherwhere of Art: Awareness, Creation, Redemption. Art and the Artistic Imagination in John Banville's Trilogy of Art', *Prospero: Rivista di culture anglo-germaniche* IV (1997b): 94–109.
Gide, Andre. *The Immoralist*. (Harmondsworth: Penguin, 1983).
Goethe, Johann Wolfgang. *Faust/Part One*. (Trans.) Philip Wayne. (Harmondsworth: Penguin, 1967).
Goffman, Erving, *The Presentation of Self in Everyday Life*. (New York: Doubleday, 1959).
Golden, Sean. 'Parsing Love's Complainte: Aidan Higgins on the Need to Name', *Review of Contemporary Fiction*, (Spring 1983): 210–19.
Graham, Colin and Richard Kirkland. (Eds) *Ireland and Cultural Theory: The Mechanics of Authenticity*. (London: MacMillan Press, 1999).
Grossvogel, David I. *Limits of the Novel: Evolutions of a Form from Chaucer to Robbe-Grillet*. (Ithaca, New York: Cornell UP, 1968).
Hand, Derek. *John Banville: Exploring Fictions*. (Dublin: The Liffey Press, 2002).
Hanly, David. 'Writer in Profile': Interview with Neil Jordan.(RTE 1, 12.8.92).
Harmon, Maurice. 'By Memory Inspired: Themes and Forces in Recent Irish Writing', *Eire* (1973): 3–19.
Harvey, David. The Condition of Postmodernity: An Enquiry into the Origins of Cultural Change. (Oxford: Basil Blackwell, 1989).
Hassan, Ihab. 'Frontiers of Criticism: Metaphors of Silence', *Virginia Quarterly*, 46.1 (1970): 81–95.
Hassan, Ihab. 'The Culture of Postmodernism', *Theory, Culture and Society* 2.3 (1985): 119–31.
Hassan, Ihab. *The Postmodern Turn: Essays in Postmodern Theory and Culture*. (Ohio: Ohio State University Press, 1987).
Healy, Dermot. 'Towards *Bornholm Night-Ferry* and *Texts For the Air*: A Rereading of Aidan Higgins', *Review of Contemporary Fiction* (Spring 1983): 181–92.
Healy, Dermot. 'A Travel Guide to the Imagination', *The Sunday Tribune* (April 23 1989): B 10.
Healy, Dermot. '"Donkey's Years": A Review', *Asylum Arts Review* Vol. 1, Issue 1 (Autumn 1995): 45–46.

Hebdige, Dick. 'The Bottom Line on Planet One', *Modern Literary Theory: A Reader*. (Eds) Philip Rice and Patricia Waugh. (London: Edward Arnold, 1989): 260–81.

Heller, Erich. *The Poet's Self and the Poem: Essays On Goethe, Nietzsche, Rilke and Thomas Mann*. (London: Athlone Press, University of London, 1976).

Higgins, Aidan. 'A Bash in the Tunnel', *James Joyce by the Irish*. (Ed.) John Ryan. (Brighton: Clifton Books, 1970).

Higgins, Aidan. 'Writer in Profile: Aidan Higgins', *RTE Guide* (Feb. 5 1971): 13.

Higgins, Aidan. 'Glancing Blows', *Books Ireland* (Oct. 1982): 174.

Higgins, Aidan. 'The Heroe's Portion: Chaos or Anarchy in the Cultic Twoilet', *Review of Contemporary Fiction* (Spring 1983): 108–14.

Higgins, Aidan. 'Fresh Horrors', *The Irish Times* (Dec. 3 1988): W9.

Higgins, Aidan. 'The Hidden Narrator', *Asylum Arts Review*, Vol 1 Issue 1 (Autumn 1995): 2–7.

Hopper, Keith. *A Portrait of the Artist as a Young Post-Modernist*. (Cork: Cork University Press, 1995).

Hughes-Hallet, Lucy. 'Visions of loveliness: *Sunrise with Sea-Monster*', *The Sunday Times* (Jan. 15, 1995): B13.

Hughes-Hallet, Lucy. 'Last tango in Dublin', *The Sunday Times* (Feb. 19, 1995): B7.

Hutcheon, Linda and Natoli, Joseph (Eds) *A Postmodern Reader*. (Albany: N.Y. State University Press, 1993).

Hutcheon, Linda. *A Poetics of Postmodernism*. (London: Routledge, 1996).

Imhof, Rüdiger. 'John Banville: A Checklist', *Irish University Review* 11.1 (Spring 1981a): 87–95.

Imhof, Rüdiger. 'John Banville's Supreme Fiction', *Irish University Review* 11.1 (Spring 1981b): 52–86.

Imhof, Rüdiger. 'My Readers, That Small Band, Deserve a Rest', *Irish University Review* 11.1 (Spring 1981c): 5–12.

Imhof, Rüdiger. '*The Newton Letter*, by John Banville: An Exercise in Literary Derivation', *Irish University Review* 13.2 (Autumn 1983): 162–67.

Imhof, Rüdiger. '*Bornholm Night-Ferry* and *Journal to Stella*: Aidan Higgins's Indebtedness to Jonathan Swift', *The Canadian Journal of Irish Studies*, 10, 2 (1984a): 5–13.

Imhof, Rüdiger and Kamm, Jurgen. 'Coming to Grips with Aidan Higgins's "Killachter Meadow": An Analysis', *Etudes Irlandaises* (1984b): 145–60.

Imhof, Rüdiger. 'German Influences on John Banville and Aidan Higgins', *Literary Interrelations: Ireland, England and the World*, Vol 2: *Comparison and Impact*. (Eds) Wolfgang Zach and Heinz Kosok. (Tubingen: Gunter Narr, 1987a).

Imhof, Rüdiger. 'Swan's way, or Goethe, Einstein, Banville – The Eternal Recurrence'. *Etudes Irlandaises* (12 Dec. 1987b): 113–29.

Imhof, Rüdiger. 'Questions and Answers with John Banville', *Irish Literary Supplement* (Spring 1987c): 13.

Imhof, Rüdiger. *John Banville: A Critical Introduction.* (Dublin: Wolfhound Press, 1989).
Imhof, Rüdiger. (Ed.) *Contemporary Irish Novelists.* (Gunter Narr Verlag: Tubingen, 1990).
Imhof, Rüdiger. 'How it is on the Fringes of Irish Fiction', *Irish University Review*, 22.1 (Spring/Summer, 1992a): 151–67.
Imhof, Rüdiger. 'Post-Joycean Experiment in Recent Irish Fiction', *Ireland and France – A bountiful friendship: Literature, History and Ideas.* (Eds) Barbara Hayley and Christopher Murray. (Colin Smythe Ltd: Buckinghamshire, 1992b):124–36.
Imhof, Rüdiger. 'Proust and Contemporary Irish Fiction', *The Internationalism Of Irish Literature and Drama: Irish Literary Studies* 41. (Ed.) Joseph McMinn, assisted by Anne McMaster and Angela Welch. (Buckinghamshire: Colin Smythe Ltd., 1992c): 255–60.
Imhof, Rüdiger. 'Review of Ghosts', *ABEI Newsletter*, Issue 8 (August 1994): 7–8.
Imhof, Rudiger. 'Review of Sunrise with Sea-Monster', *Linen Hall Review* (Spring 1995a): 23–26.
Imhof, Rüdiger. 'John Banville's *Athena*: A Love Letter to Art', *Asylum Arts Review*, Vol. 1 Issue 1 (Autumn 1995b) 27–34.
Imhof, Rüdiger. 'In Search of the Rosy Grail: The Creative Process in the Novels of John Banville', *Irish Writers and Their Creative Process: Irish Literary Studies* 48. (Eds) Jacqueline Genet and Wynne Hellegouarc'h. (Gerrards Cross: Colin Smythe, 1996): 123–36.
Imhof, Rüdiger. *John Banville: A Critical Introduction.* (Dublin: Wolfhound Press, 1997).
Imhof, Rüdiger. *The Modern Irish Novel: Irish Novelists after 1945.* (Dublin: Wolfhound Press, 2002).
Jakobson, Roman. 'The Dominant', *Readings in Russian Poetics: Formalist and Structuralist Views.* (Eds) Ladislav Matejka and Krystna Pomorska. (Cambridge, Mass: MIT Press 1971): 105–10.
Jordan, Neil. *The Crying Game*: *An Original Screenplay.* (London: Vintage, 1993a).
Jordan, Neil. 'Projecting Thoughts', *The Irish Times* (May 15 1993b): W9.
Joyce, James. *Ulysses.* London: Penguin, 1986).
Joyce, James. *A Portrait of the Artist as a Young Man.* (Introduction) Seamus Deane (Harmondsworth: Penguin, 1992).
Kafka, Franz. *The Metamorphosis* (Trans.) Stanley Corngold. (New York: Norton, 1996).
Kearney, Richard. 'A Crisis of Imagination', *The Crane Bag Book of Irish Studies* (Dublin: Blackwater Press, 1982): 390–401.
Kearney, Richard. 'The Nightmare of History', *The Irish Literary Supplement* 2.2 (1983): 24–25.
Kearney, Richard. 'Myth and Motherland', *Ireland's Field Day.* (London: Hutchinson and Co. Ltd., 1985): 59–80.

Kearney, Richard. *Transitions: Narratives in Irish Culture*. (Dublin: Wolfhound Press, 1988a).
Kearney, Richard. *The Wake of Imagination*. (London: Hutchinson, 1988b).
Kearney, Colbert. 'The Treasure of Hungry Hill', *Cultural Contexts and Literary Idioms in Contemporary Irish Literature*. (Ed.) Michael Keneally. (Gerrards Cross: Colin Smythe Ltd., 1988c): 124–37.
Kearney, Richard. 'Modern Irish Cinema: Re-Viewing Traditions', *Irish Literary Studies* 35. (Ed.) Michael Kenneally. (Gerrard's Cross: Colin Smythe Ltd., 1992a): 144–59.
Kearney, Richard. 'Modern Irish Cinema: Re-Viewing Traditions', *Irish Literary Studies* 35. (Ed.) Michael Kenneally. (Gerrard's Cross: Colin Smythe Ltd., 1992b): 144–59.
Kellaway, Kate. Behind the Curtains: Interview with J. Banville', *The Observer*, (April 4, 1993a): 59.
Kemp, Peter. 'Bewitched, baroque and bewildering', *The Sunday Times* (April 11, 1993b): B13.
Kermode, Frank. *Wallace Stevens*. (New York: Chips Bookshop Inc., 1979).
Kiberd, Declan. *Inventing Ireland*. (London: Jonathan Cape, 1995).
Kilroy, Thomas. 'Tellers of Tales', *Times Literary Supplement* (17 March 1972): 301.
Kilroy, Thomas. *The Big Chapel*. (Dublin: Poolbeg Press, 1982).
Kilroy, Thomas. 'The isle is full of noises', *The Irish Times* (March 7, 1993): W8.
Kinsella, Thomas. 'Another September' (Ed.) Augustine Martine *Soundings*. (Dublin: Gill and Macmillan Ltd.), 1969.
Koestler, Arthur. *The Sleepwalkers: A History of Man's Changing Vision*. (Harmondsworth: Penguin, 1977).
Kreilkamp, Vera. 'Reinventing a Form: the Big House in Aidan Higgins's *Langrishe, Go Down*', *The Canadian Journal of Irish Studies* 11.2 (Dec. 1985): 27–38.
Kundera, Milan. *The Unbearable Lightness of Being*. (Trans.) M.H. Heim. (New York: Harper Perennial, 1991).
Kundera, Milan. *The Book of Laughter and Forgetting*. (Trans.) Aaron Asher. (London: Faber and Faber, 1996).
Lerner, Laurence. ' A Hero of our Time' (*The Spectator*, 28 Oct. 1989): 33.
Lernout, Geert. 'Banville and being: *The Newton Letter and history*', *History and Violence in Anglo-Irish Literature*. (Eds) Joris Duytschaever and Geert Lernout. (Amsterdam: Rodopi, 1988): 67–77.
Lernout, Geert. 'Looking for Pure Visions', *Graph: Irish Literary Review* 1 (Oct. 1986): 12–16.
Liddy, James. 'Notes on the Wandering Celt: Aidan Higgins' *Balcony of Europe*', *Review of Contemporary Fiction* (Spring 1983): 166–68.
Lodge, David. *Language of Fiction. Essays in Criticism and Verbal Analysis of the English Novel*. (London: Routledge and Kegan Paul, 1970).

Lodge, David. *Working with Structuralism: Essays and Reviews on Nineteenth and Twentieth Century Literature.* (Boston: Routledge and Kegan Paul, 1981).

Lodge, David. *The Modes of Modern Writing: Metaphor, Metonymy, and the Typology of Modern Literature.* (London: Edward Arnold, 1983).

Lodge, David. *The Art of Fiction.* (London: Penguin, 1992).

Lubbers, Klaus. '*Balcony of Europe*: The Trend towards Internationalization in Recent Irish Fiction', *Literary Interrelations: Ireland, England and the World.* (Tubingen: Gunter Narr, 1987): 235–44.

Lukacs, George. *The Theory of the Novel.* (Trans.) Anna Bostock. (London: Merlin, 1971).

Lyotard, Jean-François. *The Postmodern Condition: A Report on Knowledge* (Trans.) G. Bennington/B.Massumi. (Minneapolis: University of Minnesota Press, 1989).

Lysaght, Sean. 'Review of The Book of Evidence and Rudiger Imhof's John Banville: A Critical Introduction', *Irish University Review* 20.1 (Spring 1990): 214–17.

Lysaght, Sean. 'Banville's Tetralogy: The Limits of Mimesis', *Irish University Review* 21.1 (Spring/Summer 1991): 82–100.

Mann, Thomas. *Doctor Faustus.* (Trans.) H.T. Lowe-Porter. (Harmondsworth: Penguin, 1971).

Marquez, Gabriel Garcia. *One Hundred Years of Solitude.* (Trans.) Gregory Rabassa. (Harmondsworth: Penguin, 1972).

Marquez, Gabriel Garcia. *Love in the Time of Cholera.* (Trans.) Edith Grossman. (Harmondsworth: Penguin, 1988).

Martin, Augustine. 'Banville Revealed', *Irish Independent* (May 11, 1991): 16.

Matthews, Aidan. 'A rush through the vagaries of Berlin life: Review of *Lions of the Grunewald*', *The Sunday Tribune* (Nov. 21, 1993): B12.

Meany, Helen. 'Master of Paradox: Interview with John Banville', *The Irish Times* (March 24, 1993): 12.

Meany, Helen. 'Scenes From a Receding Past: Interview with Aidan Higgins', *The Irish Times* (June 6, 1995): 8.

Molloy, Francis C. ' The Search for Truth: The Fiction of John Banville', *Irish University Review* 11.1 (Spring 1981): 29–51.

Mullen, Michael. 'Aidan Higgins: Figures in Landscapes', *Review of Contemporary Fiction* (Spring 1983): 158–61.

Murphy, Neil. *Out of the Postmodern Abyss: The Quest for Truth in the Fiction of John Banville.* (M.A. thesis, University College, Galway, 1991).

Murphy, Neil. 'Angels and Gods, and Purely Untellable Things', *The Irish Review* 17–18 (Winter 1995): 195–97.

Murphy, Neil. 'Dreams, Departures, Destinations: A Reassessment of Aidan Higgins's Fiction', *Graph*, 2nd Series, Issue 1 (1995): 64–71.

Murphy, Neil. 'Review of *Lions of the Grunewald*', *Irish University Review* (Spring/Summer 1995): 188–90.

MacLaughlin, Brigid. 'A Torrent of Nostalgia', *Sunday Independent* (July 2, 1995): 10L.
McAleese, Mary. 'Banville's Fiction Compromised by Reality?', *Alpha* (25 May 1989): 17.
McCormack, David. 'John Banville: Literature as Criticism', *The Irish Review* 2 (1987): 95–99.
McCone, Kim. *Pagan Past and Christian Present*. (Maynooth: Maynooth Monographs, 1990).
McGee, Harry. 'Freddie's back as Banville grapples with alien planet: Interview with J. Banville', *The Sunday Press* (March 28, 1993): 42.
McGrath, Patrick. 'An elegiac love letter', *The Irish Times* (Feb. 11, 1995): 9.
McHale, Brian. *Postmodernist Fiction*. (London: Routledge, 1996).
McKenna, John. 'The State of Irish Writing', *In Dublin* (Nov. 29, 1984): 8–11.
McKenna, John. 'Rage for Order', *In Dublin* (Nov. 13 1986): 17.
McKenna, John. 'Review of *The Book of Evidence*.' *In Dublin* (Feb. 15–28 1990): 67.
McMahon, Sean. 'Banville Island Worth the Trip', *Irish Independent* (April 3, 1993): W10.
McMinn, Joseph. 'Reality Refuses To Fall Into Place.' *Fortnight* (Oct. 1986): 24.
McMinn, Joseph. 'Stereotypical Images of Ireland in John Banville's Fiction', *Eire-Ireland: A Journal of Irish Studies*, 23.3 (Fall 1988a): 94–102.
McMinn, Joseph. 'An Exalted Naming: the Poetical Fictions of John Banville', *The Canadian Journal of Irish Studies* 14.1 (July 1988b): 17–27.
McMinn, Joseph. 'Disturbing Fascination', *Fortnight* (June 1989): 23.
McMinn, Joseph. *John Banville: A Critical Study*. (Dublin: Gill and Macmillan, 1991).
McMinn, Joseph. 'Naming the World: Language and Experience in John Banville's Fiction', *Irish University Review*, 23.2 (Autumn/Winter 1993): 183–96.
McMinn, Joseph. *The Supreme Fictions of John Banville*. (Manchester: Manchester UP, 1999).
Nabokov, Vladimir. *Ada*. (Harmondsworth: Penguin, 1970).
Nabokov, Vladimir. *Pale Fire*. (Harmondsworth: Penguin, 1973).
Nabokov, Vladimir. *Despair*. (Harmondsworth: Penguin, 1987a).
Nabokov, Vladimir. *Lolita*. (Harmondsworth: Penguin, 1987b).
Ní Bhrian, Doirin. Special John Banville Episode. *Bookside*. RTE (March 1989).
Nietzsche, Friedrich. *The Birth of Tragedy/The Case of Wagner*. (Trans.) W. Kaufmann. (New York: Vintage, 1967).
Nietzsche, Friedrich. *Beyond Good and Evil*. (Trans.) R.J. Hollingdale. (Harmondsworth: Penguin, 1974).
Nietzsche, Friedrich. *A Nietzsche Reader*. (Ed. and Trans.) R.J. Hollingdale. (Harmondsworth: Penguin, 1977).
Nietzsche, Friedrich. *Thus Spoke Zarathustra*. (Trans.) R.J. Hollingdale. (Harmondsworth: Penguin, 1986).

Nietzsche, Friedrich. *Ecce Homo*. (Trans.) R.J. Hollingdale. (Harmondsworth: Penguin, 1988).
Nietzsche, Friedrich. *Twilight of the Idols/The Anti-Christ*. (Trans.) R.J. Hollingdale. (Harmondsworth: Penguin, 1990).
Nye, Robert. 'Heliocentric Vision', *Hibernia*, (Dec. 3 1976): 20.
O'Brien, Flann. *At Swim Two Birds*. (Harmondsworth: Penguin, 1967).
O'Brien, George. 'Goodbye to All That', *The Irish Review* 7 (Autumn 1989): 89–92.
O'Brien, George. 'Consumed by Memories', *The Irish Times* (June 10, 1995): W9.
O'Brien, John. 'Scenes from a Receding Past', *Review of Contemporary Fiction*, (Spring 1983): 164–66.
O'Connor, Joe. 'Banville novel is beautiful and beguiling', *The Sunday Tribune*, (April 11, 1993): B4.
O'Donnell, Mary. 'Crimes of the Imagination', *The Sunday Tribune* (March 26 1989a): 22.
O'Donnell, Mary. 'Evident Success', *The Sunday Tribune* (6 August 1989b): 12.
O' Faolain, Sean. Introduction to *Night in Tunisia* (London: Vintage, 1988).
O'Neill, Patrick. 'Aidan Higgins', *Contemporary Irish Novelists*. (Ed.) Rudiger Imhof. (Tubingen: Gunter Narr Verlag, 1990a): 93–107.
O'Neill, Patrick. 'John Banville', *Contemporary Irish Novelists*. (Ed.) Rudiger Imhof. (Tubingen: Gunter Narr Verlag, 1990b): 207–23.
O'Toole, Fintan. 'Island of Saints and Silicon: Literature and Social Change in Contemporary Ireland', *Cultural Contexts and Literary Idioms in Contemporary Irish Literature*. (Ed.) Michael Keneally. (Gerrards Cross: Colin Smythe, 1988): 11–35.
O'Toole, Fintan. ' Stepping into the Limelight – and the Chaos', *The Irish Times*, (Oct. 21 1989): W5. An Interview with John Banville.
Passmore, John. *A Hundred Years of Philosophy*. (London: Duckworth, 1966).
Pernot-Deschamps, Maggie. Neil Jordan's Short Stories – A Question of Irishness', *Asylum Arts Review*, Issue 4 (Winter 1997): 19–23.
Pilling, John. *An Introduction to Fifty Modern European Poets*. (London: Pan Books, 1982).
Reiss, Hans. *The Writer's Task from Nietzsche to Brecht*. (London: Macmillan, 1978).
Rilke, Rainer Maria. *Selected Poems*. (Trans.) J.B. Leishman. (Ed.) A. Alvarez. (Harmondsworth: Penguin, 1978).
Rilke, Rainer Maria. *The Notebooks of Malte Laurids Brigge*. (Trans.) Stephen Mitchell. (London: Picador, 1988).
Rilke, Rainer Maria. *The Selected Poetry of R.M. Rilke*. (Ed. and Trans.) Stephen Mitchell. (New York: Vintage, 1989).
Rilke, Rainer Maria. *Letters to a Young Poet*. (Trans.) John Burnham. (California: New World Library, 1992).
Robbe-Grillet, Alain. 'A Future for the Novel', *20th Century Literary Criticism: A Reader*. (Ed.) David Lodge. (London: Longman, 1972): 466–72.

Robbe-Grillet, Alain. *Topology of Phantom City*. (Trans.) J.A. Underwood. (London: John Calder, 1978).
Rushdie, Salman. *Midnight's Children*. (New York: Penguin 1980).
Sartre, Jean Paul. *Nausea*. (Trans.) R. Baldick. (Harmondsworth: Penguin, 1970).
Scholes, Robert. *The Fabulators*. (New York: Oxford UP, 1967).
Share, Bernard. 'Down from the Balcony', *Review of Contemporary Fiction*, (Spring 1983): 162-63.
Shattuck, Roger. *Proust's Binoculars: A Study of Memory, Time, and Recognition in A La Recherche Du Temps Perdu*. (New Jersey: Princeton UP, 1983).
Sheehan, Ronan. 'Novelists On The Novel: Ronan Sheehan talks to John Banville and Francis Stuart', *The Crane Bag* 3.1 (1979): 76-84.
Sherwood, Peter. 'In the city of widows', *TLS*, Nov. 26, 1993: 21.
Skelton, Robin. 'Aidan Higgins and the Total Book', *Mosaic*, X/I (Fall 1976): 27-37.
Somerville Large, Gillian. 'Review of *Lions of the Grunewald*', *Irish Independent* (Nov. 20, 1993): W10.
Stambaugh, Joan. *Nietzsche's Thought of Eternal Return*. (Baltimore, Maryland: The John Hopkins University Press, 1972).
Stevens, Wallace. *The Collected Poems of Wallace Stevens*. (London: Faber and Faber, 1984).
Stevick, Philip. *The Theory of the Novel*. (New York: Macmillan, 1967).
Updale, Ellie. 'Chaos Theory: *Sunrise with Sea-Monster*', *Literary Review* (January 1995): 47.
Waugh, Patricia. Metafiction: *The Theory and Practice of Self-Conscious Fiction*. (London: Methuen, 1984).
Waugh, Patricia. (Ed.) *Postmodernism: A Reader*. (London: Edward. Arnold, 1996).
White, Harry. 'Review of Aidan Higgins's *Helsingor Station* and *Ronda Gorge'*, *Irish University Review*, 20.1 (Spring 1990): 209-12.
Widger, Tom. 'In Another World', *The Tribune Magazine* (11 June, 1995): 21.
Woolf, Virginia. *To the Lighthouse*. (London: Grafton, 1977).
Yeats, W.B. *Collected Poems*. (Ed.) Norman Jeffares. (Dublin: Gill and Macmillan, 1989).
Yourcenar, Marguerite. *Memoirs of Hadrian*. (London: Four Square Books, 1966).
Yourcenar, Marguerite. *The Abyss*. (London: Black Swan Books, 1985).

INDEX

A

Adorno Theodore, 184, 235
Art, 91, 106, 129, 138, 167, 168, 174, 182, 184, 190, 214
autobiography, 37, 64, 68, 78–81, 82, 91–7, 98, 100, 233

B

Banville John, 1, 2, 3–6, 8, 9, 10, 11, 20, 27, 29, 30, 32–3, 34, 56, 99, **103–91**, 193–4, 199, 204, 208–210, 212–15, 218, 220, 227, 228, 233, 234–6
Athena, 33, 106, 149, 168, 179, 180, 182–7, 189–90
Birchwood, 27, **107–14**, 121, 125, 126, 130, 132, 134, 144, 145, 147, 152, 159, 178, 181, 183, 184, 188, 208, 213
Book of Evidence, The, 30, 33, 80, 106, 145, 151, 155, **156–71**, 178, 179, 180, 182, 186, 190, 218
Broken Jug, The, 141 ·
Doctor Copernicus, 33, 106, 113, **114–30**, 133–4, 144, 146
Ghosts 33, 106, 149, 168, **171–82**, 184–6, 190
Kepler, 33, 106, 113, **114–30**, 133–4, 137, 143, 146
Long Lankin, 113, 145, 184
Mefisto, 31, 32, 33, 106, **132–56**, 157, 158, 172, 181, 184, 190
Newton Letter, The, 33, 106, 122, 127, **132–56**, 237
Nightspawn, 8, 107, 113, 130, 132, 133, 136, 145, 181, 210

Barry, Sebastian, 8
Barth, John, 33, 111
Barthes, Roland, 1, 152, 171, 190
Battersby, Eileen, 141
Beckett, Samuel, 1, 3–4, 6, 7, 8, 9, 10, 16–21, 22, 23, 33, 38, 50, 54, 83, 99, 100, 108, 114, 125, 126, 139, 148, 152, 171, 175, 188, 191, 195, 213, 215, 220, 221
Beja, Morris, 57
big house, 27, 43–4, 47, 49, 54, 65, 107, 108, 111, 132, 134, 147, 159, 165
Blake, William, 213–14, 217, 219
Bloom, Harold, 151
Bloom, Leopold, 12, 13
Bloom, Molly, 150
Bolger, Dermot, 8
Borges, Jorge-Louis, 30, 33
Bragg, Melvyn, 171, 177
Brautigan Richard, 22–3, 65, 202
Brown Terence, 165

C

Calvino, Italo, 1, 26, 33, 188
Camus, Albert, 158
Carty, Ciaran, 133
Catholic, 47, 65, 224
Cervantes, 9
Coleridge, S.T., 231
Conrad, Joseph, 41, 54, 199
Cook, Albert, 136
critical theory, 5
Cronin, Anthony, 5

D

Deane, Seamus, 43, 113, 115, 121, 146, 168, 214
Democritus, 153, 157
Dickens, Charles, 150
dominant, the, 2, 9, 12, 15, 24–7, 28, 30, 34, 50, 61, 81, 84, 89, 91, 105–106, 112, 130, 178, 194, 204–205, 209–10, 217–18, 229, 231–2
Donnelly, Brian, 108

E

Eagleton, Terry, 32, 232
Eliot, T.S., 1, 22, 25, 38, 88, 146, 152
epistolary novel, 69, 74

F

Faulkner, William, 16
film, 34, 58, 194, 210, 215, 224–5
Fitzgerald, F. Scott, 51

G

García Márquez, Gabriel, 30, 33, 103, 237
Gardner, Martin, 157
Garfitt, Roger, 40
Gide, André, 145, 152, 178
Goethe, Wolfgang, 138, 142, 148–52, 170, 175, 177, 191

H

Hanly, David, 209, 215
Hassan, Ihab, 21, 28–9, 31, 32
Healy, Dermot, 90, 96
Hebdige, Dick, 31–2, 232
Heidegger, Martin, 47
Heisenberg, Werner, 143, 154, 157, 216, 218
Heller, Erich, 140, 168
Hibben, J.G., 143, 155
Higgins, Aidan, 1, 2, 5, 8, 10, 21, 27, 31, 34, **37–101**, 103–106, 167, 193, 195, 199, 203, 209, 227, 233–4, 236, 237
  Balcony of Europe, 27, 31, **55–64**, 66, 68, 74, 78, 83, 88, 167, 209
  Bornholm Night-Ferry, **69–74**, 76, 79, 82
  Donkey's Years, 78, 82, **92–7**
  Felo De Se, **39–43**, 52, 77, 98
  Helsingor Station and Other Departures, 37, **74–82**
  Images of Africa, 42, **50–54**, 75, 83, 91, 98
  Langrishe, Go Down, **43–50**, 55, 65, 68, 74, 91, 93, 108, 209, 233
  Lions of the Grunewald, **82–92**, 100
  Ronda Gorge and Other Precipices, **75–82**
  Scenes From a Receding Past, **64–9**, 78
Hofmannsthal, Hugo, 20, 138, 147
Homer, 182, 233
Hopper, Keith, 5

I

Imhof, Rüdiger, 5–8, 9, 11, 15, 21, 3–3, 34, 57, 108, 119, 125, 127, 137, 139, 143, 146, 148, 150, 153, 154, 155, 186, 210
intertextuality, 146, 171, 190
Ireland, 3–5, 6–8, 11, 20, 27, 33, 39, 46, 98, 108, 115, 132, 134, 160, 195–6, 216, 222, 224, 225–6
Irish, 2–11, 15, 20, 27, 33–4, 38, 44–6, 69, 94, 98, 108, 145–6, 167, 181, 191, 194, 196–7, 205, 215–17, 221–2, 225, 229

J

Jakobson, Roman, 15, 24, 50
James, Henry, 148
Jordan, Neil,1, 2–3, 5, 9, 10, 21, 34, **193–229**, 233, 235–6
  Night in Tunisia, 194, **196–204**, 216, 217, 226
  Sunrise with Sea-Monster,194, 196, 210, **216–24**, 227–9, 236
  The Crying Game, 194–5, **224–6**, 228, 236
  The Dream of a Beast, 194–6, 209, **210–16**, 227–8, 236
  The Past, 194, **204–10**, 215, 217, 227

Joyce, James, 1, 3–4, 6, 8, 10–15, 20, 21, 23, 25, 33, 34, 38, 50, 51, 56, 77, 81, 88, 98, 104, 105, 108, 112, 123, 134, 191, 197

K

Kafka, Franz,63, 134, 138, 171, 175, 177, 194, 209, 210
Kant, Immanuel, 110, 137, 200
Kearney, Richard, 5, 7, 8, 9–12, 13, 16, 20, 33, 34, 48, 56, 63, 71, 189, 196, 205, 215, 225
Kleist, Heinrich, 140, 184, 191
Kreilkamp, Vera, 44, 108

L

Lernout, Geert, 115
Lodge, David, 15–16, 31, 33, 115, 129, 135
Lubbers, Klaus, 56
Lukacs, George, 142

M

Mann, Thomas, 138
Matthews, Aidan, 8, 91
McCone, Kim, 222
McCormack, David, 137
McGahern, John, 3, 9–10, 41
McGrath, Patrick, 183
McHale, Brian, 7, 15, 17, 24–8, 34, 50, 105, 188, 210, 218
McKenna, John, 116, 145
McLiam Wilson, Robert, 8
McMinn, Joseph, 5, 121, 129, 137, 144, 166
Meany, Helen, 178–90
memory,4, 8, 9, 12, 14, 23, 26, 28, 32, 37–8, 44–5, 46, 49–50, 55–6, 57, 60–62, 64–6, 67–8, 70, 73, 77, 79, 85, 87, 90, 92–4, 96, 97, 98–9, 103, 105, 109, 127, 149, 188, 196, 197, 199, 203, 204, 207–208, 213, 217, 218, 221, 233
Modernism, 3–5, 14–16, 17, 20–25, 26, 28–9, 30, 32–3, 37–8, 98, 99, 103, 105, 107, 114, 121, 131, 135, 187, 193, 199, 212, 221, 231–4
Molloy, Francis C, 17–19, 121

N

Nabokov, Vladimir, 31, 33, 84, 128, 147, 152, 188, 190, 213
Ní Bhrian, Doirín, 156, 158, 168
Nietzsche, Friedrich, 20, 30, 133, 138, 150–51, 154–5, **157–71**, 175, 177, 179, 191, 235, 236

O

O'Brien, Flann, 3, 4, 6, 9, 10, 38, 68, 80
O'Faolain, Sean, 6, 198
O'Neill, Patrick, 40, 49, 62
O'Toole, Fintan, 6, 205
Ossian, 46

P

paintings, 173–4, 181, 186
Passmore, John, 110
Pavel, Thomas, 26
perception, 4, 14, 17, 20, 23, 29–31, 33, 37–8, 49–50, 58, 64, 97, 105, 109, 129, 132, 134, 135, 143, 153, 204, 205, 207,211, 213–15, 217, 220, 233
Pernot-Deschamps, Maggie, 196–7
Pilling, John, 138, 148
postcolonialism, 3
Postmodernism , 3, 5, 7, 11, 14–16, 20–25, 26–7, 22–33, 99, 100, 104–105, 107, 135, 146, 159, 188, 189, 193, 212–15, 216, 218, 220, 231–2, 234, 2
Proust, Marcel, 20, 22, 57, 84, 109–10, 159

R

realism, 7, 14, 16, 26, 27, 51, 63, 66, 125, 150, 187, 216–24, 226, 233
Rilke, Rainer Maria, 20, 33, 52–3, 124–5, 129, 138–49, 150–51, 187, 191, 235
Robbe-Grillet, Alain, 31, 202
Rushdie, Salman, 190, 231, 237

S

Sartre, Jean-Paul, 147
Scholes, Robert, 7, 111
self-conscious, 22, 97, 130, 188, 195, 204, 208, 209, 229
self-reflexive, 4, 8–9, 11, 14, 17–18, 22, 63, 68, 70, 72–4, 77, 88–9, 99, 105, 108, 109, 113, 121, 129, 133, 134, 136, 139, 169, 172, 177–8, 184, 187, 188, 205–207, 208, 209, 214, 219, 231, 234
self-reflexivity, 11, 14, 34, 104, 105, 186, 217
sequential narrative, 40, 57, 69, 89, 90, 96, 202, 203, 226
Shakespeare, 9, 150, 190, 231
Share, Bernard, 8, 83
Sheehan, Ronan, 107, 128 146
Shelley, Mary, 175
Shelley, P.B., 12
Skelton, Robin, 57
spatial narrative, 40, 57, 58
Stambaugh, Joan, 168
Sterne, Laurence, 9, 20, 22
Stevens, Wallace, 124, 129, 143, 146, 175, 177, 179
Stuart, Francis, 9, 10

T

Tynjanov, Jurij, 24

W

Watteau, Jean-Antoine, 173, 175, 177
Waugh, Patricia, 7, 14–15, 22, 24, 34, 99
Wilde, Oscar, 115, 152
Wittgenstein, Ludvig von, 110
Woolf, Virginia, 16, 98, 110, 210

Y

Yeats, W.B., 1, 3, 75, 115, 150, 219
Yourcenar, Marguerite, 112, 115

Z

Zeus, 182–3

STUDIES IN IRISH LITERATURE

1. Brian Arkins, **Greek and Roman Themes in Joyce**
2. Morton Levitt, **James Joyce and Modernism: Beyond Dublin**
3. Paralee Norman, **Marmion Wilme Savage 1804-1872–Dublin's Victorian Satirist**
4. Anne MacCarthy, **James Clarence Mangan, Edward Walsh and Nineteenth-Century Irish Literature in English**
5. Marie Arndt, **A Critical Study of Sean O'Faolain's Life and Work**
6. Sarah Ferris, **Poet John Hewitt, 1907-1987, and Criticism of Northern Irish Protestant Writing**
7. Gian Balsamo, **Scriptural Poetics in Joyce's** *Finnegans Wake*
8. James Whyte, **History, Myth, and Ritual in the Fiction of John McGahern: Strategies of Transcendence**
9. Yu-Chen Lin, **Justice, History, and Language in James Joyce's** *Finnegans Wake*
10. Teresa Deevy, **Selected Plays of Irish Playwright Teresa Deevy, 1894-1963,** edited by Eibhear Walshe
11. Dawn Duncan, **Postcolonial Theory in Irish Drama From 1800-2000**
12. Neil Murphy, **Irish Fiction and Postmodern Doubt–An Analysis of the Epistemological Crisis in Modern Fiction**